Falling H...

A
MERRIE MELODIE CARTOON
IN
TECHNICOLOR

DISTRIBUTED BY
Warner Bros.

HARE FORCE

FROM THE *Warner Bros.* PICTURE

LEON SCHLESINGER PRODUCTION

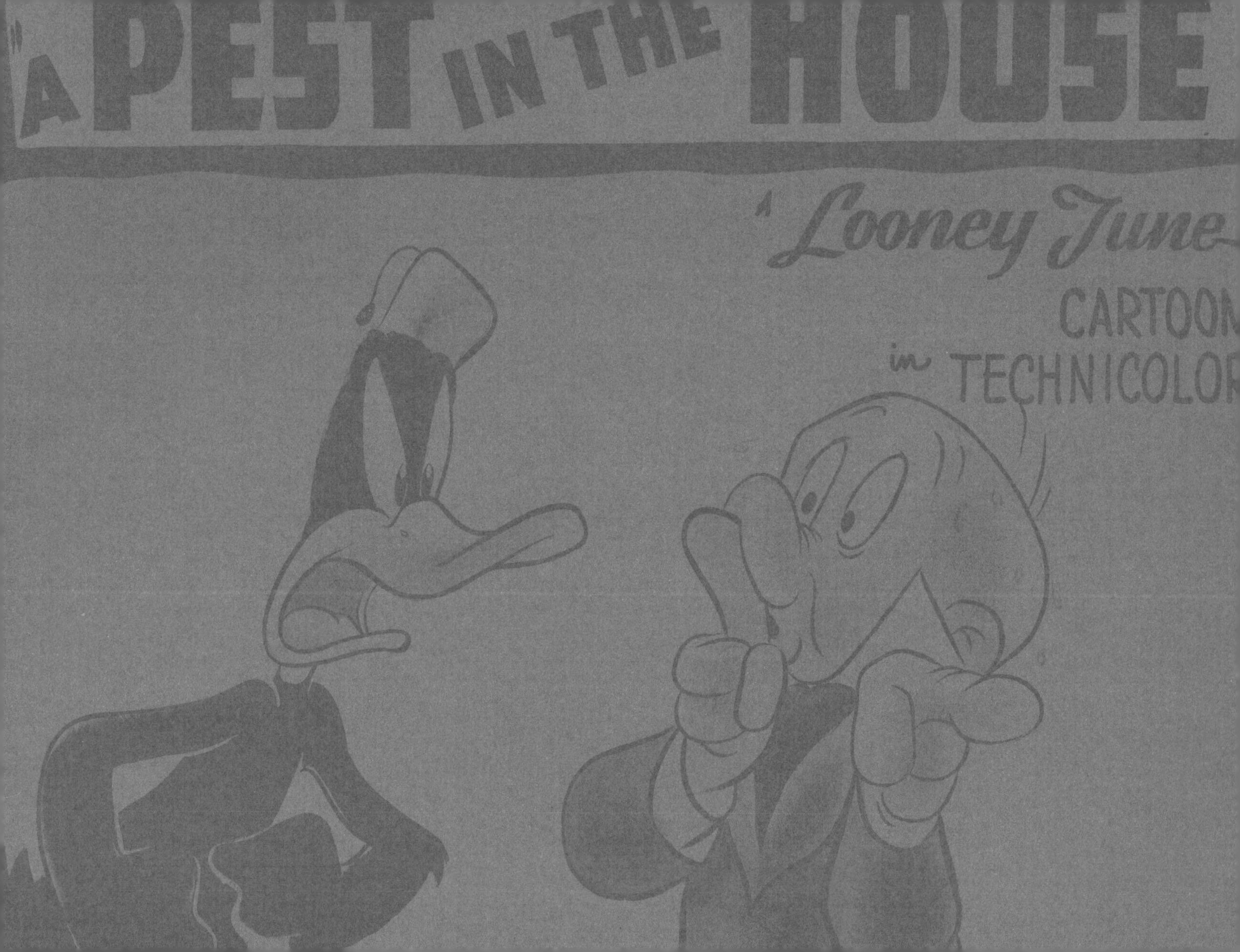
"A PEST IN THE HOUSE
A 'Looney Tune
CARTOON
in TECHNICOLOR

THE 100 GREATEST

LOONEY TUNES

Cartoons

™

INSIGHT ◉ EDITIONS

PO Box 3088
San Rafael, CA 94912

www.insighteditions.com

PALA22177

Technicolor is a trademark of Technicolor S.A.

Library of Congress Cataloging-in-Publication Data available.

ISBN: 978-1-60887-003-5

ROOTS of PEACE   ♠ REPLANTED PAPER

Insight Editions, in association with Roots of Peace, will plant two trees for each tree used in the manufacturing of
this book. Roots of Peace is an internationally renowned humanitarian organization dedicated to eradicating land
mines worldwide and converting war-torn lands into productive farms and wildlife habitats. Roots of Peace will
plant two million fruit and nut trees in Afghanistan and provide farmers there with the skills and support neces-
sary for sustainable land use.

Manufactured in China by Insight Editions

10 9 8 7 6 5 4 3

THE 100 GREATEST

LOONEY TUNES

Cartoons

™

EDITED BY JERRY BECK ★ FOREWORD BY LEONARD MALTIN

INSIGHT EDITIONS

SAN RAFAEL, CALIFORNIA

Table of Contents

Foreword

LEONARD MALTIN

I owe a lot to Looney Tunes: my knowledge of classical music, my understanding of World War II on the home front, and most of all, my sense of humor. Snippets of dialogue from these cartoons fill my subconscious, not so far beneath the surface. They were embedded there when I was young and I soaked them up like a sponge:

"The camels are coming...THE CAMELS ARE COMING!"

"You...are a gazelle." (I didn't know what a gazelle was, but the word sounded funny.)

I laughed at the drunken fish who poked his face at the camera while singing "On Moonlight Bay" and tried to imitate the furious patter of the Do-Do bird and the infectious laugh of a hysterical hippopotamus (which I now know was voiced by director Tex Avery himself).

Like millions of other kids of the baby boom era, I grew up glued to a television set at a time when TV was a living museum of movie history—including animation. Every day I got a dose of Laurel and Hardy, the Little Rascals, and cartoons of every sort. I think I'd memorized all the Betty Boop, Willie Whopper, and Van Beuren Studios shorts when the Warner Bros. cartoons of the 1930s and '40s arrived on the scene. This was a turning point in my life.

Director Chuck Jones didn't like making topical allusions in his cartoons, but he was in the minority at Warner Bros., so I grew up learning about things that a child of the 1950s might not have encountered any other way: radio comedians like Joe Penner ("You wanna buy a duck?"), kitchen and household products whose logos were ripe for visual gags (Old Dutch Cleanser, Arm & Hammer Baking Soda), and wartime songs like "We Did It Before (And We Can Do It Again)."

Sometimes I asked my parents to explain these things, but more often I put two and two together—especially since I saw some of the same references in other cartoons and comedy shorts of the period. Remember, these film libraries were played to death on local television, so even in that pre-VCR era I saw the same shorts over and over again. (Of course, I wasn't the only one having this experience. Many years later, at *Entertainment Tonight*, I asked an intern to help me locate some footage of Jimmy Durante; he had no idea who I was talking about, but after a few words of description he understood whom I meant from having seen caricatures of Durante in Warner Bros. cartoons! These Looney Tunes and Merrie Melodies entertained, informed, and influenced several generations of kids.)

As I got older, certain names and phrases periodically rang gongs in my head; I refer to them as a series of awakenings. The subtitle "The Rains Came (From the Picture of the Same Name)" always struck me as funny, but it never occurred to me that there was a genuine movie from 1939 called *The Rains Came*. Imagine

TO THIS DAY, I THINK HOLDING UP A PIECE OF PAPER WITH A DRAWING OF A SCREW AND A BALL ON IT WOULD BE AN IDEAL WAY OF DESCRIBING SOME OF THE PEOPLE I MEET.

my sense of wonderment when I realized that the Merrie Melody **A CORNY CONCERTO** was a parody of Walt Disney's **FANTASIA**—and that Elmer Fudd was a stand-in for that film's host, Deems Taylor.

A CORNY CONCERTO also introduced me to such classical-music standards as "Tales from the Vienna Woods" and "The Blue Danube." What's more, from the cartoon I even learned the names of the compositions. It took me years longer to learn the title of the exciting music inspiring the building of a skyscraper in **RHAPSODY IN RIVETS**. (It's Liszt's "Second Hungarian Rhapsody.")

Most of all, the frantic antics of Porky Pig, Daffy Duck, Bugs Bunny, and their costars helped form my sense of humor as well as my frame of reference. I may not have been able to adopt Bugs's wiseguy attitude in real life, but I reveled in it; to this day, I think holding up a piece of paper with a drawing of a screw and a ball on it would be an ideal way of describing some of the people I meet.

I never knew these cartoons were "old" when I first encountered them on television. Like the comedy shorts I loved, they were new to me.

My passion for them led me to my local library, where I found one book on Walt Disney and little else. When I launched my first "fanzine," around the age of 13, I wrote my first article about Warner Bros. cartoons, based entirely on my notes and observations. It would be several more years before Mike Barrier published his seminal interview with director Bob Clampett in *Funnyworld* and educated an entire generation of cartoon fans. Not long afterward, I got the opportunity to edit a series of film books and had a hand in publishing Joe Adamson's revelatory work *Tex Avery: King of Cartoons*.

I began teaching a course on the history of animation at the New School for Social Research in New York City. As many teachers know, the best way to learn a subject is to teach it. Giving lectures week after week, and screening 16mm prints of cartoons, caused me to articulate my thoughts about this medium and its development, and helped me when I wrote *Of Mice and Magic: A History of American Animated Cartoons*.

I'll always be grateful to that experience at the New School because I met so many terrific people there, including Jerry Beck, who has

gone on to become one of the most respected chroniclers of animation past and present.

For this volume, Jerry has solicited the opinions of animation experts to determine the hundred greatest Looney Tunes of all time—no easy task, given the number of gems the Warner Bros. team turned out. Through pictures and text you can revisit, or be introduced to, short films that represent the pinnacle of animated entertainment. You'd never dream these films were turned out on an assembly line. They feature an amazing array of characters in great scripts, with masterful voice work, music scores, artwork, and animation, all of which combine in perfect harmony—pun intended. For some of you, this will be a trip down memory lane, but my fondest wish is that this book will inspire younger animation fans to seek out these ageless cartoons.

Oh—and remember one thing: When confronted by a gwizzly bear, wie fwat on the gwound and pway dead. *Above all, wemain absowutely motionwess!*

Introduction

JERRY BECK

No doubt about it, the Looney Tunes are the funniest cartoons ever made. In fact, I'll take that statement a step further. I believe the Warner Bros. cartoons are as classic as anything in American cinema, and should be ranked alongside the likes of *The Wizard of Oz*, *Casablanca*, *Gone with the Wind*, and *Citizen Kane*.

True, we are talking about seven-minute cartoons: humorous drawings, made with ink and paint, that usually featured talking animals in impossible, hilarious situations. But the Warner Bros. cartoons created—as do all great films—original characters with believable personalities and motivations. Who doesn't know someone like Daffy Duck? Who doesn't sometimes feel like Wile E. Coyote? Who doesn't want to be Bugs Bunny?

The cartoons themselves are miniature works of art that often mix sophisticated filmmaking techniques and brilliant artwork with witty dialogue and hysterical situations.

It should be noted that, despite the popular misconception, the cartoons were never aimed exclusively at kids. In fact, the filmmakers claimed to have made them for themselves. Because of their technical brilliance and sharp-eyed humor, the Looney Tunes have stood the test of time. They've become permanent fixtures in global pop culture and, as with all fine art, can be enjoyed again and again, touching us with something new upon each viewing.

There were more than one thousand Warner Bros. cartoons produced under both the Looney Tunes and Merrie Melodies brands during the "golden age" of animation (1930 to 1969), and this book is your guide to the best of the best. We've polled animation fans online and have reached out to a number of professional cartoonists, animators, and filmmakers to pick their favorites. We also asked noted critics, historians, and scholars to contribute their thoughts—all in an effort to get a consensus of opinion as to which cartoons were the most satisfying, the most significant, and the laugh-out-loud funniest.

THE ORIGIN OF LOONEY TUNES

Warner Bros. began distributing cartoons in 1930, when producer Leon Schlesinger contracted with animators Hugh Harman and Rudolph Ising for a series of musical cartoons to compete with animated shorts from their former boss, Walt Disney. Harman and Ising's answer to Mickey Mouse was Bosko (who starred in more than three dozen Looney Tunes, including the very first, **SINKIN' IN THE BATHTUB**), and their answer to Disney's Silly Symphonies was a series called Merrie Melodies. As long as a Schlesinger cartoon had bouncing characters, humorous gags, and at least one chorus from a song owned by Warner Bros., the front office was content.

THERE WERE MORE THAN ONE THOUSAND WARNER BROS. CARTOONS PRODUCED UNDER BOTH THE LOONEY TUNES AND MERRIE MELODIES BRANDS DURING THE "GOLDEN AGE" OF ANIMATION (1930 TO 1969).

But Harman and Ising wanted to do more. After a few years, the pair left Schlesinger for bigger budgets at MGM, taking Bosko with them. In 1934, Schlesinger had no choice but to set up his own shop from scratch. He moved animator Friz Freleng into the director's chair and then allowed an emerging group of young Turks (including future directors Tex Avery, Frank Tashlin, Bob Clampett, and Chuck Jones) the opportunity to try some new things.

First they created Porky Pig, whose unique shape and signature speech impediment earned the studio its first positive buzz. Avery, Tashlin, and Clampett began to use the pig as a comic centerpiece for cartoons that were fast-paced, funny, and as contemporary as the live-action feature films Warner Bros. was producing at the time. Early versions of Daffy Duck and Bugs Bunny emerged from Porky's Looney Tunes series. Also joining the Schlesinger team at this time were musician Carl Stalling and voice actor Mel Blanc.

The Merrie Melodies series, which distinguished itself from the outset by presenting a variety of one-shot characters and situations in each cartoon, later distancing itself from the Looney Tunes with bigger budgets and Cinecolor photography (from 1934 to 1943 all Looney Tunes were in black and white), was

an incubator for new ideas. **I LOVE TO SINGA**, **PAGE MISS GLORY**, **HORTON HATCHES THE EGG**, and **A WILD HARE** are a few of classics of its early period, cartoons combining great animation and edgy humor that differentiated the Warner Bros. cartoons from their competitors.

By 1940, both Daffy Duck and Bugs Bunny were leading players and became the symbols of the new, brash Warner Bros. cartoon style. A few years later, when both Looney Tunes and Merrie Melodies were being produced in full color, rendering their series designations practically meaningless, the Looney Tunes moniker stuck with the public as the nickname for all Warner Bros. cartoons due to the studio's trademark zany humor. When the country plunged into the War, the studio fulfilled a demand for animated wise guys like Bugs Bunny to counter real-life Elmer Fudds like Mussolini. From here on out, Warner Bros. established themselves as creators of the most popular animated shorts coming out of Hollywood.

As the War wound down, Schlesinger sold his studio lock, stock, and barrel to Warner Bros. During the next decade, the cartoon department nurtured a menagerie of new characters (Sylvester the Cat, Pepé Le Pew, Foghorn Leghorn, Marvin the Martian, Road Runner, and Speedy Gonzales, to name but a

few), each one becoming a superstar in his or her own right. Jones, Freleng, and McKimson all came into their own as directors, creating the bulk of the masterpieces pictured in this tome and winning a total of seven Academy Awards.

During the next fifty years, the Looney Tunes became a staple of television programming, a ubiquitous presence on afternoon kids' shows, and a perennial favorite of network Saturday morning schedules (not to mention numerous prime-time specials and extensive runs on Nickelodeon and Cartoon Network). The Looney Tunes characters inspired Warner Bros. to produce five theatrical compilation features and two movies that combined live-action with animation, **SPACE JAM** (1996) and **LOONEY TUNES: BACK IN ACTION** (2003). No wonder the Looney Tunes have consumed our imaginations for so long, and their characters' antics have become part of our national psyche.

ON TERMITE TERRACE

Something we hope to accomplish with this book is to direct a spotlight on the incredible talent behind the scenes. One of the joys of watching classic Looney Tunes is the

REVISITING ALL THE CARTOONS LISTED IN THIS BOOK WAS LIKE A BLAST OF DYNAMITE FOR ME. EACH AND EVERY ONE IS A CINEMATIC TREASURE.

ability to note the different directors' styles. By the 1950s, each director had his creative team locked in place and his personal style strongly stamped onto his films. Chuck Jones's cartoons used strong poses and stylized animation to play up both his sense of design and his characters, who all had capital-A Attitude. Friz Freleng emphasized broad gags, appealing personalities, and strong musical timing. Robert McKimson leaned toward bombastic characters (think Foghorn Leghorn or the Tasmanian Devil) with strong stories and solid draftsmanship.

Each unit had a dedicated story man (Warren Foster, Michael Maltese, and Tedd Pierce during the heyday of the 1940s and '50s), but before each cartoon went into production, the entire staff would review the storyboard, and everyone was encouraged to add gags to the picture. This review was called a "no 'no' session," as no gag was too crazy to suggest, allowing a creative atmosphere open to all.

As uniquely gifted as the directors, animators, and story men were, there were several constants in all Warner Bros. cartoons with which we've become familiar: the voice actors, led by Mel Blanc; the musical scores from Carl Stalling and Milt Franklyn; and hilarious sound effects from film editor Treg Brown.

These constants were the glue that held the Warner Bros. cartoon universe together. What would the cartoons sound like without them? It's unimaginable.

Mel Blanc was integral to 95 percent of the cartoons listed herein. (The remaining 5 percent include several pantomime shorts without dialogue: those starring the Road Runner, musical shorts like 1960's **HIGH NOTE** and 1957's **THE THREE LITTLE BOPS**, and one-shots like **ROCKET-BYE BABY**.) Blanc was known as "The Man of a Thousand Voices" because his voice alone defined the Warner Bros. cartoons. However, voice actors Stan Freberg, June Foray, Arthur Q. Bryan, Bea Benaderet, Frank Graham, and Robert Bruce, among many others, never got the credit—literally—that they richly deserve. Their contributions in bringing to life the Looney Tunes supporting players cannot be overstated.

Obviously, I'm a huge fan of the Warner Bros. cartoons, and putting this book together was a lot of fun. However, I discovered a big problem early on: One hundred slots weren't nearly enough to cover all the greats! The ultimate choices here are bound to disappoint some—not for what is included, but for what was left out. Warner Bros. has simply made too many good cartoons. After due consideration,

we decided to list the Looney Tunes alphabetically instead of ranking them by number. It's our opinion that all of them deserve equal celebration. Since comedy is subjective, we'll leave it to you to determine which ones you think better than others.

Each entry contains production information, including release dates and screen and voice-over credits (historian Keith Scott provided special research on vocal characterizations). A plot synopsis is followed by a guest commentary that explains why each cartoon rates being in this book.

Revisiting all the cartoons listed in this book was like a blast of dynamite for me. Each and every one is a cinematic treasure—and if you didn't know that already, now you'll find out why. Pass them on to your friends, family, and children, or just watch 'em yourself over and over again—for the first time or the hundredth, perhaps in date order or simply **FROM A TO Z-Z-Z**.

"That's not all folks—it's only the beginning!"

Episode List

FROM A TO Z-Z-Z-Z

ACROBATTY BUNNY

ALI BABA BUNNY

THE ARISTO-CAT

BABY BOTTLENECK

BACK ALLEY OPROAR

BASEBALL BUGS

A BEAR FOR PUNISHMENT

THE BIG SNOOZE

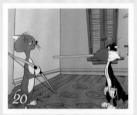

BIRDS ANONYMOUS

BOOK REVUE

BUCCANEER BUNNY

BUGS AND THUGS

BUGS BUNNY GETS THE BOID

BULLY FOR BUGS

BUNNY HUGGED

CANNED FEUD

CHOW HOUND

CINDERELLA MEETS FELLA

COAL BLACK AND DE SEBBEN DWARFS

42

A CORNY CONCERTO

45

DEDUCE, YOU SAY

46

DOG GONE SOUTH

49

DOG POUNDED

50

DOUGH RAY ME-OW

53

THE DOVER BOYS AT PIMENTO UNIVERSITY

54

DRAFTEE DAFFY

57

DRIP-ALONG DAFFY

58

DUCK AMUCK

61

DUCK DODGERS IN THE 24½TH CENTURY

62

DUCK! RABBIT, DUCK!

65

EASTER YEGGS

66

EATIN' ON THE CUFF

69

8 BALL BUNNY

70

FALLING HARE

72

FAST AND FURRY-OUS

74

FEED THE KITTY

77

GORILLA MY DREAMS

78

THE GREAT PIGGY BANK ROBBERY

81

A GRUESOME TWOSOME

82 GUIDED MUSCLE

84 HAIR-RAISING HARE

86 A HAM IN A ROLE

89 HAREDEVIL HARE

90 A HARE GROWS IN MANHATTAN

93 THE HEP CAT

94 HIGH DIVING HARE

97 HIGH NOTE

98 HILLBILLY HARE

100 HOLLYWOOD STEPS OUT

103 HONEY'S MONEY

104 THE HYPO-CHONDRI-CAT

107 I LOVE TO SINGA

108 AN ITCH IN TIME

111 KITTY KORNERED

112 LITTLE RED RIDING RABBIT

115 LONG-HAIRED HARE

116 MEXICALI SCHMOES

119 MUCH ADO ABOUT NUTTING

120 NASTY QUACKS

122 OLD GLORY

126 THE OLD GREY HARE

129 ONE FROGGY EVENING

130 OPERATION: RABBIT

132 PAGE MISS GLORY

135 A PEST IN THE HOUSE

136 PIGS IN A POLKA

139 PIGS IS PIGS

140 PLANE DAFFY

142 PORKY IN WACKYLAND

145 PORKY PIG'S FEAT

146 RABBIT FIRE

150 RABBIT OF SEVILLE

153 RABBIT SEASONING

154 RHAPSODY IN RIVETS

157 ROBIN HOOD DAFFY

158 ROCKET-BYE BABY

160 RUSSIAN RHAPSODY

162 SATAN'S WAITIN'

165 SCAREDY CAT

166

THE SCARLET PUMPERNICKEL

169

SCRAP HAPPY DAFFY

170

SHOW BIZ BUGS

172

SLICK HARE

174

STEAL WOOL

177

THE STUPID CUPID

178

THE STUPOR SALESMAN

180

SWOONER CROONER

182

A TALE OF TWO KITTIES

185

THE THREE LITTLE BOPS

186

THUGS WITH DIRTY MUGS

188

TIN PAN ALLEY CATS

191

TORTOISE WINS BY A HARE

192

TREE FOR TWO

194

WABBIT TWOUBLE

197

WALKY TALKY HAWKY

198

WHAT'S OPERA, DOC?

201

WHOLLY SMOKE

202

A WILD HARE

204

YOU OUGHT TO BE IN PICTURES

THE **100** GREATEST

LOONEY TUNES
Cartoons

™

From A to Z-Z-Z-Z

Most pupils at Valley View School are busily reciting their math lesson—but Ralph Phillips dreamily stares out the window, imagining he can fly like a bird. Teacher Miss Wallace snaps Ralph to attention, asking him to solve a towering sum on the blackboard. Ralph's spirit is willing, but his imagination is strong; soon the chalk numbers are warriors, and Ralph is fighting a duel. Miss Wallace sends the boy to get some fresh air and put a letter in the school mailbox. But the errand starts Ralph fantasizing again; in his mind he's a Pony Express rider, braving a fierce Indian attack. Later, Ralph sits mesmerized by the classroom fish tank, perceiving a goldfish as a "saber-tooth tiger shark" and a toy boat as a stranded sub. Heroic Navy man Ralph dives without a suit and slices the shark in two—while back in real life, Miss Wallace makes our hero stand in the corner. Or...is it the corner of a boxing ring? And is that the boxing-ring bell or the end-of-school bell? In the end, Ralph leaves for home, only to become General MacArthur on his way out the door, proclaiming, "I shall return!"

DIRECTOR: CHARLES M. JONES **STORY:** MICHAEL MALTESE **ANIMATION:** KEN HARRIS, BEN WASHAM, LLOYD VAUGHAN **LAYOUT:** MAURICE NOBLE **BACKGROUNDS:** PHIL DEGUARD **VOICES:** RICHARD BEALS (RALPH PHILLIPS), MARIAN RICHMAN (TEACHER), NORMAN NESBITT (CAPTAIN, MATE), MEL BLANC (LAUGHTER) **MUSIC:** CARL STALLING

DARRELL VAN CITTERS, former Warner Bros. creative director Of all the Warner Bros. directors, Chuck Jones seems to have relied least on conventional formulas for his story material. Part of this was probably due to his personal preferences and part of it was due to his ace story man, Mike Maltese. It's unlikely that a film such as this would have been made under Friz Freleng, Maltese's previous director. Credit goes to Maltese for suggesting such a gentle cartoon in a studio that relied heavily on adversarial relationships in its films, and credit to Jones for agreeing to make it. Not only is the story charming, it also provided rich material for production designer Maurice Noble's vision of the role of animation design in a cartoon. For a film to work as well as this one does means that the material has to resonate with all members of the creative team.

This cartoon focuses on the imagination of a young boy, Ralph Phillips. In his Walter Mitty–like daydreams, Ralph sees every situation as more adventurous than his schoolroom reality. The boy's flights of fancy lead to flights of fancy in the design work, and this film seems to provide the first real clues on where Maurice Noble would take animation design. Maurice felt that flat characters should inherently exist over flat environments, and vigorously shunned the use of airbrush or rendering in the final execution. He would get involved early in the story process with staging and concepts that would often end up greatly influencing the final product. Noble's presence can be felt in every frame—the exaggerated

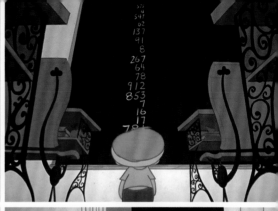

perspective highlighting the child's view of the world, the stylized cascade of arrows that cowboy Ralph rides through, the flashes of red emphasizing each punch. In fact, as the 1950s wore on, his contributions to Chuck's output became ever greater, so much so that Jones eventually gave him co-director credit. The 1957 follow-up to this film, **BOYHOOD DAZE**, shows Maurice's influence even more strongly in its exaggerated stylization and bolder color palettes.

"EVEN THOUGH I GOT A 'C' IN ARITHMETIC, YOU CAN...I MEAN, YOU MAY DEPEND ON ME, YOUR CAPTAINSHIP, SIR."

JERRY SAYS Apart from his most famous roles in **FROM A TO Z-Z-Z-Z**, **BOYHOOD DAZE**, and the TV pilot **ADVENTURES OF THE ROAD-RUNNER** (1962), Ralph Phillips led two other lives—as a teenager in Chuck Jones's army recruitment shorts, **90-DAY WONDERING** (1956) and **DRAFTY, ISN'T IT?** (1957), and in **LOONEY TUNES** comic books, as a Tubby-like antagonist to Suzanne, the destructive little girl from the Sylvester classic **A KIDDIES KITTY** (1955).

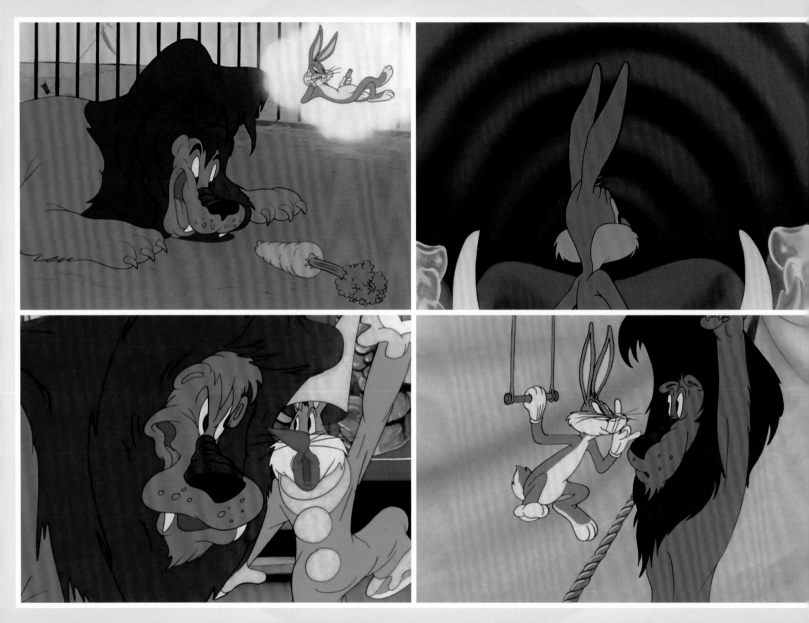

Acrobatty Bunny

"IRON BARS DO NOT A PRISON MAKE—BUT THEY SURE HELP, EH, DOC?"

DIRECTOR: ROBERT MCKIMSON **STORY:** WARREN FOSTER **ANIMATION:** ART DAVIS, CAL DALTON, RICHARD BICKENBACH **LAYOUTS AND BACKGROUNDS:** CORNETT WOOD, RICHARD H. THOMAS **VOICES:** MEL BLANC (BUGS BUNNY, NERO LION) **MUSIC:** CARL STALLING

The circus comes to town, and the roustabouts place the lion's cage directly over Bugs Bunny's rabbit hole. Nero Lion sniffs the rabbit out, which soon leads to a chase around the Big Top. First Bugs taunts the lion from outside his cage, then frustrates the beast by switching places with him. When the lion uses an elephant to break the cage, Bugs retaliates with a mouse to scare the pachyderm—who in turn uses Nero to swat the rodent. Bugs runs into a clown's dressing room and emerges as Pagliacci, urging Nero to "laugh, clown, laugh," then whacking him with a two-by-four. Next, they hit the trapeze and swing into high-wire action—with and without a net. Finally, Bugs tricks the lion into climbing into a lit cannon and blows him into a dizzy state. The dazed Nero becomes a dancing girl for the rabbit's new act, "Bugs Bunny and His Hula Hula Lion."

HARRY MCCRACKEN, editor of *Animato!* With **ACROBATTY BUNNY,** like other early McKimson cartoons, it's not individual gags that stand out as amusing so much as the overall feeling of exuberantly corny, kinetic fun. But it does feature one of the greatest Disney references ever, when Bugs peers into Nero Lion's mouth and bellows "PINNNNOCCHIOOOOO!"

JERRY SAYS Nonstop action and gags, **ACROBATTY BUNNY** is a pure Bugs Bunny cartoon, demonstrating what the rabbit does best: using his brains to heckle an aggressive bully and stay one step ahead of his opponent. Robert McKimson's very first Bugs Bunny cartoon is one of the funniest ever made.

Ali Baba Bunny

"HASSAN CHOP!"

In search of Pismo Beach, Bugs and Daffy accidentally tunnel their way into Ali Baba's cave of treasures. Daffy reverts to his greedy self and starts carting off the jewels. He mistakes the scimitar-wielding guard, Hassan, for a baggage porter but is chased away. Bugs pretends to be the genie of the lamp and removes Hassan from the cave with a rope trick. The real genie emerges and takes revenge on Daffy as Bugs makes a clean getaway. Later, at Pismo Beach, Bugs finds a pearl in an oyster—which is immediately grabbed by the now-miniature version of Daffy Duck.

LINDA SIMENSKY, vice president of children's programming, PBS When I was growing up, the Looney Tunes package that ran on television in the New York area featured a number of older cartoons, mostly from the 1950s. Consequently, while I was not that familiar with director Bob Clampett's cartoons, I knew the early 1950s Chuck Jones ones by heart. Of those cartoons,

DIRECTOR: CHUCK JONES **STORY:** MICHAEL MALTESE **ANIMATION:** RICHARD THOMPSON, KEN HARRIS, ABE LEVITOW, BEN WASHAM **EFFECTS ANIMATION:** HARRY LOVE **LAYOUT:** MAURICE NOBLE **BACKGROUNDS:** PHILIP DEGUARD **FILM EDITOR:** TREG BROWN **VOICES:** MEL BLANC (BUGS, DAFFY, HASSAN) **MUSIC:** CARL STALLING, MILT FRANKLYN

my all-time favorite as a kid was **ALI BABA BUNNY**. As an adult, I know that the stars of this short are the layouts, the backgrounds, and the color styling. The modern styling of these cartoons works perfectly for depicting the natural vistas, the insides of the caves, and of course, Pismo Beach.

ALI BABA BUNNY was produced in an era when Bugs and Daffy were often paired up, and while that didn't always work, in this cartoon they seem to be formidable opponents. In the early 1950s, Daffy Duck was no longer just daffy. He had progressed to being greedy, cheap, and without a

trace of empathy. When put in the right circumstances, this worked. Bugs, as paired up with Daffy, lost a little of his ability to incite conflict, being given the job of mostly reacting and politely suffering Daffy's outbursts. But in this cartoon Bugs has his classic moments, too—too cool to care about riches, he is able to provide some fake genie assistance to Daffy ("Ickety, ackety, oop!"), who unfortunately can't be helped.

What I remember most about this particular cartoon is the quotable dialogue. The list of lines is long: "Hassan chop!" "Open, Sasparilla! Open, Saskatchewan!" "We should have turned left at Albuquerque." "I'm rich, I'm wealthy, I'm independent, I'm socially secure." And, of course, "Consequences, shmonsequences, as long as I'm rich."

The Aristo-Cat

"MEADOWS...MEADOWS!...MEADOWS!...MEADOOOWS!"

DIRECTOR: CHARLES M. JONES **STORY:** TED PIERCE* **ANIMATION:** RUDY LARRIVA, JOHN MCGREW, KEN HARRIS, BOBE CANNON **BACKGROUNDS:** GENE FLEURY, BERNICE POLIFKA **VOICES:** MEL BLANC (PUSSY, MEADOWS, BERTIE, ROVER), TED PIERCE* (HUBIE) **MUSIC:** CARL STALLING

Pussy is a cat that has it all: a posh home, drawn baths, breakfast in his own Louis XVI bed, not to mention Meadows, the butler. While the mistress is gone, this very British wage slave must humor Pussy's every whim, even putting up with the cat's schoolboyish pranks. But after slipping on a well-placed bar of soap, Meadows resigns, and no amount of screaming will bring him back. Without a caretaker, Pussy fears he'll starve. Luckily, a book on cats that Pussy discovers in the library suggests a food source: mice. Unfortunately, Pussy doesn't know a mouse when he sees one. Spotting house mice Hubie and Bertie, the cat flees in terror—and the rodents see

a sucker. Hubie and Bertie direct Pussy to what they claim is a mouse: Rover, a giant bulldog, whom the cat actually tries to eat. Barely escaping with his life, Pussy learns Hubie and Bertie's true identities, then chases them hungrily—only to land in Rover's doghouse again. The battle rages until the cat wakes up in bed. "What a terrible dream!" Pussy sighs. "Yeah, wasn't it?" gasp Rover, Hubie, and Bertie, all sharing the sheets with him.

MICHAEL SPORN, animator John McGrew is certainly one of my favorite layout and background designers in animation. His work on **DOVER BOYS** in 1942 set new highs for animation. He followed **DOVER BOYS** with daring work on **CONRAD THE SAILOR**, **INKI AND THE MINAH BIRD**, **THE CASE OF THE MISSING HARE**, and others—all for Chuck Jones, who was no slouch himself in

encouraging exciting innovation in design and film cutting.

THE ARISTO-CAT was probably the first of McGrew's works that I saw when I was a kid. It made my eyes pop, even though I watched it originally in black and white. His dynamic wallpaper decoration, combined with the outrageous pans and camera work, took me by force; the violently repeating patterns jump out of the background and reach the forefront of this short. All of this exuberant design acted to support the main character's anxiety, fear, and terror—the fine character animation of Ken Harris, Rudy Larriva, and Bobe Cannon.

Working with Jones and painter Gene Fleury, McGrew sure-footedly set the way for United Productions of America (UPA) cartoons and Ward Kimball's **TOOT WHISTLE PLUNK & BOOM** (1953). Maurice Noble and other stylized designers of the 1950s couldn't have broken through if McGrew hadn't been there first, supporting and pushing Chuck Jones.

* We have standardized Mr. Pierce's name to "Ted," although he was sometimes credited as "Tedd."

JERRY SAYS Not only is **THE ARISTO-CAT** an impressive cartoon—funny, aesthetically progressive, and important—it introduces Hubie and Bertie to the Looney Tunes menagerie. Chuck Jones would go on to make several great cartoons with this pair of mischievous mice (**THE HYPO-CHRONDRI-CAT**, also in this book, is another). In addition, this cartoon represents another milestone in Jones's transition from his earlier, slow-paced, Disney-styled films to faster, funnier, more artistically experimental cartoons. Working with layout artist John McGrew and the husband-wife team of background painters Eugene Fleury and Bernice Polifka, Jones depicts the action from the pussycat's point of view. His flat, sparse, graphic backgrounds—a feast for the eyes—were a departure from the standard Hollywood cartoon look at the time. The checkerboard floors and zigzagged wallpaper are just as memorable as the story itself. In fact, the cartoons Jones made at this time would go on to influence the "modern art" movement that fueled the UPA studio a few years later.

THE ARISTO-CAT also makes use of Carl Stalling's great musical range. Stalling first uses Raymond Scott's "In an Eighteenth-Century Drawing Room" to set up the initial pampered cat sequences. Scott's "Twilight in Turkey," as well as Chopin and Rossini cues, are perfect melodies to underscore wild chases around a wealthy estate.

But the cartoon is all about the cat and his paranoia over being alone and potentially starving, then being duped by two con-artist mice. Despite the abstract settings and classical music, the characters are realistic, their feelings are realistic, and the situation is hilarious.

Baby Bottleneck

When the postwar baby boom overburdens a baby-delivering stork, he drinks away his troubles. Meanwhile, the drunk stork's "help" does his job badly, sending baby gorillas to kangaroos and baby cats to mice. Storks Inc. needs new traffic managers, and finds them in the "Pig and Duck Nip and Tuck Delivery Service." Alas, Porky and Daffy are hardly better than the klutzes they've replaced. In the orders office, Daffy makes smart-mouthed remarks to parents who call in their requests. And Porky's assembly line powders, diapers, feeds, and burps the new babies. But the action stops when an orphan egg is discovered. "You'll have to sit on this egg," Porky tells Daffy, "and hatch it out to see who it belongs to." Daffy refuses to play mama. The ensuing pig-duck chase finally lands Porky and Daffy on their own assembly line, where they're powdered, diapered, and sent off to be a mother gorilla's babies.

One of Bob Clampett's looniest 'toons, **BABY BOTTLENECK** once included a scene that has been cut from surviving prints. When a toothy baby alligator tries to nurse at Mama Pig's teat,

"OH, YES, MR. CANTOR! YOU SAY YOU HAVEN'T GOT THAT BOY YET? WELL, IF AT FIRST YOU DON'T SUCCEED … WOO-HOO-HOO-HOO!"

DIRECTOR: ROBERT CLAMPETT **STORY:** WARREN FOSTER **ANIMATION:** ROD SCRIBNER, MANNY GOULD, ROBERT MCKIMSON, J. C. MELENDEZ* **LAYOUT AND BACKGROUNDS:** THOMAS MCKIMSON, DORCY HOWARD **VOICES:** MEL BLANC (DAFFY, PORKY, NARRATOR, STORK, BABY), SARA BERNER (MOTHER GORILLA) **MUSIC:** CARL STALLING

she originally reprimands him, "Don't touch that dial!"

MIKE BARRIER, animation and comics scholar
BABY BOTTLENECK, like **BOOK REVUE** (1946), reveals just how great Bob Clampett's impact was on the Warner Bros. cartoons in the early 1940s. The starting point here is a "cute factory" like those in any number of Warner cartoons from a decade and more earlier—for example, the baby factory in the Merrie Melody **SHUFFLE OFF TO BUFFALO** (1933). But there the resemblance ends, because **BABY BOTTLENECK**'s factory is run by Porky Pig and Daffy Duck. As so often in Clampett's best cartoons, there is a prevailing air of hysteria and madness: The stork is drunk, inexperienced help is delivering babies to the wrong mothers, everything is a mess—and all is bliss.

* Animator José Cuauhtémoc "Bill" Meléndez, who went on to later fame with the *Peanuts* gang, was in these cartoons credited either as "J. C." or "C." Melendez, which we have standardized to "J. C."

Back Alley Oproar

"YOU'RE JUST AN ANGEL IN DISGUISE."

Elmer Fudd is so sleepy that he rushes into bed before his lamp even shuts off. Alas, Sylvester has chosen Fudd's fence to perform his nighttime concert on, starting with a rendition of "Largo al factotum" from **THE BARBER OF SEVILLE**. Elmer shuts the cat up with a boot, and Sylvester returns the favor by stomping out Liszt's Second Hungarian Rhapsody on Fudd's back stairs—before he is bound and gagged. Soon enough, Sylvester is back on the fence singing "Some Sunday Morning," so Elmer launches a copy of **THE THIN MAN** at him, but it is thrown right back as **RETURN OF THE THIN MAN**. Elmer shuts the window, and immediately receives a phone call: It's Sylvester, finishing the song. Elmer goes for his golf club, while Sylvester covers the stairs in grease and sprinkles tacks on the ground below. Elmer falls for the trap not just once, but a second time, going back to his house to retrieve his rifle, then a *third* time coming back out. Sylvester continues with "You Never Know Where You're Going Till You Get There" until he spots Elmer. At this point he calls in his stand-in: a dopey orange tabby who sings "Carissima" from the 1903 opera **RED FEATHER** in an unexpectedly lyrical soprano voice; Elmer bashes the tabby on the head, and he falls off the roof. Elmer corners Sylvester, but is lulled

DIRECTOR: I. FRELENG **ANIMATION:** GERRY CHINIQUY, MANUEL PEREZ, KEN CHAMPIN, VIRGIL ROSS **STORY:** MICHAEL MALTESE, TED PIERCE **LAYOUT:** HAWLEY PRATT **BACKGROUNDS:** PAUL JULIAN **VOICES:** MEL BLANC (SYLVESTER), ARTHUR Q. BRYAN (ELMER), GLORIA CURRAN (OPERA SINGER), TUDOR WILLIAMS (BASS SINGER IN HEAVEN) **MUSIC:** CARL STALLING

to sleep by the cat's variation on Brahms' Lullaby. His rest is short-lived, and he is immediately woken up by the cat's one-man band. Back on the fence, Sylvester sings "On Moonlight Bay" until Elmer sabotages his performance by feeding him some alum-laced milk, which causes Sylvester's head (and voice) to shrink. Returning to normal, Sylvester is once again singing, this time "Angel in Disguise," starting off like Sinatra and finishing off like Spike Jones, complete with ear-splitting sound effects. Elmer decides to blast the cat to kingdom come with a crate of dynamite, but the explosion kills him, too. In an angel outfit, Elmer attempts to finally get some rest, but is awoken by Sylvester's nine lives singing (badly) the sextet "Chi mi frena in tal momento" from **LUCIA DI LAMMERMOOR**. One of them nabs Elmer's halo, causing him to jump to his doom—again.

GREG FORD, animation historian After Robert Clampett left Warner Bros. in the mid-1940s, director Friz Freleng had exclusive dibs on the Tweety and Sylvester stories. Freleng would often open these cartoons with the grubby, unkempt scrounge Sylvester using a garbage-can lid to elegantly serve himself trash and fish bones foraged from the ashcan heap—probably the only explanation why Sylvester would even find the measly Tweety palatable. Freleng's "hobo kitty" Sylvester contrasts markedly with Chuck Jones's later portrayal of Sylvester as a spineless, craven domestic pet in shorts such as **SCAREDY CAT** (1948) and **CLAWS FOR ALARM** (1954).

BACK ALLEY OPROAR is perhaps Sylvester's finest hour. It finds him caterwauling in his typical environment—a back alley—as Freleng combines his postwar Sylvester with his earlier musical themes. Instead of producing the usual feline yowling, Sylvester dances a sailor's hornpipe, sings the Jule Styne–Sammy Cahn standard "You Never Know Where You're Going till You Get There" in march time, and does an "Angel in Disguise" number that must have been inspired by Spike Jones's bandsman (he accompanies himself by lighting firecrackers and clunking himself in the head with bricks).

Whereas Tweety was initially developed under Robert Clampett's supervision, Sylvester's early evolution in cartoons like **LIFE WITH FEATHERS** (1945) and **PECK UP YOUR TROUBLES** (1945) was overseen by Friz Freleng himself, and **BACK ALLEY OPROAR** best showcases this primal incarnation. Sylvester's design, as envisioned by Friz, incorporated circus clown attributes: a big red nose, a low crotch evocative of baggy pants, and a low waistline and squatty legs, which lent a screwball dimension to the character (later downplayed). **BACK ALLEY OPROAR**'s Sylvester exudes enormous appeal as he tunefully harasses Fudd, his merry medley aided and abetted by Carl Stalling's score, Mel Blanc's virtuosic vocalizations, and Freleng's A-list animation team, here led by song-and-dance impresario Gerry Chiniquy.

Freleng's ambitious black-and-white cartoon **NOTES TO YOU** (1941) depicted an anonymous pussy on a nearly identical backyard fence belting out a similarly exhaustive repertoire with similarly improbable high production values. However, that performance now registers as a rough draft for the later Freleng masterwork, whose greatness is largely ascribable to Sylvester's charisma and the tremendous star power that he radiates. Whether studiously consulting his sheet music to better splutter "Figaro!" or resorting to a huge prop rowboat to complement his crooning of "On Moonlight Bay," Sylvester the Cat triumphs as a dauntless purveyor of showbiz pizzazz, a courageous patron of the arts, and unlikely exemplar of a commitment to musical expressiveness against all odds.

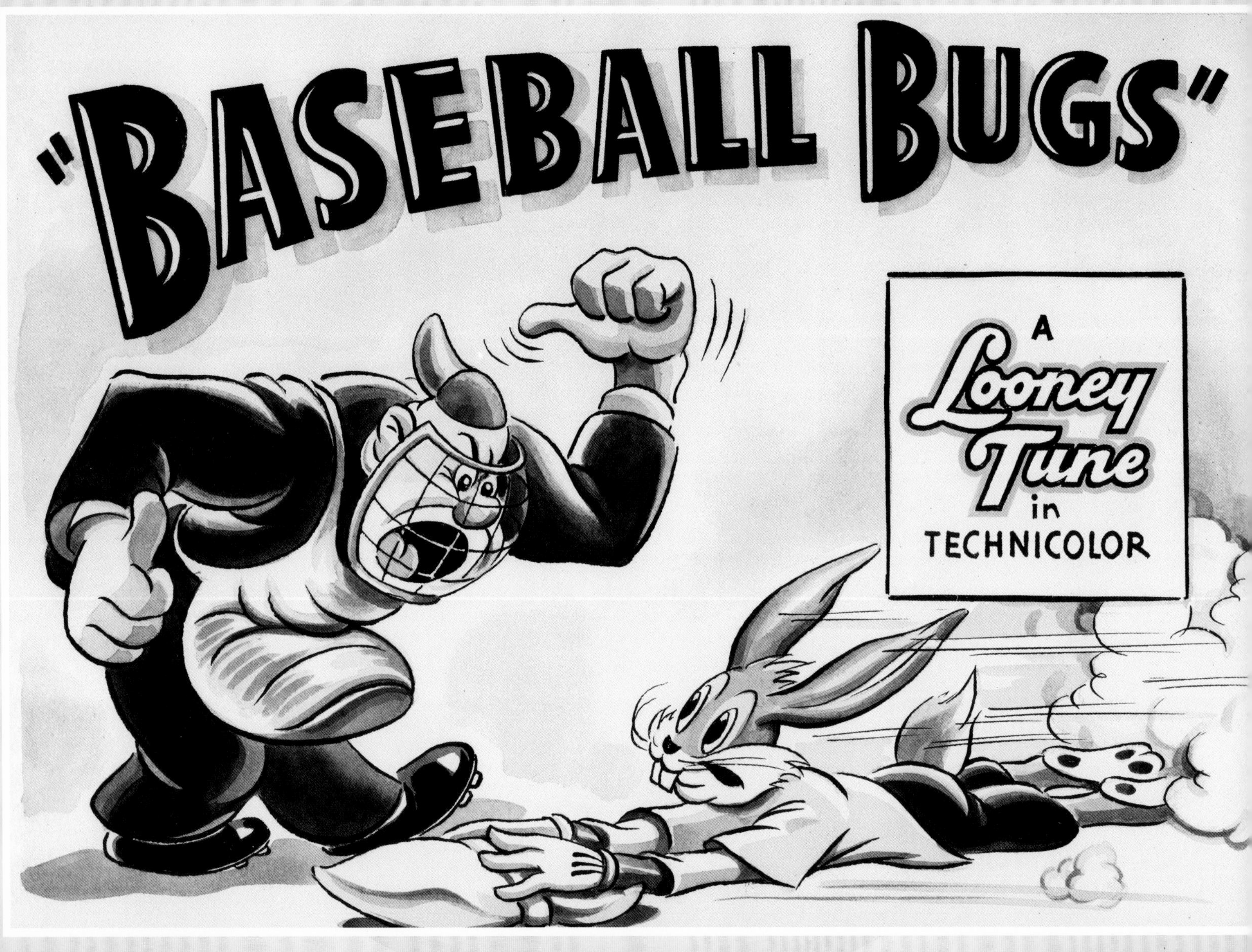
"BASEBALL BUGS"
A
Looney
Tune
in
TECHNICOLOR

Baseball Bugs

"WATCH ME PASTE THIS PATHETIC PALOOKA WIT' A POWERFUL, PARALYZING, POIFECT, PACHYDOI'MOUS, PERCUSSION PITCH."

It's a one-sided baseball game when the dirty Gas-House Gorillas, a gang of burly thugs, take on the Tea Totallers, whose star player is "only ninety-three and a half years old!" The Gorillas have the umpire in their pocket, too. Spectator Bugs Bunny is outraged with this poor sportsmanship and boasts that he could beat the Gorillas all by himself. Angered, they decide to take the rabbit up on his challenge. In the next scene, we see that a few changes have been made to the Tea Totaller lineup: "Catching: Bugs Bunny! Left field: Bugs Bunny! Pitching: Bugs Bunny!" As pitcher, Bugs perplexes most of the Gorillas with his slow ball, which moves at such a slothlike pace nobody can hit it. Running bases, the rabbit distracts one Gorilla with a pinup poster and snookers the Gorilla posing as the umpire into making a call in Bugs's favor ("I say you're safe!" the umpire finally shouts. "If you don't like it you can go to the showers!"). His hits drive one player to an early grave and turn the Gorillas into a human pinball machine. At the bottom of the ninth, Bugs Bunny has 96 runs and the Gas-House Gorillas, 95; a home run will win the game for the Gorillas. To ensure that this happens, the Gorilla at bat

uses a whole tree. Bugs chases the ball out of the park, almost sabotaged by a Gorilla posing as a taxi driver. But the rabbit makes it to the top of the Umpire State Building and catches the ball, winning the game. When the batter argues with the umpire's declaration of "Out!" the Statue of Liberty scolds him, saying, "That's what the man said, you heard what he said, he said that!"

> **DIRECTOR:** I. FRELENG **STORY:** MICHAEL MALTESE **ANIMATION:** MANUEL PEREZ, KEN CHAMPIN, VIRGIL ROSS, GERRY CHINIQUY **BACKGROUND AND LAYOUT:** PAUL JULIAN, HAWLEY PRATT **VOICES:** MEL BLANC (BUGS, OLD MAN), FRANK GRAHAM (COMMENTATOR, GAS-HOUSE GORILLA), BEA BENEDERET (STATUE OF LIBERTY), THE SPORTSMEN QUARTET **MUSIC:** CARL STALLING

DAVID GERSTEIN, animation historian The great American pastime meets the great American cartoon character—and finds him at a, er, striking disadvantage. An avid fan of the fair-playing—though decrepit—Tea Totallers, Bugs gets uncharacteristically carried away on their behalf, bragging that he could beat the opposing

Gas-House Gorillas "with one hand tied behind my back." When the humongous, cigar-smoking players confront Bugs, who genuinely seems a little scared, we really aren't quite sure which way the result will go—and it makes our emotional investment in Bugs's fate more trenchant than usual. The uncertainty is especially troubling given his position on the side of justice. A less fair, more heckler-minded Bugs might lose to Cecil Turtle and we wouldn't care; in **BASEBALL BUGS**, his loss matters.

This, then, is this classic cartoon's secret: Cool as Bugs may act at times during the story, our hero is unusually vulnerable this time—only one point ahead of the bad guys at the climax—and it makes his final win that much more satisfying. The victory is actually no mean feat, given the wacky circumstances of the story. In a more realistic ball game, "screaming" fastballs wouldn't actually scream, nor would the Gorillas' dirty plays be tolerated. But the flawless emotional setup of **BASEBALL BUGS** allows us to enjoy the impossibility as we root for our hero.

A Bear for Punishment

When a 21-alarm-clock salute blasts Henry Bear out of bed, he clobbers Junyer for having set the clocks up—until Maw explains that it's Father's Day. Paw is getting honored, whether he likes it or not. Breakfast in bed is spilled on Henry's noggin; a "good old shave" from Junyer cuts Paw up badly. Junyer can't even fill Henry's favorite pipe—"G-U-N-P-O-W-D-E-R. Deh…tobacco!"—without blasting him halfway across the cave. The big day ends with a show unmatched in stage history. Junyer recites a dopey poem for Paw, then Maw performs the world's most deadpan tap dance. By the grand finale, which involves singing, firing off shotguns, and costuming Henry as the Statue of Liberty, Paw is too shell-shocked to protest.

GREG FORD, animation historian Surely no Hollywood cartoon director has ever inserted so many of his own character poses into the action, calculatedly interrupting the flow, as did animation director Chuck Jones. Jones merges broad comedy with the utmost understatement, and never more so than in the idiosyncratic spin-off characters that comprised the bear family, one of which was the idiotic infant often voiced by the humorist Stan Freberg.

> "WHEN MY LITTLE PINK CHEEKS ARE PALE WITH FRIGHT / WHO IS IT THAT LIFTS ME AND HOLDS ME TIGHT / AND SAYS, 'THERE, THERE, LITTLE MAN, EVERYTHING IS ALL RIGHT'? / MY PAW!

DIRECTOR: CHARLES M. JONES **STORY:** MICHAEL MALTESE **ANIMATION:** KEN HARRIS, PHIL MONROE, LLOYD VAUGHAN, BEN WASHAM **LAYOUT:** ROBERT GRIBBROEK **BACKGROUNDS:** PHILIP DEGUARD **VOICES:** BILLY BLETCHER (PAW), BEA BENADERET (MAW), STAN FREBERG (JUNYER) **MUSIC:** CARL STALLING

The family's rough graphic likenesses were originally fashioned by Art Heinemann, character designer extraordinaire. However, Jones quickly made the Three Bears his own and sustained them over five exceptionally raucous films. **BUGS BUNNY AND THE THREE BEARS** (1944) gave a royal send-off to this ongoing portrait of a dysfunctional clan: the pitiable, diminutive, and always irked Papa Bear, who erupts in violent tantrums; the frazzled and frumpish Mama Bear, who seems to possess some untapped erotic reserves; and the diapered, frighteningly overgrown, cretinous Baby Bear, with his uncontrollable jags of bawling. The capstone of the series is **A BEAR FOR PUNISHMENT**, a tour de force depicting Maw and Junyer Bear's overzealous salute to Father's Day. No sooner has the slow-witted son performed a preposterously gooey poetry reading ("'My Paw,' by Junyer Bear, age seven and a half") than the normally low-key wife sashays onstage, straw hat and cane in hand, to do a fancifully choreographed tap-dance routine. But as outrageous as Ken Harris's animation of this pageant is, Jones's drawings of Paw, in intercut reaction shots, are even funnier. They eloquently capture the frustration of the poor father bracing himself in the

"A BEAR FOR PUNISHMENT"

1173

chair, a captive one-bear audience, watching the celebration in stunned disbelief. It is typical of Jones's direction that, even in the midst of one of the most energetic, floridly animated scenes in cartoon history, the primacy of the single drawing should reassert itself.

JERRY SAYS We're not sure why Junyer loves his raging dad so much, but Chuck Jones's final Three Bears cartoon peerlessly expresses the fact. Carl Stalling's score adds to the fun with ditties such as "What's the Matter with Father?" and "Father, Dear Father."

The Big Snooze

The cartoon begins with Elmer Fudd chasing Bugs Bunny all over the countryside. When Elmer follows him through a hollow log perched near a cliff, Bugs maneuvers the log to let Fudd out midair. After falling for this gag three times (animation for this sequence is reused from Tex Avery's 1941 cartoon ALL THIS AND RABBIT STEW), Fudd has a nervous breakdown. He quits, breaks his rifle in half, and rips up his contract with "Mr. Warner." He walks off the picture with his fishing gear, heading for a life of retirement. Bugs begs Fudd to reconsider, but he'll hear none of it. His mind is made up: "West and welaxation, at wast! And no more wabbits!" But as Fudd takes a nap at the fishin' hole, Bugs—who was hiding in the tackle box—decides to look into Fudd's "heavenly dream."

The rabbit downs a whole bottle of sleeping pills (labeled with the Brooklynese motto "Take Dese and Doze") and slips into Elmer's subconscious. He coats the fluffy pink clouds of Fudd's dreamscape with nightmare paint and sends the hunter into several surreal situations. First, Elmer is tied to a railroad track, and hundreds of abstract rabbits run over him. Next, the hunter, dreaming himself naked except for a ring of leaves around his waist, is given a makeover by Bugs—who dresses Fudd up as a sexy femme fatale and sets him on the corner of Hollywood and Vine. There, Fudd is quickly noticed and chased by a pack of love-hungry wolves. Bugs and Elmer run right off the

"THINK WHAT WE'VE BEEN TO EACH OTHER! WHY, WE'VE BEEN LIKE RABBIT AND COSTELLO . . . DAMON AND RUNYON . . . STAN AND LAUREL! . . . YOU DON'T WANT TO BREAK UP THE ACT, DO YA?"

dreamland clouds, now apparently falling to their deaths. Fudd crashes into his own sleeping body and awakens from his nightmare. Quickly pasting his contract back together, he happily resumes his eternal fate—chasing Bugs Bunny into the hills.

DIRECTOR: ROBERT CLAMPETT **ANIMATION:** ROD SCRIBNER, T. ELLIS, MANNY GOULD, J. C. MELENDEZ **LAYOUTS AND BACKGROUNDS:** THOMAS MCKIMSON, PHILIP DEGUARD **VOICES:** MEL BLANC (BUGS), ARTHUR Q. BRYAN (ELMER) **MUSIC:** CARL STALLING

MARK NEWGARDEN, underground cartoonist There is enough pure id embedded in THE BIG SNOOZE to keep a rumpus room of psychoanalysts deconstructing this cartoon for the next 63 years. But, in the meantime, we can just laugh at it.

JERRY SAYS This is the last cartoon Bob Clampett directed for Warner Bros. before embarking on his independent producing career, which included creating the Emmy Award–winning TIME FOR BEANY, 1949–55. Almost every cartoon Clampett directed in his final year at Warner has made it onto this "hundred greatest" list. He left the studio at his peak, having defined what a Warner Bros. cartoon is and having created numerous classic characters, including Tweety, Beaky Buzzard, and the Do-Do. In THE BIG SNOOZE, Clampett, who has drawn up imaginary worlds several times before, outdoes himself with the imagery in Elmer's nightmare. The abstract rabbits foreshadow the minimalism of United Productions of America (UPA) cartoons, and the surreal landscape combining clouds, yellow skies, and musical notes is the closest we'll come to visualizing a Looney Tunes acid trip. Clampett goes out with a bang.

Birds Anonymous

"ONCE A BAD OL' PUTTY TAT, ALWAYS A BAD OL' PUTTY TAT!"

In an opening scene that would do Hitchcock proud, Sylvester draws every blind and curtain in the house, putting the scene in total darkness so he can eat Tweety without any witnesses. One shade opens, though, and an orange feline named Clarence warns Sylvester of the hazards of bird-stalking ("Before you know it...the end of the road," Clarence mournfully says). He invites Sylvester to join B.A., or Birds Anonymous. Seeing what fulfilling lives the cats in B.A. are leading by not stalking birds, Sylvester vows to do the same. Upon returning home, Tweety is stupefied at Sylvester's joyful, non-predatory tendencies, scribbling, "Deaw Diawy, I know you won't bewieve this, but today...."

Television doesn't help Sylvester kick his habit, though, as the first thing he sees is a poultry cooking show. Nor does the radio help by playing "Bye, Bye, Blackbird" and "Red Red Robin." Sylvester tries to force himself to behave by handcuffing himself to the radiator, but his appetite proves strong enough to cause him to rip the radiator out of the wall to get Tweety! Clarence arrives just in time, launching a plunger in Sylvester's face. ("I was afraid you might be weakening." "Yeth, I did weaken. Thankth a lot.") Sylvester is unable to sleep due to his cravings and is driven out of his mind. He goes for Tweety again, but Clarence arrives in time to pour alum in Sylvester's mouth, rendering him unable to gobble Tweety, even with a straw. When Sylvester breaks down and sobs on the floor, Clarence shows him how easy cat-bird love can be by kissing Tweety—which proves too much for *him*. In the end, Sylvester has to stop Clarence from giving in to his own feline instincts.

SHAENON K. GARRITY, webcomics author and writer Sylvester the Cat was one of Friz Freleng's trademark characters. Freleng directed dozens of the cat's shorts, including the first Sylvester cartoon, **LIFE WITH FEATHERS** (1945), as well as **TWEETIE PIE** (1947), the first cartoon pairing him with Tweety Bird. No animator was better equipped to handle this deft deconstruction of the Sylvester-and-Tweety formula.

BIRDS ANONYMOUS starts as a typical Sylvester and Tweety cartoon, complete with Tweety's catchphrase, "I tawt I taw a puddy tat!" But then the plot veers into a spot-on parody of

DIRECTOR: FRIZ FRELENG **STORY:** WARREN FOSTER **ANIMATION:** ART DAVIS, VIRGIL ROSS, GERRY CHINIQUY **LAYOUT:** HAWLEY PRATT **BACKGROUNDS:** BORIS GORELICK **FILM EDITOR:** TREG BROWN **VOICES:** MEL BLANC (TWEETY, SYLVESTER, CATS) **MUSIC:** MILT FRANKLYN

Tweety and Sylvester in "BIRDS ANONYMOUS"

TECHNICOLOR®

a MERRIE MELODIE CARTOON

© 1957 WARNER BROS. PICTURES INC.

A WARNER BROS. CARTOON

Alcoholics Anonymous, which, at the time, had recently transitioned from an informal Christian support group to an international organization. "I was a three-bird-a-day pussycat until B.A. helped me," one cat testifies against a background of revival-tent music. Alas, both Sylvester and his sponsor succumb to the craving for bird, causing Sylvester to sob, lispingly, "I'm weak! But I don't care! After all, I *am* a pussycat!"

Mel Blanc's amazing vocal performances—it was reputedly the Warner Bros. short of which he was proudest—rank high among the many joys of this lovingly crafted, hilariously self-aware cartoon. Freleng and his team went all out to give **BIRDS ANONYMOUS** a film noir look, with dramatic camera angles drawn by layout artist Hawley Pratt and moody backgrounds by Boris Gorelick. Small wonder **BIRDS ANONYMOUS** won that year's Academy Award for best animated short subject. (When producer Eddie Selzer died, he willed his **BIRDS ANONYMOUS** Oscar to Mel Blanc.)

Above all, **BIRDS ANONYMOUS** satirizes Warner Bros. cartoons themselves. The structure of the standard Sylvester and Tweety cartoon—and all chase cartoons—is threatened by Sylvester's resolution to walk away from the conflict and be a better cat. In the Looney Tunes world, of course, this can't be allowed. By the end of the cartoon the balance has been restored, and Tweety delivers the fatalistic moral, "Once a bad ol' puddy tat, always a bad ol' puddy tat!"

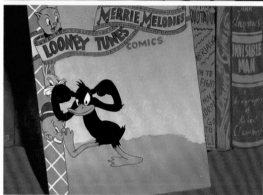

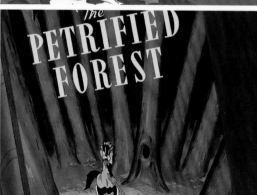

Book Revue

"STOP THAT DANCING UP THERE...YOU SILLIES!"

At midnight in a bookshop, the characters on the covers of volumes and magazines come to life. Caricatures of Harry James, Gene Krupa, and Tommy Dorsey perform a jam session, and Frank Sinatra (**THE VOICE IN THE WILDERNESS**) causes the ladies—including Mother Goose—to swoon. Daffy Duck jumps off the cover of a Looney Tunes comic book and does a song number in the eccentric style of Danny Kaye. Daffy warns Little Red Riding Hood of the Big Bad Wolf, who, after a chase through **THE PETRIFIED FOREST**, is swiftly brought to justice by **THE LONG ARM OF THE LAW**. He is sentenced to **LIFE** (magazine) but escapes, only to fall into **DANTE'S INFERNO**.

STEVE SCHNEIDER, animation historian Sad to say, **BOOK REVUE**—produced at the pinnacle (dare I say "Acme"?) of director Bob Clampett's last years with Warner Bros., one of the great runs in all of world cinema—has grown dated.

DIRECTOR: ROBERT CLAMPETT **STORY:** WARREN FOSTER **ANIMATION:** ROBERT MCKIMSON, ROD SCRIBNER, MANNY GOULD, J. C. MELENDEZ **LAYOUT AND BACKGROUNDS:** THOMAS MCKIMSON, CORNETT WOOD **VOICES:** MEL BLANC (DAFFY, CUCKOO CLOCK, SEA WOLF), SARA BERNER (HENRY'S MOTHER), ROBERT BRUCE (HENRY ALDRICH), DICK BICKENBACH (FRANKIE), THE SPORTSMEN QUARTET **MUSIC:** CARL STALLING

The waterfall of references to Jimmy Durante, Edna Ferber, Danny Kaye, Henry Aldrich, and other well-known figures of their time only speak to the most nostalgic among us, and not knowing who they are pulls much of the film's comedic punch.

But who cares? All kinds of folks take delight in Claude Lorrain's classical landscapes or Pieter Brueghel's folk pageants without knowing the characters or the tales that are being alluded to.

Instead, they're wowed by the artistry. Better simply to revel in **BOOK REVUE**'s headlong brio, overlapping settings, meticulous economy of gesture, intertwining narratives, resourceful color effects, super-efficient use of screen space—and a great, great turn by a duck called Daffy, as he dances, scat-sings, cavorts, and distorts in one of his true moments of glory (thank you for the animation, Rod Scribner!). **BOOK REVUE** is an encyclopedia of what can be done in the animated medium if you're brilliant enough.

Both killing off and pushing to unanticipated heights Warner's long tradition of "books come to life" cartoons, this undeniable masterwork has yet another elegiac quality: Within a few years, will anyone even remember what books are?

Buccaneer Bunny

"I'M A PIRATE, SEA-GOIN' SAM, THE BLOODTHIRSTIEST, SHOOT-'EM-FIRSTIEST, DOGGONE WORSTIEST BUCCANEER THAT EVER SAILED THE SPANISH MAIN."

Sea-goin' Sam is on a desert island burying his booty, but unfortunately, he chooses to bury it in close proximity to Bugs Bunny's home. When Bugs emerges from his hole, clad in some serious bling, Sam tells him that nobody's going to know the location of his treasure. "Dead rabbits tell no tales!" he growls. Bugs corrects him that it's dead *men* and almost gets Sam to shoot his own head off. Bugs is chased by the vengeful Sam and rows to Sam's pirate ship so fast he paddles without the boat under him. When Sam realizes Bugs has taken the paddles, he swims to his ship, grabs the paddles, swims back to the boat with the paddles between his teeth, and rows to the ship properly.

Onboard, Bugs is dressed as "Captain Bligh" (mimicking Charles Laughton in the 1935 MUTINY ON THE BOUNTY), and addresses Sam as "Mister Christian," giving him orders. Sam eventually sees through the ruse and continues to chase the hare, helped by his obnoxious parrot, who points out all of Bugs' hiding places. Bugs subdues Polly with a

DIRECTOR: I. FRELENG STORY: MICHAEL MALTESE, TED PIERCE ANIMATION: MANUEL PEREZ, KEN CHAMPIN, VIRGIL ROSS, GERRY CHINIQUY LAYOUT: HAWLEY PRATT BACKGROUNDS: PAUL JULIAN VOICES: MEL BLANC (BUGS, SAM) MUSIC: CARL STALLING

(fire)cracker that leaves the bird featherless ("Me and my big mouth! *Rawk!*") and then tricks Sam into sticking his head into a live cannon, blasting the pirate. Bugs takes the crow's nest elevator up beyond Sam's reach, throwing an anvil down to Sam's waiting arms and sinking the whole ship—save Bugs. Bubbling curses, Sam tosses the anvil overboard, and the ship emerges from the water ("Have a nice dip, drip?" Bugs asks him). The chase continues, and Sam keeps opening the wrong door, only to be blasted by cannons. Sam eventually corners Bugs by the gunpowder room. Bugs nonchalantly tosses a match into it, making Sam rush after it. After chasing down a second match, Sam claims if Bugs does it again, "I ain't a-goin' after it!" He keeps his word, and this time

the ship is blasted to smithereens, launching the two back to the island. Sam corners the rabbit in his hole, only to get blasted by a cannon one final time. "I have not even begun to fight!" exclaims Bugs, donning an admiral's hat.

DAVID GERSTEIN, animation historian Yosemite Sam: His very name suggests the Wild West outlaw he was first created to portray. Yet soon after cowboy Sam arrived, there were other Sams: the Saudi Sam, the Hessian Sam, even the space alien Sam. The character's bluster made any role equally funny. Sea-goin' Sam the pirate is arguably the greatest Sam role, and **BUCCANEER BUNNY** establishes why.

Let's start with what a pirate is and a cowboy isn't. A cowboy, even a villainous cowboy, needn't necessarily be a loud, furious, bellowing character. Cowboys could be subtle, strong, and silent. But pirates had to be rowdy and scary to attack ships on the high seas, and had to outdo one another in scariness to make names for themselves. Making Sam a pirate, then, put him into a role in which acting "Sam-like" was already what audiences would expect. To carve out a unique place in the pirate realm, Sam would have to out-Sam himself. The results couldn't help but be good.

In **BUCCANEER BUNNY**, Sam out-Sams himself by turning a sea shanty into a rhumba and by gritting his teeth so hard that they break. The trappings of piracy become part of the show, with booming cannons, ascending crow's nests, and stoolie parrots, all of which deliver an in-your-face impact that few other Sam stories could offer. The pirate world's high ham factor even affects Bugs, who takes on an unforgettable Captain Bligh disguise.

So memorable was Sam's sea-goin' persona, in fact, that in the early 1950s, when Looney Tunes comics made Sam into a regular character, his default role became a buccaneer rather than a cowboy. There's just something about a pirate who can't swing a sword without falling down.

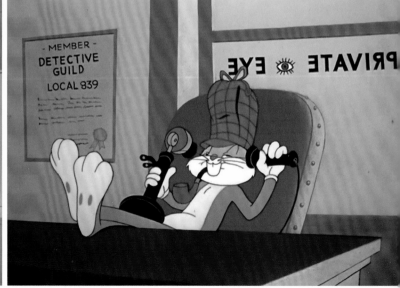

Bugs and Thugs

"OKAY, CLANCY, TAKE THE BOYS AND SURROUND THE HOUSE!"

City dweller Bugs Bunny, en route to make a withdrawal at his downtown carrot bank, is reading about hunting season and is grateful he lives in the less violent metropolis. Unfortunately, the cab he grabs for a spin around Central Park happens to be the getaway car for bank robbers Rocky and Mugsy. They take him for a ride because he "knows too much" (facts like two and two is four and Carson City is the capital of Nevada). When Rocky orders the chatty rabbit to "Shaddup!" the bunny complies by explaining at length how well he shuts up. Rocky alters the order to "Shut up shutting up!" When Bugs directs the car into an oncoming train, he is forced to rebuild the vehicle and become its fourth wheel. At the hideout, Bugs convinces Mugsy that when Rocky said to "let him have it!" he meant to give the rabbit the gun. Bugs tricks the hoods into thinking the cops have found their hideout and hides them in the gas oven. He then proceeds to demonstrate what he would never do to the stove if his pal Rocky were hiding in there—like turning on the gas and lighting it. Rocky and Mugsy are soon begging the real cops to arrest them. The rabbit returns to the city in a new role: Bugs Bunny, "private eyeball."

DIRECTOR: I. FRELENG **STORY:** WARREN FOSTER **ANIMATION:** MANUEL PEREZ, KEN CHAMPIN, VIRGIL ROSS, ARTHUR DAVIS **LAYOUT:** HAWLEY PRATT **BACKGROUNDS:** IRV WYNER **VOICES:** MEL BLANC (BUGS, ROCKY, MUGSY, POLICE) **MUSIC:** MILT FRANKLYN

ROB COLEMAN, animation director I have to say **BUGS AND THUGS** remains one of my all-time favorites. Not only are the timing and camera angles perfect, the cartoon contains one of Freleng's best callback gags—hiding Rocky and Mugsy in the stove—and even lets us in on the joke!

Realizing that he is trapped at the hideout, Bugs invents a police raid through voice and sound effects. The cops have not arrived, but Bugs is so convincing that the pair takes the rabbit's suggestion and dive for cover in the oven. I love that when Mugsy begins to bawl, Bugs pauses to enjoy the absurdity of the moment with the audience. "I must be dreaming," he says. "It couldn't be this easy." Known for his awareness that he is in a cartoon (which perhaps reached its quintessence in 1953's **DUCK AMUCK**), Bugs here again breaks the "fourth wall" with his remarks.

Bugs could make his escape after the bank robbers are in the oven, but he stays to playfully take revenge. Look for his sideways glance to the camera as he turns on the gas; he wants to make sure that we are watching. After the explosion, Bugs announces that the coast is clear, but immediately the gag escalates as the police do, in fact, arrive. Back into the oven Rocky and Mugsy scramble. We watch in glee as the real policeman bursts into the kitchen. Bugs leads us back through the lighting-the-gas gag again, word for word. It's priceless.

JERRY SAYS A remake of director Friz Freleng's earlier crime classic **RACKETEER RABBIT** (1946), which featured caricatures of Edward G. Robinson and Peter Lorre as the gangsters, **BUGS AND THUGS** is faster and funnier, has a great modern design (thanks to Hawley Pratt's layouts), and introduces two great new foils—Rocky and Mugsy—for Bugs Bunny.

Bugs Bunny Gets the Boid

"YUH KNOW SOMETHIN'? I, UH, THINK HE'S A-TRICKIN' ME."

When Mama Buzzard assigns her boys to bring home horses, cattle, and moose for dinner, bashful Beaky Buzzard wants no part of the job. But Mama kicks him out of the nest anyway, insisting he at least catch a rabbit. Dorkily scat-singing to "The Arkansas Traveler," Beaky approaches Bugs Bunny's hole. Bugs sees him coming and broadcasts fake radio landing instructions, causing Beaky to crash. Recovering, Beaky is dumb enough to let Bugs take a shower before coming with him. Bugs emerges from the shower in drag, flustering bashful Beaky before snapping the bird with his towel. Catching the rabbit in the ensuing chase, Beaky lifts Bugs skyward, but gets tickled until he lets the rabbit go. Bugs plummets back to earth at such speed that he's half-buried among some cattle bones. Mistaking them for his own, Bugs panics—then, upon finding he's okay, manipulates Beaky into being buried in the bones instead. Now Beaky thinks *he's* the one who has been skeletonized. When Beaky hollers for Mama, Bugs's future looks bleak. But when the rabbit "rescues" an intact Beaky from the bones, Mama declares Bugs a hero instead! "Uhhh…nope, nope, nope," Bugs blushes in bashful Beaky style.

> **DIRECTOR:** ROBERT CLAMPETT **STORY:** WARREN FOSTER **ANIMATION:** ROD SCRIBNER **VOICES:** MEL BLANC (BUGS), SARA BERNER (MAMA), KENT ROGERS (BEAKY) **MUSIC:** CARL STALLING

CHARLES CARNEY, former Warner Bros. writer and editor Actually, the trickin' started the other way around: The young buzzard, Killer (later called Beaky and voiced by Kent Rogers), is supposed to be getting Bugs Bunny, but we all know *that's* not going to happen. Not even two years into his development, Bugs, in the hands of director Bob Clampett and writer Warren Foster, is evolving in ways that would within a year make him America's number-one cartoon star, as popular with audiences as live action stars like Humphrey Bogart and Errol Flynn. Mama Buzzard (played in a braying Italian accent by actress Sara Berner) orders her "Keell-a" to bring home "at least a rabbit," and he reluctantly goes on a search that leads him to, of all the rabbits in the world, Bugs Bunny. Bugs lets the goofy predator off fairly easy for a few moments, trying to escape rather than taking him on, but when Killer persists, Bugs ramps it up, confusing the dimwitted buzzard by going drag ("You naughty, naughty boy!"), tickling, and—in a masterful five seconds of animation by Virgil Ross—jitterbugging with him in the midst of a furious wrestling match.

Clampett, one of the midwives of Bugs's deepening character, proceeds at his trademark breakneck speed. He allows the rabbit a moment of error—the tickling makes Killer release him in midair—and terror as Bugs crashes into the ground beneath a skeleton of a dead animal. Bugs, dazed, wails at his fate for a moment, only to break the drama with an aside to the audience ("Gruesome, isn't it?") that's pure Bugs—still in control. Bugs would go on to outwit a catalog of adversaries throughout the years, from the merely dumb (Elmer Fudd, Gossamer, The Crusher) to the diabolical (Yosemite Sam, Witch Hazel, Marvin the Martian). But his struggles with Killer, whom Clampett would later use in the less interesting Beaky solo outing

THE BASHFUL BUZZARD (1945), remain a classic of two memorable young characters in a comic battle for survival.

Bully for Bugs

"OF COURSE YOU REALIZE, THIS MEANS WAR!"

It's *corrida* time in Spain, and El Toro is making mincemeat out of a dweebish matador. After making another wrong turn at Albuquerque in an attempt to tunnel to the Coachella Valley Carrot Festival, Bugs Bunny pops into the arena. Bugs can't get directions out of the fleeing matador and only gets annoyance from the bull ("Stop steamin' up my tail!" he yells at the bull. "What are ya tryin' to do, wrinkle it?"). When El Toro rams Bugs out of sight, he promises, "This means war." The hare returns, in matador garb, and gets the bull's attention with his red cape. There's an anvil hidden behind it, which the bull smashes into headfirst. With his cape, Bugs is then easily able to entice the dazed bull to smash into a wooden fence (a sequence hilariously animated by Ben Washam). "What a nin-cow-poop!" the rabbit crows—prematurely.

After some war games that involve using the bull's horns as a slingshot for a boulder, Bugs dons a sombrero and teases the bull while smacking him, dancing to "Las Chiapanecas" (beautifully animated by Ken Harris). Bugs pushes his luck by trying to use a rifle, which the bull swallows and is able to operate, shooting bullets out of his horns. When he runs out of ammo, he swallows a box of Acme Elephant Bullets, which only succeed in blowing him up. Bugs gets the bull to run so fast that he overdoes it, going into the countryside, giving Bugs enough time to set up a Rube Goldberg–style booby trap. The trap sends the bull flying into the air, covering his stomach with glue and then sandpaper, and striking a match next to a fuse, which leads to a keg of TNT that explodes as the bull soars over it. El Toro crashes into one final fence, and Bugs covers the bull's rear with a cape reading "The End."

> **DIRECTOR:** CHARLES M. JONES **STORY:** MICHAEL MALTESE **ANIMATION:** BEN WASHAM, LLOYD VAUGHAN, KEN HARRIS **LAYOUT:** MAURICE NOBLE **BACKGROUNDS:** PHILIP DEGUARD **VOICES:** MEL BLANC (BUGS) **MUSIC:** CARL STALLING

DARRELL VAN CITTERS, former Warner Bros. creative director This film hits squarely in director Chuck Jones's sweet spot and features most of the creative team we've come to associate with his best work. According to Jones, studio production head Eddie Selzer saw a drawing of a bull on Jones's sketchpad and told him bullfights weren't funny. Story man Mike Maltese figured if Selzer was against the idea, there must be something to it.

Jones had matured as a director by this point. Not only were the cartoons funnier than his earlier efforts, they had become more deft and sophisticated. Mike Maltese was adept at writing for personality, which gave Chuck the perfect platform from which to perform via his expressive layout drawings. Mike had begun giving a different shading to Bugs Bunny's character, and this cartoon shows it off to its best advantage, with a rabbit that's more sly and confident in his response to provocations.

The bull, designed by Chuck himself, manages to be both threatening and appealing while always seeming like a bull. The play of the bull's mass against its small legs, the way the fur is rendered, and the handling of the runs, low to the ground and with no up-and-down movement, all contribute greatly to the bull's weight and menace. Jones, no stranger to stylizing motion, made good use of it here: The bull's zip-offs leave dozens of hooves dangling in midair.

Both the writing and directing are self-assured, and there is no wasted effort anywhere in the film. Jones was a master of timing and the expressive hold. Often his holds would be followed up by the movement of one body part, such as an eyebrow raise, making the statement even more effective. In his best films, such as **BULLY FOR BUGS**, his timing revealed character, making the moment all the funnier.

Bunny Hugged

"IT'S A LIVIN'!"

BUNNY HUGGED is the second time in the ring for Bugs Bunny and director Chuck Jones. In **RABBIT PUNCH** (1948) Jones put Bugs in a furious boxing match. Here, at the height of wrestling's popularity on television, he casts the rabbit as mascot to fey Ravishing Ronald (a takeoff on real-life wrestler Gorgeous George) in a contest for the world heavyweight championship. When Ronald is quickly (and literally) turned into a punching bag by his opponent, The Crusher, Bugs steps in as the "Masked Terror" to challenge the victor. After several rounds of bunny-ball bowling, ear-propeller flying, needle poking, and bank vault door slamming, Bugs (literally) pins Crusher's shoulders to the mat.

Jones and writer Mike Maltese hit their stride in this cartoon with a nonstop collection of gag situations that show off Bugs' versatility as a character: one moment living in the lap of luxury as a mascot, the next aggressively putting the corner post in a headlock, the next disguising himself as "Stychen Tyme," a tailor, in the ring to stitch the Crusher's trunks (which Bugs made him think were ripped).

DIRECTOR: CHARLES M. JONES **STORY:** MICHAEL MALTESE **ANIMATION:** KEN HARRIS, PHIL MONROE, BEN WASHAM, LLOYD VAUGHAN **LAYOUT:** PETER ALVARADO **BACKGROUNDS:** PHILIP DEGUARD **VOICES:** MEL BLANC (BUGS), JOHN T. SMITH (THE CRUSHER) **MUSIC:** CARL STALLING

PAUL DINI, TV animation producer Many good cartoons feature realistic human animation. But a great cartoon features humans so wildly caricatured that their every motion strikes us as real. **BUNNY HUGGED** is one such cartoon. In this parody of early TV wrestling shows, director Chuck Jones displays a skill for human caricature not seen since his completely different—but equally brilliant—take in **THE DOVER BOYS** (1942). From the doughy announcer and the doe-eyed slave girl to the ringlet-tressed but rubber-armed Ravishing Ronald, Jones deftly captures each human character with the same ease he might render Wile E. Coyote or Pepé Le Pew.

Jones' masterpiece, of course, is the unshaven mass of sadistic muscle who tangles with Bugs Bunny and lives to regret it. Though the galoot began his animated existence as "Battling McGook" in Jones' earlier **RABBIT PUNCH**, Bugs's dirty opponent was rechristened "The Crusher" in **BUNNY HUGGED** and has been known by that name ever since.

John T. Smith, the uncredited voice of Crusher, also growled for such memorable heavies as the bullying mutt in **CHOW HOUND** (1951), the construction worker Hercules in **HOMELESS HARE** (1950), and the Vincent Price–inspired Evil Scientist in **WATER, WATER, EVERY HARE** (1950). However, Crusher's punch-drunk ramble after colliding with Bugs' strategically placed vault door may be Smith's most fondly remembered performance: "Yeah, well, I wuz jus' passin' by...."

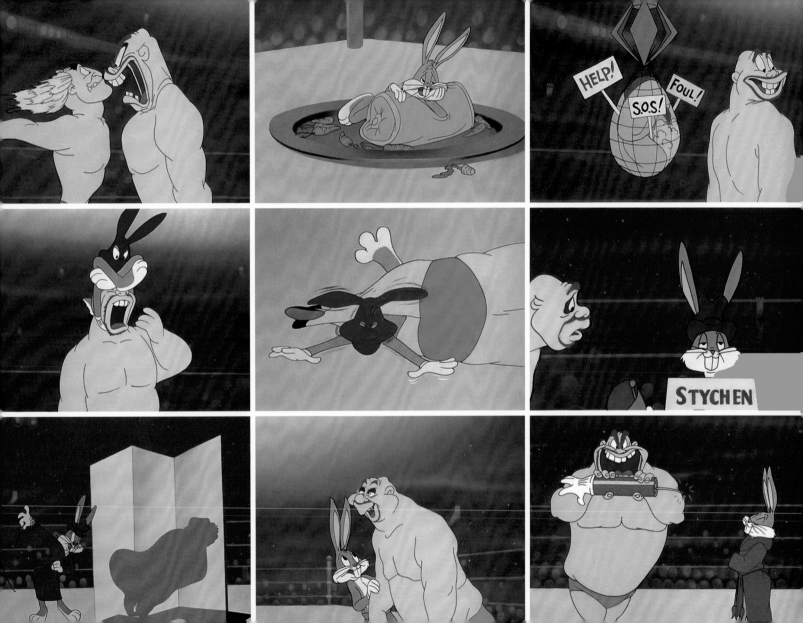

Canned Feud

"GIMME, GIMME, GIMME, QUICK, QUICK, QUICK, GIMME THE CAN OPENER!"

Mr. and Mrs. Champin (an in-joke referring to animator Ken Champin) go on vacation but forget to let the cat out. Sylvester awakens from a nap, finding himself home alone with nothing to eat. The cat also discovers he's locked in the house and, according to a note left for the milkman, that his owners will be gone for two weeks. Panic sets in as the cat frantically starts going through the kitchen in search of edible food. He is relieved to find a cabinet filled with canned tuna, salmon, and sardines. Unfortunately, the only way to get at the food is with a can opener—the only one of which is in the hands of a clever little mouse.

Sylvester first tries stomping on the cans, but no luck. He needs the can opener. The mouse withholds the opener and drives the cat to desperate measures—the kind that get Sylvester electrocuted, pummeled with a piano, and blown up. When Sylvester uses a vacuum cleaner to suck the can opener out of the mouse's hole, the rodent maneuvers the vacuum to swallow Sylvester into its bag instead. For good measure, the mouse then sucks hot coals from the fireplace into the vacuum bag to give the cat a particularly painful experience. Fed up, Sylvester grabs TNT from the basement and literally blows the house to bits to obtain the can opener. Grabbing it at last, he races to the pantry where the cans are—only to find it now bolted shut with a padlock! The mouse whistles to get Sylvester's attention, holding up his latest prize: the padlock key. Sylvester faints.

DIRECTOR: I. FRELENG **STORY:** WARREN FOSTER, CAL HOWARD **ANIMATION:** KEN CHAMPIN, VIRGIL ROSS, ARTHUR DAVIS, MANUEL PEREZ, JOHN CAREY **LAYOUT:** HAWLEY PRATT **BACKGROUNDS:** PAUL JULIAN **VOICES:** MEL BLANC (SYLVESTER, SAM, MOUSE), MARIAN RICHMAN (VI) **MUSIC:** CARL STALLING

LINDA SIMENSKY, vice president of children's programming, PBS This cartoon, which stars Sylvester the Cat, is a showcase of masterful comic timing, pantomime acting, and sustained hysteria. Thanks to the limited dialogue and simple narrative, Friz Freleng focuses on letting Sylvester act, react, and completely panic at the thought of no food for two weeks. To some degree, this cartoon does come off as a Warner Bros. version of a simple **TOM AND JERRY** cartoon, but is so strong and character-driven that it demonstrates how a simple chase cartoon can be more than a sequence of funny gags. Sylvester seems to have access to every tool he might need—except a can opener, which is in the hands of his foe. Unlike watching a **TOM AND JERRY** episode, here the viewer roots for the cat.

Chow Hound

"DON'T FORGET THE GRAVY!"

"**B**utch" the cat leaves his house for the night after dinner, looking mortified. "Hand it over!" a gruff dog orders—"it" being the steak the cat has tucked away in his sweater. "What! No gravy?" the bulldog shrieks, but devours it regardless. The dog then carries his unwitting accomplice off to the next stop in his address book. He dolls the cat up with a bow, and now he is "Harold," pet of a lady who orders him to eat and fall right asleep. The cat attempts to make the best of it but is grabbed by the dog from the window. No gravy again. The next stop is in a dilapidated section of town, where the dog is keeping a mouse prisoner in a sardine can so he can make the cat (now named "Timothy") pretend he's caught a rodent to earn his keep with an old man. ("Oh, sir, I beg you to spare me the indignity!" the mouse complains.) The mouse is knocked out with a teeny hammer to keep him in line.

At the zoo the next morning, a new addition to the exhibits arrives just in time for feeding: the saber-toothed alley cattus, our hero with fake fangs. He tries to pay the dog back by adding dynamite to this steak, but it only causes the hound slight indigestion. Nevertheless, the dog is fed up with this rut and gets the idea to hold the cat hostage, waiting for "lost cat" ads to appear in the newspaper. He collects the reward for the cat from his various owners, dressing as a safari hunter with a pygmy companion (the mouse) to return the alley cattus to the zoo. The dog spends his fortune on a meat market and eats himself sick.

DIRECTOR: CHARLES M. JONES **STORY:** MICHAEL MALTESE **ANIMATION:** PHIL MONROE, BEN WASHAM, LLOYD VAUGHAN, KEN HARRIS **LAYOUT:** ROBERT GRIBBROEK **BACKGROUNDS:** PHILIP DEGUARD **VOICES:** MEL BLANC (DOCTOR, CAT, MOUSE), JOHN T. SMITH (CHOW HOUND, ZOO KEEPER), BEA BENEDARET (WOMAN) **MUSIC:** CARL STALLING

ERIC GOLDBERG, animator and director This is one of my all-time favorite Chuck Jones cartoons for a variety of reasons, not the least of which is that it may be the darkest film he ever made (in collusion, of course, with writer Mike Maltese). The story concerns a perpetually hungry dog (perhaps a mutt cousin of the bulldog Marc Anthony, with the same voice as construction worker Hercules in 1950's **HOMELESS HARE**) who employs a beleaguered cat to go house to house to get food for him. The ruse is ingenious.

When the dog carries out his scheme to extract reward money from all of the cat's owners, watch for a couple of sly in-jokes as the dog reads the want ads looking for reward postings: the names of several animators, including one who lives at "12 Termite Terrace" (the nickname for the Warner Bros. animation studio). There is some terrific animation here as well, especially from Ken Harris, but frankly, the real star here is the story.

Spoiler alert! The darkest part of the plot comes at the payoff: After gorging himself, the dog lies bloated and belly-up in the animal hospital, unable to move under his enormous girth. After the doctors exit, we see the doorknob turn. The cat, joined by the mouse, peers in with an evil grin on his puss: "*This* time, we didn't forget the gravy!" he crows. The dog starts to plead pathetically while beads of sweat form on his head. The cat enters the frame with an industrial-size canister of gravy, and the mouse pops a funnel into the dog's mouth. Just as the cat starts to pour it in, and we start to hear the hapless dog swallow, iris out. Boy, talk about a morality play! I don't think I've ever seen comic retribution played out with such devilish, and deserved, relish. A masterpiece.

Cinderella Meets Fella

"YOO-HOO! IT'S PRINCE CHOW MEIN, CINDY— COME OUT, COME OUT, WHEREVER YOU ARE!"

DIRECTOR: FRED AVERY **STORY:** TED PIERCE **ANIMATION:** VIRGIL ROSS **VOICES:** DAVE WEBER (EGGHEAD), BERNICE HANSEN (CINDERELLA), MEL BLANC (CUCKOO CLOCK, COPS), ELVIA ALLMAN (FAIRY GODMOTHER), FRED AVERY (POLICE RADIO), PAUL TAYLOR CHORUS **MUSIC:** CARL STALLING

GREG FORD, animation historian The feverish fairy tale adaptations that famed director "Tex" Avery concocted at MGM in the mid-1940s may constitute Avery's fastest-paced, most outrageous series of cartoons, with their big-city settings, snakelike limousines, and sexy nightclub

As Cinderella sweeps the floor, her ugly stepsisters brag that they're going to the king's ball. Left alone, Cindy expects her fairy godmother to appear—but the old girl is absent, forcing Cindy to sic the police on "every beer joint" in the area. When a tipsy Fairy Godmother is finally found, she waves a gin bottle instead of her magic wand. Then, trying to give Cindy a coach, she produces Santa and reindeer before settling on a Wild West wagon and horses. At the ball, Cindy meets "Prince Charming." Revealed as a geeky, early version of Elmer Fudd, he tips his entire head to onlookers, then dances with Cindy to "Boy Meets Girl." But midnight strikes, and Cindy must flee, leaving the prince to search her out. Cindy's house, bedecked with neon signs, is easy to locate, but a note inside explains that Cindy "got tired of waiting—went to a Warner Bros. show." She's in a theater watching this very cartoon, and Elmer joins her there!

"CINDERELLA MEETS FELLA"

featuring
ELMER
A MERRIE MELODIE CARTOON
IN TECHNICOLOR

VITAPHONE # 4566
REL 3-4-17

A LEON SCHLESINGER *Production*

and altogether traditional, also posts an extraneous "No Cover Charge" sign above its drawbridge. And the formal invitation to this royal hoedown, as shown in the opening insert shot, is followed by a flashing postscript advertising the cheeseburgers at Sweeney's Drive-In.

There are visual and aural incongruities aplenty: The fairy godmother doesn't arrive on schedule, since the old crone was out gallivanting at some bar the night before. Cindy initiates a police dragnet to haul the fairy figure back in a contemporary-looking paddy wagon; the unexpected cop-action montage is edited like something lifted out of Warner's feature-film vaults. And once the fairy godmother is bum-rushed in at last, her maladroit magic wand conjures up Santa Claus and reindeer instead of a posh pumpkin coach.

The effect of this deliberate inappropriateness—the allusions to advertising, modern technology, and other myths, as well as the less-than-perfect way the actors read their lines—removes the viewer from the immediate story line and comically reminds him or her that there's a real world out there with a million things extrinsic to this fairy-tale milieu. The payoff is terrific: Prince Charming (played by Egghead) finds his Cinderella not in her humble cottage but out here, along with the rest of us. In fact, she's waving to him from the fifth row of the very theater projecting the cartoon.

songstresses. Generally speaking, however, each of those updated fables was antedated by a more subdued yet equally hilarious version he dreamed up when he was on the Warner Bros. cartoon staff. Tex's scorchy MGM item **RED HOT RIDING HOOD** (1943) was preceded by **LITTLE RED WALKING HOOD** (1937), his **SHOOTING OF DAN McGOO** (1945) by **DANGEROUS DAN McFOO**

(1939), and his sassy **SWING SHIFT CINDERELLA** (1945) by **CINDERELLA MEETS FELLA**.

CINDERELLA certifies Avery's standing as a modernist in its distanced refurbishing of the hoary old Cinderella narrative. Indeed, the director's wisecracking rewrite has all kinds of ill-fitting modern variations—the regal castle housing Prince Charming's royal ball, moated and turreted

JERRY SAYS Elmer Fudd's second appearance finds him in his early, squinty-eyed phase, billed in promo literature as "Egghead's brother." Both proto-Elmer and toupéed, wide-eyed Egghead had voices that mimicked comedian Joe Penner.

Coal Black and de Sebben Dwarfs

"I'M WACKY OVER KHAKI NOW!"

Here's the fairy tale of a mean old queen who hoards wartime luxuries like sugar and tires and tirelessly envies her pretty stepdaughter, So White. When the queen asks her magic mirror to "Send me a prince, about six feet tall," and Prince Chawmin' falls for the jitter-bugging princess instead, a line in the sand is crossed: "Queenie" calls for assassins to "black out So White." But after sexy So smothers the Murder Inc. reps with kisses, they wind up freeing her in the forest, unharmed. There she meets the Sebben Dwarfs, now an Army platoon, and takes a job as their cook. The queen invades the camp disguised as an apple saleslady, and—just like her Grimm inspiration—puts So White to sleep with her poison fruit. In the end, though, Prince

DIRECTOR: ROBERT CLAMPETT **STORY:** WARREN FOSTER **ANIMATION:** ROD SCRIBNER **VOICES:** VIVIAN DANDRIDGE (SO WHITE), DANNY WEBB (WICKED QUEEN), LILLIAN RANDOLPH (MAMMY, HONEYCHILE), LEO L. "ZOOT" WATSON (PRINCE CHAWMIN'), MEL BLANC (DWARFS, WORM) **MUSIC:** CARL STALLING, EDDIE BEAL TRIO

Chawmin's kisses fail to wake the princess up, while the littlest dwarf's kiss works instead. How come? "That is a military secret!" he squeaks.

MIKE BARRIER, animation scholar COAL BLACK AND DE SEBBEN DWARFS is one of the most famous Looney Tunes, because it's a masterpiece—but it's also one of the least seen because of what we perceive today as racial stereotypes. Bob Clampett uses those stereotypes so inventively, though, that the cartoon almost transcends them. **COAL BLACK**'s roots are in African-American culture: Clampett got the idea for the cartoon when he saw a Duke Ellington revue, **JUMP FOR JOY**, and he and his animators visited black nightclubs so that the animators could study the fashions and the dancing. **COAL BLACK** invites us to respond not to the stereotypes themselves—there's not a trace of hatred or contempt in them—but to the energy that Clampett and his animators, led by Rod Scribner, poured into those stereotypes as they responded to the vitality of black dancers and musicians.

QUEENIE   COAL BLACK   DE PRINCE

JERRY SAYS This cartoon may be the most controversial film listed in the book—and for good reason. The portrayal of its characters is based on black stereotypes that were commonplace in the 1930s and '40s, primarily seen in the entertainment media of the time: movies, stage, radio, and comic strips. This was insulting then, even more so today, but it is part of American history, and it cannot be ignored.

Created in 1942, this is perhaps the ultimate example of a cartoon of its time, as can be seen in its references to the war and wartime shortages, and its being rife with racism, violence, implied sexuality, sexism, and characters who smoke—attitudes totally unacceptable in cartoons made for children today.

COAL BLACK was never reissued to theaters. It played on TV only in the 1950s and early '60s and was forever withdrawn from television distribution in 1969. Warner Bros. has never put this film on videotape, laser disc, or DVD. Nonetheless, this cartoon is nearly unanimously praised by animation historians and critics as one of the all-time best. Judged on its animation, humor, and manic energy— and in the context of its times—it is seen as the quintessential example of Warner Bros.' trademark cartoon lunacy. And as a parody of Disney's **SNOW WHITE**, it is spot on. Despite the stereotyped images, Clampett did not set out to make a film to offend anyone. If anything, the use of actual black musicians and voice actors inform us that they were in on the joke.

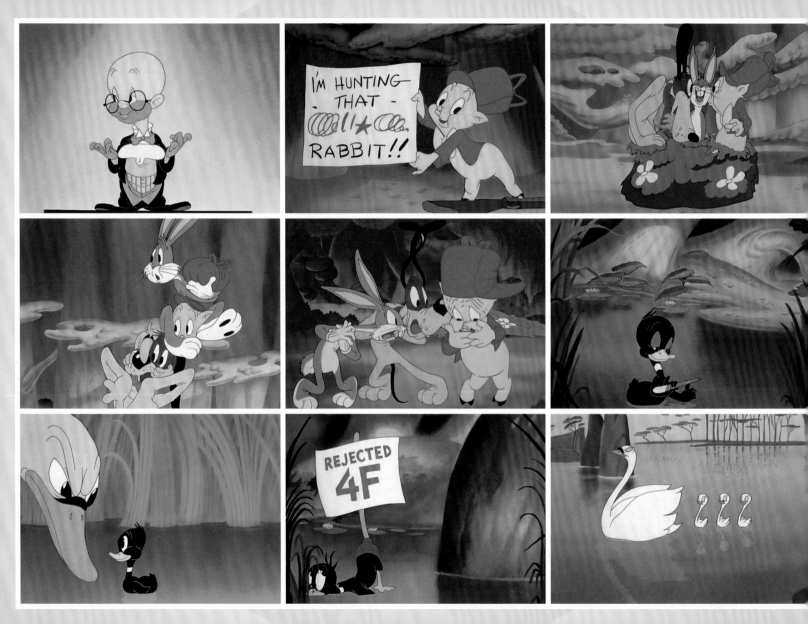

A Corny Concerto

"LISTEN TO THE WHIPPERING WHYTHM OF THE WOODWINDS AS IT WOLLS AWOUND ANA AWOUND...AND IT COMES OUT HERE!"

At Corny-Gie Hall, Elmer Fudd (mocking composer Deems Taylor) is the master of ceremonies in this biting mockery of Disney's **FANTASIA**, all set to music by Johann Strauss (save for Tchaikovsky's First Piano Concerto over the opening credits). Elmer has some trouble with his dickey as he tells us to "wisten to the wippling whythm of the woodwinds." The first act is set to "Tales from the Vienna Woods," where we find Porky Pig out hunting with his dog. Through signs, we see that Porky is "Hunting that @@!!@@ rabbit!!" (Dog: "Ditto.") We come across Bugs Bunny, who is disposing of his carrot scraps in a rabbit rubbish can. The dog spots Bugs, who shows him a page of **EMILY POST ETIQUETTE** titled "It Ain't Polite to Point!" Bugs disposes of Porky's gun in a nearby tree, angering a trigger-happy squirrel that blasts all three of them. Porky and the dog rejoice that they are not harmed, but Bugs is apparently wounded, and he faints, literally deflating. Porky and the dog mourn for the rabbit and try to dress his wounds. They quickly find that Bugs is wearing

a bra, and he shrieks like a girl. Bugs, now in a ballerina outfit, smacks Porky for his freshness, placing the bra over the two boobs' heads and prancing off into the sunset.

> **DIRECTOR:** ROBERT CLAMPETT **STORY:** FRANK TASHLIN **ANIMATION:** ROBERT MCKIMSON **VOICES:** ARTHUR Q. BRYAN (ELMER), ROBERT CLAMPETT (VOCAL EFFECTS) **MUSIC:** CARL STALLING

After we see Elmer lose his pants, we come to the next act, set to "The Blue Danube." It tells the story of the ugly duckling—namely, Daffy. Daffy tries to join a mother swan and her cygnets but is scorned. A vulture spies the tasty morsels and joins the swim, nabbing each of the cygnets but leaving Daffy (and, adding insult to injury, marking his rear with a "4F" rejection card). The mother faints into the lake when she finds her children missing, and Daffy tries to revive her by throwing more water on her head. Daffy spots the villain and makes off like a warplane to rescue his

friends. The vulture turns yellow and tries to make a run for it, but Daffy stops him, gives him a TNT keg, and pulls a cloud out from under him, causing the vulture's demise. Daffy is taken in by the mother and happily swims and sings on his merry way until his watery reflection misses a turn and crashes into a tree.

MICHAEL SPORN, animator A CORNY CONCERTO was a milestone in that it was the first Warner Bros. cartoon ever to feature more than two major characters in starring roles (Elmer, Bugs, and Porky, as well as a prototype of a young Daffy). This formula would be used repeatedly in cartoons such as **THE SCARLET PUMPERNICKEL** (1948). Other than Porky hunting a Bugs Bunny prototype in **PORKY'S HARE HUNT** (1938), this is the pig's sole outing as a rabbit hunter. The film contains no dialogue, the only spoken words being the introductions, and features lots of action synchronized tightly to the musical score.

Deduce, You Say

"I MAY BE DOWN, BUT THE JIG IS UP!"

Watkins (Porky Pig), partner of famous London detective Dorlock Homes (Daffy Duck), shares his recollections of the "Case of the Shropshire Slasher." As the story opens, we find Dorlock enjoying his favorite pastime: deducting—his taxes, that is. Dorlock mistakes a falling deliveryman for dead, until the man gets up, telling the detective he "best get that step fixed, Guvnah!" ("Just for that, you receive no gratuity," Dorlock replies.) The telegram is from the Slasher, who boasts that he's escaped from prison and is going to "start slashing innocent citizens again."

Dorlock's detecting leads him and Watkins to a pub, Henry the Eighth's Fifth, a known haunt of the Slasher. Dorlock collects clues from the patrons within, annoying Lady Ashtebula, who has her lover, Alfie, load Dorlock's beak with darts. The Slasher arrives on the scene, but Homes can't even phase the oversize thug and only gets his own neck twisted. Watkins takes over and manages to get Slasher to give his name ("Shropshire Slasher") and occupation ("Shropshire Slasher"). Dorlock tells Watkins to knock off his bumbling

DIRECTOR: CHUCK JONES **STORY:** MICHAEL MALTESE **ANIMATION:** ABE LEVITOW, RICHARD THOMPSON, KEN HARRIS, BEN WASHAM **LAYOUT:** MAURICE NOBLE **BACKGROUNDS:** PHILIP DEGUARD **FILM EDITOR:** TREG BROWN **VOICES:** MEL BLANC (DAFFY, PORKY, SLASHER), JUNE FORAY (LADY ASHTABULA, SLASHER'S MOTHER) **MUSIC:** MILT FRANKLYN

("Buh-buh-bumbling upsets Homes no end") and yet again attempts to fight the Slasher, getting himself tied up in his own shorts. Watkins convinces the Slasher to go back to prison quietly ("Yes, sir, I want to do what's right, I do," he says meekly). Meanwhile, an irate Homes lashes out at a little old lady for "hocking dandelions without a license." She turns out to be the Slasher's mother, and Dorlock is given one final beating. The Slasher leaves the pub with his mom to return to jail, leaving Watkins to ask a dazed Homes at which school he learned to be a detective. The duck's answer: "Elementary, my dear Watkins! Elementary!"

JERRY BECK DEDUCE, YOU SAY is an outrageously witty film that parodies both the original Sherlock Holmes books by Conan Doyle and the Hollywood movie versions. Chuck Jones loved placing Daffy in places he simply didn't belong. Here the duck's hilarious overconfidence is overmatched by the Victorian surroundings (handsomely designed by Maurice Noble) and oversized brutes and thugs. Porky is, of course, cast as his Watson—Watkins in this case—a clever caricature of screen actor Nigel Bruce. Writer Mike Maltese has as much fun mocking Cockney slang here ("You fancy yourself quite a toff, but I'll show you I'm toffer than you are") as he does with his faux French in the Pepé Le Pew films. The title, by the way, is a play on a British expression "The deuce [devil] you say," their way of saying "No kidding!" The premise allowed Jones to combine Daffy's frantic animated action with Porky's subtle attitudes, facial expressions, and posing, which get just as many laughs. A class act, and a first-rate cartoon.

Dog Gone South

"OH, BELVEDEAH!"

DIRECTOR: CHARLES M. JONES **STORY:** MICHAEL MALTESE **ANIMATION:** BEN WASHAM, LLOYD VAUGHAN, KEN HARRIS, PHIL MONROE, EMERY HAWKINS **LAYOUT:** ROBERT GRIBBROEK **BACKGROUNDS:** PHIL DEGUARD **VOICES:** MEL BLANC (CHARLIE DOG, COLONEL, BELVEDERE) **MUSIC:** CARL STALLING

When homeless Charlie Dog gets booted off a freight train, he finds himself in Platt Falls, south of the Mason-Dixon Line. He tries to get adopted by a proper Southern colonel, but his rendition of "Yankee Doodle" doesn't please his potential new master. The colonel's current pet dog, Belvedere, is another obstacle. First, Charlie dresses the dog in a Union cap and sticks a banner in his mouth reading "The North Forever!" Later, Charlie dresses Belvedere in a New York Yankees uniform. Eventually Charlie takes over from the ousted Belvedere and almost immediately gets another offer from a red-bearded colonel to live a more pampered life. Charlie goes off with his new master—Belvedere in disguise—who boots him back to the next freight train going north.

MARK MAYERSON, animator It's surprising to realize, given the strong impression that he makes, that Charlie Dog only appeared in five cartoons—all of them written by Mike Maltese and directed by Chuck Jones. The first three had Charlie, a conceited, conniving deadbeat, trying to con Porky Pig into taking care of him. **DOG GONE SOUTH** is Charlie's fourth appearance, and it takes him in two new directions: Charlie has a new patsy, Colonel Shuffle, and the conflict is complicated by a third party, a bulldog named Belvedere, who is so top-heavy that his back legs rarely touch the ground.

DOG GONE SOUTH parodies extreme Southern pride, as the colonel can't stand anything with a whiff of Yankee to it. Charlie ruthlessly exploits the colonel's prejudices while he sabotages poor Belvedere. Charlie is so transparently out for himself that his downfall can't evoke anything but laughter.

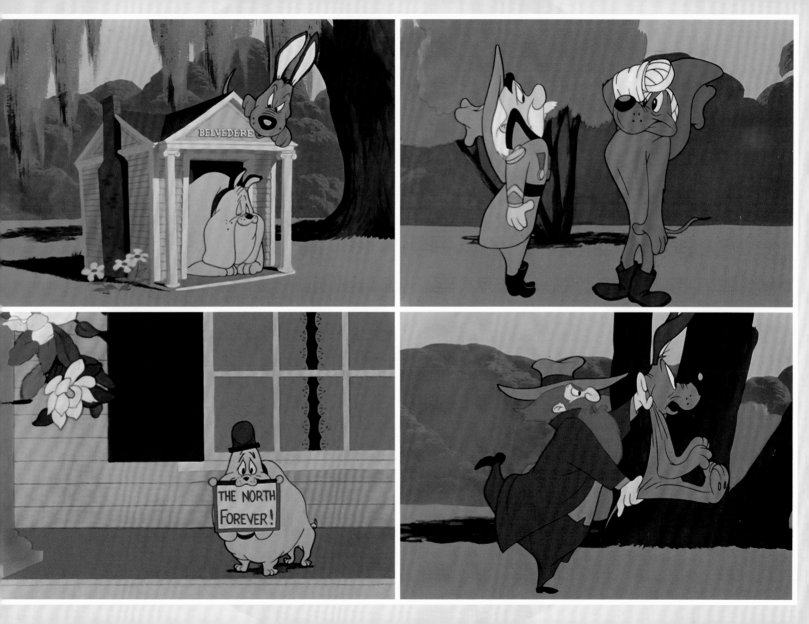

Dog Pounded

"DAT PUTTY TAT IS TURNIN' OUT TO BE AN AWFUL STINKER!"

Sylvester, downtrodden and hungry, spies Tweety in a nest singing "On Moonlight Bay." The cat rushes into things too fast, not realizing that Tweety's tree is in the middle of a dog pound, full of vicious bulldogs that he will have to get past. Sylvester tries a tightrope routine, but the dogs easily blow a gust of wind at him, causing him to fall down. He next tries tunneling underground, but the dogs are waiting down there for him, decked out in mining gear. The cat then disguises himself as a mongrel (hilariously animated by Art Davis, with Blanc ingeniously doing a "Woof! Woof!" with the cat's lisp), but the pack sees through it. Sylvester escapes, only to be brought back by a dog catcher, who tells him, "We can't have you dogs roaming the streets, you know, so we'll just put you back where you'll be safe and sound!").

More gags follow: Sylvester's technique of mass hypnotism works until Tweety awakens the dogs out of their trance with a police whistle; a rocket only blasts off Sylvester's fur; and he makes his trapeze too low, causing the mutts to dog-pile on him midair. Finally, Sylvester paints a stripe on his back, posing as a skunk, and scares them off. He finally catches Tweety—until Pepé Le Pew catches Sylvester, mistaking him for a "femme fatale" skunk.

> **DIRECTOR:** I. FRELENG **STORY:** WARREN FOSTER **ANIMATION:** MANUEL PEREZ, KEN CHAMPIN, VIRGIL ROSS, ARTHUR DAVIS **LAYOUT:** HAWLEY PRATT **BACKGROUNDS:** IRV WYNER **VOICES:** MEL BLANC (TWEETY, SYLVESTER, PEPÉ LE PEW) **MUSIC:** CARL STALLING

EARL KRESS, comic book and animation writer By 1954 Tweety cartoons had become, if not exactly predictable, then at least formulaic. However, **DOG POUNDED** is a very clever twist on the Tweety-Sylvester-Granny-Hector quadrangle. Down-and-out Sylvester hears Tweety singing in a high tree behind a fence. He dashes inside the fence, only to find it is the city dog pound and contains about a hundred bulldogs. Sylvester can't even peek through a knothole without getting his fur torn off.

Typical of this series, the rest of the cartoon is taken up by try-fail gags. As Sylvester attempts to tightrope walk across the phone lines, Tweety proclaims, "Here comes the dawing young cat on the fwying twapeze!" Musical director Carl Stalling, not usually one to miss a cue, is actually playing the song "She Was an Acrobat's Daughter" in the underscore. ("Acrobat's Daughter" was written by the team of Bert Kalmar and Harry Ruby, who had many hit songs, such as "Three Little Words" and "Hooray for Captain Spaulding," which they wrote for the Marx Brothers.)

Appropriately, the final gag is the funniest of the cartoon. Sylvester finally gets Tweety, but is interrupted by a surprise cameo from Pepé Le Pew, who proceeds to woo the "female" skunk. I wonder if director Friz Freleng needed to get permission from Chuck Jones to use his character?

Dough Ray Me-Ow

"IF I CAN'T TAKE IT WITH ME, I'M NOT GOING!"

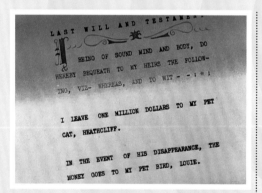

Heathcliff, an oversized, dumb housecat, stands to inherit a million dollars from his owner. Louie, a scheming pet parrot and Heathcliff's housemate, learns he is next in line for the money—and begins doing whatever he can to rid the cat of his nine lives. Unfortunately for Louie, Heathcliff's great strength and sheer dumb luck prevent the cat from succumbing to any of Louie's tricks, which include having Heathcliff play "radio" with live wires, getting shot at with arrows à la William Tell, playing "train" on real railroad tracks, and, in a sustained bit, consuming a birthday cake with explosive candles.

> **DIRECTOR:** ARTHUR DAVIS **ANIMATION:** BASIL DAVIDOVICH, J. C. MELENDEZ, DON WILLIAMS, EMERY HAWKINS **STORY:** LLOYD TURNER **LAYOUT:** DON SMITH **BACKGROUNDS:** PHILIP DEGUARD **VOICES:** MEL BLANC (LOUIE, HEATHCLIFF) **MUSIC:** CARL STALLING

MIKE MALLORY, animation historian If **DOUGH RAY ME-OW** weren't so damned funny, it would be horrifying. Of all the George-and-Lennie parodies (after Steinbeck's *Of Mice and Men*) turned out by the Warner Bros. cartoon operation, **DOUGH RAY ME-OW**'s Louie and Heathcliff are the most extreme. Louie the parrot is not simply a fast-talking cynic, he's a homicidal menace. Heathcliff the cat, meanwhile, is so colossally stupid that he forgets to inhale, forcing the parrot to slap him around while screaming, "Breathe, stupid, breathe! You forgot to breathe again!" Only after saving the cat does Louie learn that Heathcliff is set to inherit a million bucks from his owner, all of which will go to the parrot if the cat happens to disappear, thus setting an outrageous murder plot into action.

Director Arthur Davis, who habitually played things unsafely, and story man Lloyd Turner pile the gags sky high: Heathcliff cracks walnuts by putting them in his mouth and hitting his head with a mallet, and later confirms his age by referring to his birth certificate, which reads, "You're four." In turn, the animators, several of whom came from Warner Bros.' former Robert Clampett unit, present a remarkably malleable squash-and-stretch environment. Attempted murder has rarely been such a riot!

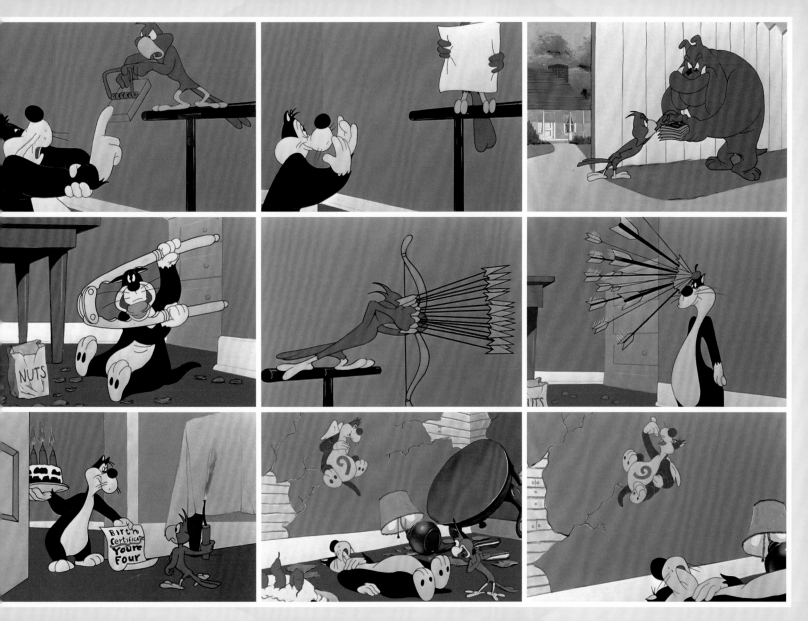

The Dover Boys at Pimento University

(Or, the Rivals of Roquefort Hall)

At "good old P.U.," the most popular guys are the clean-living Tom, Dick, and Larry Dover (parodies of Tom, Dick, and Sam, heroes of the Rover Boys series of children's books). They're off for an outing with their mutual fiancée, dear Dora Standpipe (a play on the Rovers' Dora Stanhope). Alas, they're being trailed by their seedy archenemy, "coward, bully, cad, and thief" Dan Backslide! While the boys play hide and seek, Dan kidnaps Dora in his stolen runabout and whisks her to his hideout. Alerted by telegram, the Dovers rush there to save her, but by now she's beaten up Dan so badly that he needs their help more than she does. The boys attack him anyway and manage to knock one another out—leading Dora to stroll away with an incidental character, the mustachioed sailor with a funny walk who has sauntered across the scene several times throughout the picture.

MIKE BARRIER, animation scholar Is **THE DOVER BOYS** the first "modern" cartoon, even though it

"A RUNABOUT! I'LL STEAL IT! NO ONE WILL EVER KNOW!"

parodies melodramas of the 1890s? It would be hard to find another candidate in the Hollywood mainstream with a stronger claim to that title. Chuck Jones stylized the animation in this cartoon in a way that anticipated what self-consciously modern studios like UPA would be

DIRECTOR: CHARLES M. JONES **STORY:** TED PIERCE **ANIMATION:** ROBERT CANNON **LAYOUT AND BACKGROUND:** GENE FLEURY, JOHN MCGREW **VOICES:** MEL BLANC (DAN BACKSLIDE, DICK), TED PIERCE (TOM), JOHN MCLEISH (NARRATOR), MARJORIE TARLTON (DORA), PAUL TAYLOR CHORUS **MUSIC:** CARL STALLING

doing a decade later. There's none of the realistic, Disney-like movement that Jones sought in his early Merrie Melodies; instead, he burlesques the stiffness of early photographs by throwing his characters into outlandish poses and holding them on the screen for much longer than usual. Then, when those characters move, they whip from pose to pose. The all-human cast was a novelty in early 1940s Warner Bros. cartoons, too. Future UPA luminaries like animator John Hubley noticed, and approved.

JERRY SAYS Chuck Jones's immortal send-up of the Rover Boys, the first of Edward Stratemeyer's series of novels for juveniles (Stratemeyer later created Tom Swift, the Hardy Boys, and Nancy Drew), is also a general spoof of 1900s social mores. With its pioneering use of abstract design, it marked a milestone in cartoons.

Draftee Daffy

"WHAT'S ALL THE HUBBUB, BUB?"

DIRECTOR: ROBERT CLAMPETT **STORY:** LOU LILLY **ANIMATION:** ROD SCRIBNER, MANNY GOULD **VOICES:** MEL BLANC (DAFFY, LITTLE MAN) **MUSIC:** CARL STALLING

Daffy Duck is the consummate patriot, singing an exuberant medley of flag-waving tunes—until he gets a phone call from "the little man from the draft board," which causes a 360-degree change in attitude. Daffy spends most of the remainder of the short fleeing in terror (in a hilarious run cycle animated by Manny Gould), trying to escape the diminutive, bespectacled dweeb sent to his house to deliver the duck's draft card. But no matter where in the house Daffy tries to hide—and it's amazingly large—the little man is there. Daffy finally traps the man in a safe, plasters it behind a wall, and escapes via sky rocket ("Use in Case of Induction Only," its sign reads); the rocket immediately plummets the duck to Hades. Though dead, has Daffy finally put one over on that little man from the draft board? "Well, now, I wouldn't say that!" he soon hears.

JERRY BECK Though the film is clearly Clampett's, this short's premise of the little guy who is always there owes much to Tex Avery, who used the gag before in **THE BLOW OUT** (1936, Warner Bros.) and **DUMB-HOUNDED** (1943, MGM) and would again in his tour de force, **NORTHWEST HOUNDED POLICE** (1946, MGM). In **DRAFTEE DAFFY**, however, Clampett twists the idea into a new direction: taking aim at those who would dare not serve their country during wartime. He also gives Daffy Duck the first nuance to his zany personality—something Chuck Jones would expand upon in later shorts—by making the duck an out-and-out coward. Even funnier, the little man from the draft board is portrayed by a nerdy 4F reject, who personifies government intrusion in our lives. Ironically, if Daffy used all his evasion techniques (bombs, rockets, barbed wire) against America's actual enemies, he'd be hailed a hero (as he dreams himself in director Frank Tashlin's

SCRAP HAPPY DAFFY and is portrayed in Freleng's **DAFFY THE COMMANDO**, both from 1943). **DRAFTEE DAFFY** is one of Clampett's fastest paced, most frantic cartoons, aided immeasurably by music director Carl Stalling's use of J. S. Zamecnik's rousing chase music "In the Stirrups." I love it!

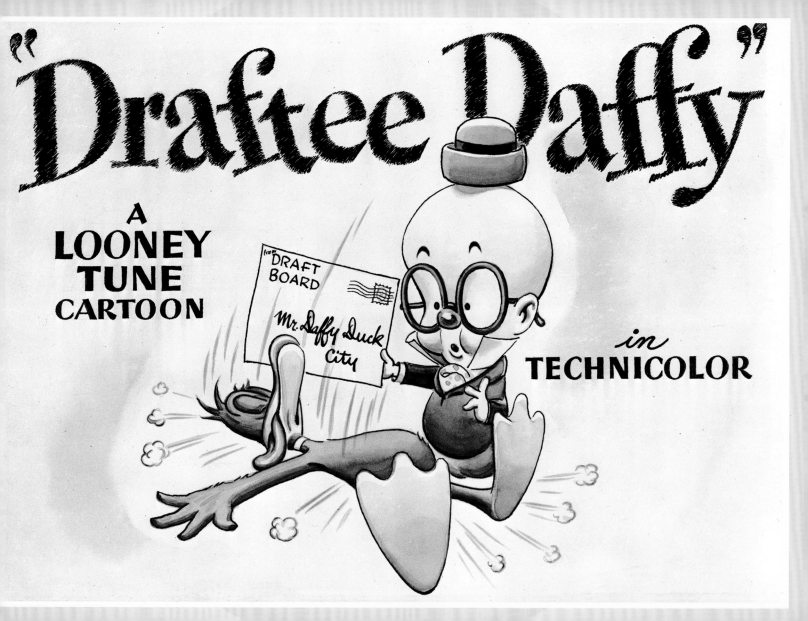

WESTERN-TYPE HERO

$ 5,000,000 00
REWARD (DEAD)

NASTY
CANASTA

Drip-Along Daffy

"THERE'S GONNA BE A SNEAK PREVIEW, AND THE SNEAKS AIN'T GONNA LIKE IT!"

O ver the opening credits, we see Daffy Duck riding into town with his assistant, Porky Pig, who is singing the hilarious original song, "The Flower of Gower Gulch." In the nearby "lawless Western town" of Snake-Bite Center, we see that the post of sheriff is vacant and that everyone is trigger-happy and looting, even the horses. Only the business of Rigor O'Mortis, "the smiling undertaker," is profiting from this bloodshed.

Daffy takes the vacant post and vows to clean up this one-horse town. He enters the saloon, quick-drawing his pants off along with his guns. The patrons give Daffy no notice, so he orders a milk shake, which is shattered by a bullet fired by Nasty Canasta, local rustler, bandit, and square-dance caller. He takes a bite out of Daffy's gun ("Probably didn't have his iron today," Daffy surmises) and forces the duck to share a drink: a concoction of cobra fang juice, hydrogen bitters, and old panther. Canasta is unaffected by it, and so is Daffy's guinea pig, Porky. So Daffy indulges, and immediately both he and Porky turn green, freaking out and singing "Mary Had a Little Lamb." When Daffy snaps out of it, he challenges Canasta to draw at sundown. During the final

DIRECTOR: CHARLES M. JONES **STORY:** MICHAEL MALTESE **ANIMATION:** PHIL MONROE, LLOYD VAUGHAN, BEN WASHAM, KEN HARRIS **BACKGROUNDS:** ROBERT GRIBBROEK **LAYOUT:** PHILIP DEGUARD **VOICES:** MEL BLANC (DAFFY, PORKY, NASTY CANASTA) **MUSIC:** CARL STALLING

showdown, Porky sends out a windup toy soldier after Canasta, which the villain laughs at—before it blasts him. Porky is hailed as the town hero and its new sheriff, to Daffy's displeasure ("Carry me! Give me the cheer! Give me the…give me one dozen roses," he whines). But Daffy is cheerful that his new job will be cleaning up after all—as a street sweeper. "Lucky for him it is a one-horse town," Porky says, winking.

ANDREW FARAGO, curator, Cartoon Art Museum
The prevailing theory about acting has always been that an absolutely great actor will lose himself in any role he plays. Olivier, Welles, Brando…all actor's actors, giants in their field, respected by virtually everyone in the business for their prowess. Daffy Duck, on the other hand, didn't get where he is today by playing by the rules. Whether he's a bellhop, a talent scout,

a beloved pet, a space-faring adventurer, a scarlet-clad swashbuckler, or a cowboy, Daffy Duck is Daffy Duck is Daffy Duck.

Here, our intrepid duck rides into the lawless Western town of Snake-Bite Center to clean it up the only way he can: full of self-assured (and self-delusional) swagger, tempered with just a bit of complete and total cowardice. The "comic relief" to Daffy's "Western-type hero" is Porky Pig, who found new life as a supporting actor once his own star began to fade. **DRIP-ALONG DAFFY** marks an important turning point in their careers, as the Warner Bros. animation stable realized that the eternally optimistic, steadfast, and—dare we say it, competent—sidekick role made Porky the perfect foil for a certain irrepressible duck.

And what better challenge for our intrepid duo than Nasty Canasta, the most physically intimidating and nastiest character in Jones's stable? Put him in a cowboy hat, dress him as a wrestler, pack him off to the Yukon, and he's always the same no-nonsense, humorless brute. Maybe he's a fellow graduate of the Daffy Duck School of No-Method Acting.

Duck Amuck

Musketeer Daffy is dueling in medieval times, when suddenly the medieval world vanishes around him! Daffy finds himself at the mercy of a prankish animator, and no matter what scene he prepares to act in, another takes its place. A farmyard becomes a snowscape, then a tropic atoll; at first Daffy gets into a new costume each time, but then the animator starts experimenting on *him*. He's repainted in bizarre colors, then redrawn as a gremlin with a flower for a head. Daffy is set on a faraway island, yelling for a close-up; the close-up comes one inch from his bloodshot eyes. The frame's edge falls in on Daffy; the vertical hold slips until two Daffys appear—and fight. After Daffy is dropped from a plane with an anvil replacing his parachute, he demands that the animator show himself. The animator does—after closing a door so Daffy can't see him. "Ain't I a stinker?" asks Bugs Bunny, artiste.

GREG FORD, animation historian Aware of its modernity at a time when Disney still clung to a nineteenth-century sense of illustrational art, Chuck Jones's masterpiece **DUCK AMUCK**, during its remarkable opening right-to-left pan, trots out a series of deliberately flattened-out and dressed-down backdrops. They not only acknowledge their own artificiality but also, in their willful inappropriateness (an igloo-graced snowscape

> "IT ISN'T AS THOUGH I HAVEN'T LIVED UP TO MY CONTRACT, GOODNESS KNOWS. AND GOODNESS KNOWS, IT ISN'T AS IF I HAVEN'T KEPT MYSELF TRIM, GOODNESS KNOWS. I'VE DONE THAT."

sliding in when Daffy is costumed as a farmer, a brightly colored Hawaiian setting clashing with Daffy's winter-wardrobed skier), frustrate Daffy

DIRECTOR: CHARLES M. JONES **STORY:** MICHAEL MALTESE **ANIMATION:** KEN HARRIS, BEN WASHAM, LLOYD VAUGHAN **LAYOUT:** MAURICE NOBLE **BACKGROUNDS:** PHILIP DEGUARD **VOICES:** MEL BLANC (DAFFY, BUGS) **MUSIC:** CARL STALLING

Duck to no end and start the picture down its path toward dislocation and comic deconstruction. And while Disney's people, even in at their most frenetic, created storms only to celebrate their attendant calm, promoting a sort of God's-in-his-heaven, all-is-one, divine-natural-order-of-things mentality, **DUCK AMUCK** offers no such quaint reassurances. When daubed with polka dots by a phantom paintbrush or reimagined as a mutant platypus, Daffy protests the unchecked capriciousness of his higher power.

The facial expressions and body language of the duck, as drawn by director Jones in highly evocative "extreme poses," convey Daffy's reactions to these grievous insults to his person. The duck glowers directly at the camera, the eye contact always implicating us, the viewers, in the cartoon's gleeful sadism. While Mel Blanc's voice-acting is masterful, writer Michael Maltese's gags are great, Maurice Noble's mismatched backgrounds are hilarious, and the Disney-derived yet highly refined "stop and start" animation executed by Ken Harris is extra crispy here, the film belongs to Chuck Jones. It's as if the misadventures that Jones customarily plunged Daffy into throughout the decade have all converged in **DUCK AMUCK**. And in this, Daffy's ultimate confrontation with an all-powerful offscreen animator-God—an absurdist study on the level

of Beckett or better—the duck emerges as half laughingstock and half existential antihero, lashing out against the ultimate void in all its grotesque derision.

While **DUCK AMUCK** (nicknamed "Daffy's Book of Job" by critic Rick Thompson) is often praised by well-meaning film scholars as a chillingly nihilistic enterprise, I have always found it a thoroughly joyful one. The film could only be perceived as a bleak torture chamber if one takes it literally and disallows the cathartic power of laughter. It's wonderful to see the slapstick tradition of Buster Keaton and Charlie Chaplin so brilliantly sustained as late as 1953. That year saw a format-crazed Hollywood in a state of turmoil, eagerly inaugurating 3-D, Cinerama, Cinemascope, and several less-enduring gimmicks. Jones's own witty plays with format in **DUCK AMUCK** seem to say that the comic indignities suffered by Daffy would remain universally funny even should the screen be reduced to the size of a postage stamp (which, at one point in the film, it is). The film's message is heartening to any lover of short-film comedy facing the ongoing artistic upheaval and technological flux of our new millennium.

JERRY SAYS This fourth-wall-breaking tour de force was a perfect vehicle for the ever-frustrated Daffy—so much so that when Jones recreated it for Bugs in **RABBIT RAMPAGE** (1956), the bunny was less believable in the fall-guy role.

Duck Dodgers in the 24½th Century

"HAPPY BIRTHDAY, YOU THING FROM ANOTHER WORLD, YOU!"

ACME DISINTEGRATING PISTOL

On the 12,000th floor of a skyscraper, hero of the future Duck Dodgers (Daffy) takes orders from Dr. I. Q. Hi, secretary of the stratosphere. The world supply of illudium phosdex, "the shaving cream atom," is alarmingly low. The one source left is way-out Planet X, which Dodgers vows to find. But aboard his rocket, Dodgers is confused by his own super-complex flight plan, while Dodgers' eager young space cadet (Porky) locates Planet X the easy way: by following Planets A, B, and C! Alas, just as Dodgers claims Planet X for Earth, Marvin the Martian arrives to claim it for Mars. Marvin zaps Dodgers with his disintegrating pistol, leaving only Dodgers' disintegration-proof vest behind. After Porky restores Daffy with his integrating pistol, Dodgers fires his own disintegrating pistol on Marvin. But "when it disintegrates," warns Daffy, "it disintegrates!"

The eager young space cadet decoys Marvin with a gift-wrapped firecracker, then Dodgers uses his "ultimatum dispatcher" gun to demand Marvin's surrender. But the Martian continues to shoot at Daffy, first with a bullet from his ultimatum answerer, then from the video screen in Dodgers's cockpit. In the end, Dodgers and Marvin use giant cannons to surround each other

with dynamite. One big boom later, Dodgers pushes Marvin off Planet X and claims it for Earth. "B-b-big deal," says Cadet: All that's left of the planet is a football-size chunk.

DIRECTION: CHARLES M. JONES **STORY:** MICHAEL MALTESE **ANIMATION:** LLOYD VAUGHAN, KEN HARRIS, BEN WASHAM **LAYOUT:** MAURICE NOBLE **BACKGROUNDS:** PHILIP DEGUARD **EFFECTS ANIMATION:** HARRY LOVE **VOICES:** MEL BLANC (DAFFY, PORKY, MARVIN MARTIAN, DR. I. Q. HI) **MUSIC:** CARL STALLING

MARK EVANIER, comic book writer I get to write about **DUCK DODGERS IN THE 24½TH CENTURY**? Oh, boy. Great cartoon. Hilarious. Eminently quotable. The obnoxious, braggadocio Daffy rubs a lot of viewers the wrong way, but that's almost the point. Director Chuck Jones and writer Mike Maltese inverted the usual cartoon convention of having the hero conquer the villain. Here, Daffy pretty much conquers himself with faulty disintegration rays and faultier personal swagger. As with the other times Jones handled the duck, the Oliver Hardy principle prevails: The joke is never the destruction that befalls the luckless character but their loss of dignity afterward.

A parody of no particular science fiction franchise—and, therefore, all of them—the cartoon has been seen as a commentary that was timely and relevant to audiences when it was released in 1953. The subtext is the futility of an arms race, and I guess you could see it as that—though I must admit, it didn't dawn on me until someone else mentioned it after my 99th (at least) viewing. Yeah, sure. That could have been on someone's mind—as an afterthought to being funny. The Duck Dodgers adventure made for a memorable cartoon that spawned a number of sequels, one or two of which some people have seen. There was also a TV series from 2003 to 2005, which often built happily on the momentum.

JERRY SAYS The quintessential Marvin the Martian cartoon features careful consistency: Daffy's space weapons are always Acme products, while Marvin's are A-1s. It's no surprise that most of the Acme gadgets backfire. What's surprising is that the Acme integrating pistol works flawlessly—maybe because relatively competent Porky is using it!

Duck! Rabbit, Duck!

"FUNNY, I DIDN'T THINK MOLASSES WOULD RUN IN JANUARY!"

In the bitter cold, Daffy is burning all of the "Duck Season" signs to fool Elmer Fudd into thinking that it's rabbit season—leading the hunter, natch, to Bugs Bunny. Daffy gets Bugs out of his hidey-hole by asking for a cup of blackstrap molasses, which Elmer riddles with bullets. Bugs plays killjoy and tells Elmer that he's not a stewin' rabbit, he's a fricasseein' rabbit, and can't be shot without the proper license. Helplessly annoyed, Daffy draws up the papers, with Bugs contributing a little spelling assistance so that Daffy makes the license out for shooting "fricasseeing ducks." After realizing he's been had, Daffy claims "I guess I'm the goat," to which Bugs replies by holding a "Goat Season Open" sign. Daffy calls Bugs a dirty dog, and Bugs calls him a dirty skunk. Appalled by this, Daffy shouts "I'm a dirty skunk?" making Bugs procure a "Dirty Skunk Season" sign. Daffy is blasted, sighing, "Brother, am I a pigeon"—and is shot again once Elmer reads Bugs's "Pigeon Season" sign.

DIRECTOR: CHARLES M. JONES **STORY:** MICHAEL MALTESE **ANIMATION:** KEN HARRIS, BEN WASHAM, LLOYD VAUGHAN, RICHARD THOMPSON, ABE LEVITOW **LAYOUT:** MAURICE NOBLE **BACKGROUNDS:** PHILIP DEGUARD **VOICES:** MEL BLANC (BUGS, DAFFY), ARTHUR Q. BRYAN (ELMER) **MUSIC:** CARL STALLING

Daffy calls Elmer aside for a briefing, while Bugs makes a decoy of himself out of snow. Elmer immediately shoots the snow rabbit, and Bugs emerges in an angel outfit. ("Golly, Mister Wabbit, I hope I didn't hurt you too much when I killed you," Elmer tells him.) Daffy exclaims, "If he's dead, then I'm a mongoose!" Bugs holds up a "Mongoose Season" sign. BLAM!

Time for more briefing. Daffy tells Elmer to not pay attention to any more signs and to only listen to him. So when Bugs emerges dressed as a duck, Daffy tells Fudd, "Shoot the duck!" and is shot himself. Daffy has a nervous breakdown and tells Elmer to keep shooting ("I'm a fiddler crab! Why don't ya shoot me? It's fiddler crab season!"). Bugs, now dressed as the game warden, tells a disoriented Elmer that it's baseball season and sends Fudd on his way, shooting a single baseball into the distance. Now alone, Bugs asks Daffy what season it is really, and Daffy replies that it's of course duck season. Daffy is immediately shot by a hoard of hunters. Panting and smoking, he crawls to a smug Bugs to utter, "You're desthpicable."

DAVID GERSTEIN, animation historian "I'm a wed-hot sportsman after wild game," says Elmer Fudd, unconvincingly—for whatever a red-hot sportsman might be, the naive, inept Elmer is not it. "I'm a duck bent on self-preservation," says Daffy Duck, unconvincingly too, for preserving oneself hardly requires destroying someone else. But Daffy is at least as adamant about promoting rabbit season as he is about concealing duck season. Daffy is so obstinate that, apparently just for laughs, he'll try to get Bugs killed in the act of doing an everyday favor. "Shoot him! Shoot

him!" he shouts at Elmer. Daffy is a villain here as in no earlier short. But where some cartoons with evil Daffy fail, **DUCK! RABBIT, DUCK!** succeeds because the exaggeration of the villain role blends perfectly with the cartoon's exaggeration of Bugs, its exaggeration of Elmer—and its exaggeration of logic.

    DUCK! RABBIT, DUCK! is a cartoon that derives its entire mood from pushing gags past conventional Looney Tunes limits. Bugs often puts on disguises, but here his body simply transforms

to suit his needs (the "fricasseeing rabbit" label is just *there*). Daffy is often gullible, but here he can write out "fricasseeing duck" without seeing it. It is as if by ratcheting up an atmosphere of tension and extremes, director Chuck Jones and writer Mike Maltese can put anything over on us—and succeed by openly celebrating the fact. You think Elmer is easy to fool? They crank it up a notch, making Elmer less a character and more a destruction engine. Any hunting season sign, raised under any pretense, becomes a license

to kill. Later, as a quasi-logical extension of the conflict, when Daffy tells Elmer that appearances mean nothing—"You're just going to listen to me" —Elmer instantly agrees, and we instantly accept it. Extreme characters can reshape their world, and ours, through willpower alone. It's the shock doctrine of animated cartoons.

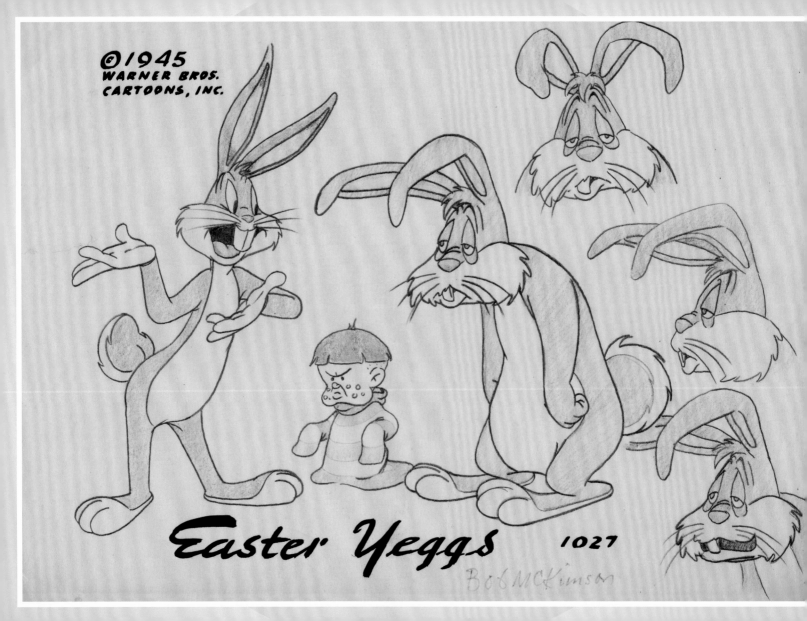

Easter Yeggs   1027

Bob McKimson

Easter Yeggs

"I WANNA EASTA EGG! I WANNA EASTA EGG!"

little kid into pounding it with a hammer. In the end, Bugs dispatches the Easter Rabbit with an explosive Easter egg.

DIRECTOR: ROBERT MCKIMSON **STORY:** WARREN FOSTER **ANIMATION:** CHARLES MCKIMSON, RICHARD BICKENBACH, I. ELLIS **LAYOUT:** CORNETT WOOD **BACKGROUNDS:** RICHARD H. THOMAS **VOICES:** MEL BLANC (BUGS, EASTER RABBIT, DEAD END KID), ARTHUR Q. BRYAN (ELMER) **MUSIC:** CARL STALLING

Bugs Bunny meets up with the sobbing Easter Rabbit, who is complaining of sore feet, and volunteers to take over his one and only chore—delivering Easter eggs. Bugs's first stop is the home of a vicious little kid who promptly attacks the rabbit. After escaping, Bugs visits the house of Elmer Fudd, who is at first disguised as a baby and later, with the help of his Dick Tracy hat, sets a series of traps for the purpose of making Easter Rabbit stew. Bugs winds up painting Elmer's head like an Easter egg, and tricks the

EARL KRESS, comic book and animation writer **DAFFY DOODLES** (1946), Robert McKimson's directorial debut, and **EASTER YEGGS** are two of the director's very best. This short begins with a beautifully painted title card and the folk song "Some Sunday Morning," which is used as underscore throughout. Warren Foster's script shows that even the lines in a cartoon that don't set up gags should have character, like when Bugs calls the basket of eggs "technicolor hen fruit" or when the Easter Rabbit says, "Every year I get some dumb bunny to do my job."

Bugs takes over for the Easter Rabbit and meets up with a "dead end kid," a play on the group of kid actors called the Dead End Kids, who debuted in the 1938 Warner Bros. movie *Angels with Dirty Faces*. It's the beginning of the period of McKimson's chubby Bugs, although the rabbit gets even plumper by the time of **A-LAD-IN HIS LAMP** (1948) and **BOWERY BUGS** (1949). There are plenty of gags and nice pacing here that make this cartoon one of my favorites.

Eatin' on the Cuff

(Or, The Moth Who Came To Dinner)

"CONFIDENTIALLY...SHE STINGS!"

A live-action, piano-playing narrator (Leo White, with vocals by Mel Blanc) tells the story, in song, of the moth and his flame (his fiancée, a honeybee). The moth is on his way to get married but is distracted by a bar full of delicious pants ("Pre-war cuffs!" he exclaims), leaving his darling tearful at the altar. Realizing he's late, the moth scurries for the church, but is halted by a nymphomaniacal black widow, who tries to woo the little guy by dressing as Veronica Lake, though she can't quite hide her bulbous

DIRECTOR: ROBERT CLAMPETT **STORY:** WARREN FOSTER **ANIMATION:** VIRGIL ROSS **STARRING:** LEO WHITE (NARRATOR) **VOICES:** MEL BLANC (NARRATOR VOCALS, MOTH) SARA BERNER (BEE, BLACK WIDOW) **MUSIC:** CARL STALLING, DAVE KLATZKIN (PIANIST) **SONG:** MICKEY FORD

nose. After chasing the moth around, the widow uses a flame to put him in a trance. Then she captures him and brings him to her place for a rendezvous. Hearing the moth's screams for help, the bee comes to his rescue and battles the widow with her stinger. Reunited, the couple embraces. But our narrator isn't quite satisfied, wondering "what that cute little bee could see in that silly moth! What a dope!" The moth replies to this by eating the narrator's pants, leaving him to run through the studio set in his shorts, knocking into everything in sight as he flees.

MARK KAUSLER, animator EATIN' ON THE CUFF was Bob Clampett's last black-and-white Looney Tune. The short has a real story, unlike the two

he made before it, **NUTTY NEWS** and **WACKY BLACKOUT** (both released earlier that year), which are spot-gag cartoons. **EATIN'** has the strong streak of comic vulgarity that informs the best of Bob's stories. There are many wonderful scenes in the picture, especially the little moth's enthusiastic reaction to the fabric sample he tries in the barroom scene (animated by Rod Scribner). After he eats a lot of the men's pants, the moth sits slumped in a chair in a characteristic Scribner pose as he slowly pulls a zipper out of his mouth and displays it to the camera, a suggestive gag made funny by the wonderful flexibility of the Moth's face as he mouths, "Darn those zippers," his face suggesting that the zipper tastes bad.

Clampett assigned most of the comic character close-ups in the picture to Rod Scribner, such as when the black widow says, "Confidentially, she stings!" to the audience, or "I don't want to set the world on fire. . . ." In that scene, her mouth moves way over to the side of her head; as it moves around within her head shape, realistic teeth and jaw structures emerge behind the plasticity of her flesh, the contrast between hard and soft giving even more illusion of flexibility to Scribner's animation. Scribner also handled the close-ups in which the widow disguises herself in a peekaboo blonde wig. The animation of her huge nose slowly emerging from behind her tresses and vibrating to a stop makes one of the funniest (and filthiest) Clampett-Scribner scenes ever.

Virgil Ross animated effectively the duel between the honey bee and the widow, who brandish the stingers in their tails like foils. I love the squash and stretch Virgil put into the ladies' abdomens as they duel as if they're in an Errol Flynn picture.

The live-action wraparounds with Leo White draw the audience into the cartoon. White had acted in Charlie Chaplin comedies, and his silent-film background comes into play in the cartoon's final shot. After the moth eats the narrator's pants, Leo scrambles into the sound stage in the background, camera undercranked to speed up his apparent motion. As he tangles with props and wrestles with a big stepladder, Mel "woo-woos" on the soundtrack.

8 Ball Bunny

"PENGUINS IS PRACTICALLY CHICKENS!"

When a Brooklyn theater's big ice skating show closes, the touring company accidentally leaves star performer Playboy Penguin behind. The mute little bird toddles after his troupe's vans, but falls into Bugs Bunny's rabbit hole instead. A sympathetic Bugs offers to help Playboy get home—only to learn too late that penguins come from the South Pole. The trip starts on a train, where Bugs must protect Playboy from a hungry hobo. Next comes a ship headed out from New Orleans—but it's actually headed back to Brooklyn, requiring another rescue. Bugs and Playboy swim to Martinique, where a two-man boat is built—and where a panhandling Humphrey Bogart appears. Bogie keeps turning up over the duration of Bugs's trek: They travel through the Panama Canal, into a cannibal village, through crocodile-infested swamps, and over stormy seas. But upon reaching the Pole, Bugs finds out that this isn't actually Playboy's home. He is, in fact, "the only Hoboken-born penguin in captivity!" When panhandling Bogie walks back into the picture, a desperate Bugs gives him the penguin to resettle this time.

> **DIRECTOR:** CHARLES M. JONES **STORY:** MICHAEL MALTESE **ANIMATION:** PHIL MONROE, BEN WASHAM, LLOYD VAUGHAN, KEN HARRIS, EMERY HAWKINS **LAYOUT AND BACKGROUNDS:** PETER ALVARADO **VOICES:** MEL BLANC (BUGS, HOBO), DAVE BARRY (HUMPHREY BOGART) **MUSIC:** CARL STALLING

JEFF SMITH, cartoonist A small black penguin in a top hat crying ice-cube tears in the snow—it's probably one of my favorite sight gags in a Looney Tunes cartoon. Bleeding-heart Bugs promises to get the penguin safely home and begins to rifle through a book to find out where penguins live. The answer comes as quite a shock: the South Pole. The title of the cartoon may be about this very moment, when, having already made his promise, Bugs suddenly finds himself in an impossible position—behind the 8 ball. But true to his word, Bugs Bunny takes the penguin by the flipper and sets off on a southward journey filled with adventures and strange encounters.

There are a couple of brilliant gags along the way, like the hungry hobo they meet on their boxcar ride to New Orleans, who plans to eat the tiny bird because "pen-goo-ins is prac-tic-ally chickens," and a recurring gag that features a memorable caricature of Humphrey Bogart showing up at the most unexpected times and asking (as he does in the movie *Treasure of the Sierra Madre*), "Pardon me, but could you help out a fellow American who's down on his luck?"

8 BALL BUNNY feels more like one of Chuck Jones's one-shot cartoons, such as **FEED THE KITTY** (1952) or **ONE FROGGY EVENING** (1955), than the standard Bugs vs. Elmer outing. **8 BALL BUNNY** involves long time spans, days of travel, very few blackout gags, and a story with an actual beginning, middle, and end. Also, the little performing penguin is a bit of a cross between Michigan J. Frog and Marc Anthony's adorable kitten: He's a performer with a top hat, and he's so cute, he's unbearable. In a perfect Chuck Jones kind of way, of course.

> **JERRY SAYS** One of the few Bugs cartoons to treat an adventure theme semiseriously, **8 BALL BUNNY** is proudly inconsistent with Playboy Penguin's other classic-era appearance: **FRIGID HARE** (1949) finds the penguin happily at home in the Antarctic.

Falling Hare

"HEY! COULD THAT HAVE BEEN A GREMLIN?"

DIRECTOR: ROBERT CLAMPETT **STORY:** WARREN FOSTER **ANIMATION:** ROD SCRIBNER, BOB MCKIMSON **VOICES:** MEL BLANC (BUGS BUNNY, GREMLIN), BOB CLAMPETT (VOCAL EFFECTS) **MUSIC:** CARL STALLING

Bugs Bunny is sitting on a blockbuster bomb underneath an airplane at a military base, laughing while reading about gremlins "and their die-a-bull-i-cull sab-o-tay-gee" (the scene is superbly animated by Bob McKimson). A little gremlin then appears, not only trying to set off the very bomb Bugs is sitting on, but convincing Bugs to do the job himself! Bugs gets wise and tries to nab the hijacker, but instead the gremlin gives him some substantial abuse with a monkey wrench. As soon as the rabbit is aboard the plane, the gremlin successfully gets it running. The little saboteur attempts to crash the plane into a few towers for sport, but Bugs foils these plans, sending the plane up a few thousand feet and then to the earth at a record-breaking speed ("Incredible, ain't it???" reads the air speedometer). The gremlin remains nonchalant as the plane loses its wings and Bugs loses his mind. But, alas, the plane sputters and comes to a halt before crashing—when it runs out of gas. "You know how it is with these 'A' [gasoline rationing] cards," confides Bugs to us, now in complete control again.

DAVID BOWERS, animator and director FALLING HARE is wonderful for many reasons, but the most fun to be had is seeing someone finally get the better of Bugs Bunny. The usually unflappable rabbit is outwitted and terrorized by a tiny gremlin with a dopey disposition. I have a real soft spot for director Bob Clampett; for me, he is, hands down, the funniest of the Warner Bros. directors. I love the way he has Bugs look and act in this cartoon—all teeth and wild poses.

Aside from containing possibly the best use ever of banana peels in a cartoon—and that's saying something—the final big joke is a masterpiece of comic staging. Clampett pours on the suspense as Bugs and the gremlin hurtle toward the earth in a crashing bomber. **FALLING HARE** is filled with great sight gags, but it is also exciting, edge-of-your-seat stuff, decades ahead of its time in terms of action staging and cutting. It builds and builds until…well, the fantastic punch line: They run out of gas a few feet from the ground. It's surreal, inspired, and, best of all, hilarious.

JERRY SAYS Originally titled **BUGS BUNNY AND THE GREMLIN**, the title was changed shortly before release to appease Disney's interests regarding its quickly abandoned gremlin feature film.

Fast and Furry-Ous

"BEEP! BEEP!"

ROAD RUNNER
(ACCELLERATII INCREDIBUS)

A dazzling blur rushes through the desert— so fast he tears the main title and credits signboards out of the ground. Frozen via still-frame, the speedster turns out to be the Road Runner, with the hungry Coyote watching him through binoculars. Coyote chases Road Runner with a knife and fork and seems to catch up, but the bird puts on an extra burst of speed, leaving slack-jawed Coyote far behind. Defeated, Coyote decides to halt Road Runner through strategy.

But a pot lid held out as a barrier fails to stop his prey, and when Coyote throws a boomerang, Road Runner throws his own. Coyote thinks a phony school crossing will force the bird to slow down, but Road Runner bowls over his schoolgirl-costumed foe.

DIRECTOR: CHARLES M. JONES **STORY:** MICHAEL MALTESE **ANIMATION:** KEN HARRIS, PHIL MONROE, BEN WASHAM, LLOYD VAUGHAN **LAYOUT:** ROBERT GRIBBROEK **BACKGROUNDS:** PETER ALVARADO **EFFECTS ANIMATION:** A. C. GAMER **VOICES:** PAUL JULIAN ("BEEP, BEEP!"), MEL BLANC (COYOTE SOUNDS) **MUSIC:** CARL STALLING

The try-fail gags continue: Coyote next tries a ride-on rocket, only to have it ram him upward into a ledge. A painted cliffside tunnel turns real when Road Runner darts into it; a TNT blockade fails to blow up, but the TNT plunger does. The Coyote dons an Acme Super Outfit to fly after the bird, and instead soars off a cliff. Finally, jet-propelled tennis shoes make Coyote as fast as his prey, except he loses Road Runner on a looping cloverleaf highway. In the end, thinking he hears the bird returning, Coyote raises an axe to attack—only to get hit by a beep-beeping truck instead. Need we mention who is riding in the back seat?

CHARLES CARNEY, former Warner Bros. writer and editor The greatness of this first pairing of Coyote and the object of his desire, the Road Runner, is obvious to any Looney Tunes fan. From the first frames, as the great bird of the Southwest blasts past the credit signs in a whirl of dust and wind, it's clear that something big is happening here. This cartoon lights the fuse for what audiences would come to expect over the run of dozens of Wile E. Coyote–Road Runner shorts. From Wile E.'s (initial) optimism to Road Runner's nonchalance in the face of a determined predator, **FAST AND FURRY-OUS** has the symphonic, witty sense of timing that Chuck Jones and his writer, the bountifully funny Mike Maltese, were developing as a team at Warner Bros.

From the soon-to-be-trademark Latinate species labels (here, *Accelleratii incredibus* vs. *Carnivorous vulgaris*) to the sequence of Wile E.'s exquisitely paced, painful efforts to bag a meal, this initial outing created in seven minutes a timeless screen legend as durable as Charlie Chaplin, Buster Keaton, and Oliver Hardy. Coyote's basic "humanity" in simply following his instincts—with the help of an arsenal of devices that defy the laws of physics and momentum but always, eventually, yield to gravity—makes him a character of great sympathy. (Jones himself was, he would admit, flummoxed by all things mechanical.) The would-be predator's imploring looks to the audience bring the humor from the cinematic to the personal. Who among us hasn't seen our best plans go south at exactly the wrong time? And the Road Runner—a force of nature in his ability to turn the highway into a flapping ribbon in the wind—reminds us of our own futile attempts to harness something beyond our control. The painted tunnel on a mountain wall, misfiring rockets, faulty flying suits, and rebellious boulders are all here, prototypes for a canon of immortal, Sisyphean comic gags.

JERRY SAYS Called simply "Coyote" in this debut appearance, Wile E. wouldn't receive his official first name and middle initial for a couple of years, when they appeared in a Bugs Bunny cartoon, **OPERATION RABBIT**. In the meantime, Looney Tunes comic books briefly called him Kelsey Coyote.

Feed the Kitty

"DON'T YOU DARE BRING ONE MORE THING INTO THIS HOUSE!"

When the bulldog Marc Anthony confronts Pussyfoot the kitten, the kitty responds to his barking by climbing onto the dog's back, ripping at his fur, and then curling up to sleep. Marc Anthony's paternal instinct kicks in, and he kisses the kitten good night, walking home carefully so he won't wake the cat. Meanwhile, the dog's mistress is furious over the mess the dog has been making and warns him not bring another thing into the house. So Marc Anthony hides Pussyfoot under a soup bowl, and the kitten scurries away under it into a mouse hole. Marc Anthony tries to retrieve Pussyfoot but only ends up with a confused mouse. He later finds the kitty attacking a ball and driving a toy car, and has to pass the little guy off as a windup toy and then a powder puff to get him by the lady of the house.

Later on, hearing his mistress, Marc Anthony hides Pussyfoot in the flour bin, doing it just when she plans on baking some cookies. The dog naturally tries everything to prevent his buddy from being baked, including passing himself off as a rabid dog, but it only angers her further ("My whipped cream!" she shouts upon seeing his foaming mouth) and gets him thrown out of the house. Pussyfoot, covered in cookie batter, climbs out of the bowl just in time for Marc Anthony to think she's used the egg beater on him. The dog is in further agony as he thinks his pal is being rolled, shaped, and baked. The hound finally breaks down and cries for the allegedly dead kitten (a powerfully effective scene animated by Ken Harris).

Marc Anthony is later allowed back in the house, and his owner tries to cheer the sad mutt up with a kitten-shaped cookie. He places it on his back like old times and has another good cry, only to be shocked to find that Pussyfoot is still alive and purring. But his mistress finally gets wise. The dog's jaw drops when she tells him that he can keep Pussyfoot as long as he takes care of him. Reunited, Pussyfoot curls up for another nap, and Marc Anthony covers the kitten with a tuft of his fur.

DAVID GERSTEIN, animation historian How do you do sentimentality right? So many cartoons have tried—and so many cartoons have failed. In fact, many classic 1930s Disney and Fleischer cartoons were hailed as sentimental classics in their era but come across as overcooked ham today. Certain emotion-grabbing ploys simply feel too calculated, too melodramatic, in the context of our more cynical age.

DIRECTOR: CHARLES M. JONES **STORY:** MICHAEL MALTESE **ANIMATION:** KEN HARRIS, PHIL MONROE, LLOYD VAUGHAN, BEN WASHAM **LAYOUT:** ROBERT GRIBBROEK **BACKGROUNDS:** PHILIP DEGUARD **VOICES:** BEA BENADERET (WOMAN), MEL BLANC (MARC ANTHONY) **MUSIC:** CARL STALLING

Into the mix comes **FEED THE KITTY**—a story that still resonates fifty-odd years on. What is its secret? Not melodrama, for its melodrama isn't entirely unlike that of mushier animated predecessors. Not conscience, for many earlier shorts also meant well. No, **FEED THE KITTY**'s secret is its wonderful mixing of these elements with flawlessly timed humor and awesome character designs: Director Chuck Jones's visuals were simply at the peak of their power when they came together with this story, and they make all the difference.

When Marc Anthony initially tries to intimidate Pussyfoot, he is a raw, roaring force of nature; when Pussyfoot balks, Marc Anthony's one-eye stare is the essence of distilled befuddlement. When Pussyfoot settles down on Marc's back for the first time, the big dog enters a sleepwalk-like bliss that represents happiness to a T—but is also impossible to view without laughing. And when Marc Anthony unwittingly transports not Pussyfoot but a mouse on his back, the bulldog's momentarily bloodshot

eyeballs shoot beyond shock to suggest anger at a trauma level.

When a story of big-brotherly love can feature a dog at various times fainting, playing mad, and growing dishpan eyes upon grabbing his owner's ankle—yet still captivate us with its believably real emotions—we know that that story has accomplished something outstanding.

Gorilla My Dreams

"I AIN'T AN APE! I'M A RABBIT! LOOK: LONG EARS, FLUFFY TAIL, TECHNICALLY KNOWN AS A RODENTUS RABBITUS!"

In a parody of the then-popular jungle movie genre, shipwrecked Bugs Bunny washes up in Bingzi-Bangzi and is immediately adopted by love-starved Mrs. Gruesome Gorilla. Bugs decides to play along, but Mr. Gorilla isn't very happy with the new arrival. "Daddy" takes "Junior" for a little walk and begins to play rough with the lad, starting with a game of oopsy-daisy—which propels Bugs into the stratosphere—and leading to a wild back-and-forth rumble in the jungle, all to the tune of Raymond Scott's "Dinner Music for a Pack of Hungry Cannibals." Bugs ultimately wears out the gorilla by allowing himself to be beaten to a pulp, a strategy that perhaps inspired Muhammad Ali in the boxer's 1974 "Rumble in the Jungle" against George Foreman.

DIRECTOR: ROBERT MCKIMSON **STORY:** WARREN FOSTER **ANIMATION:** CHARLES MCKIMSON, MANNY GOULD, JOHN CAREY **LAYOUT:** CORNETT WOOD **BACKGROUNDS:** RICHARD H. THOMAS **VOICES:** MEL BLANC (BUGS BUNNY, GRUESOME GORILLA, MRS. GRUESOME) **MUSIC:** CARL STALLING

MIKE MALLORY, animation historian Bugs Bunny is at his brashest and most fearless in **GORILLA MY DREAMS**, a drivingly funny romp staged with breathless energy and flawless timing by director Robert McKimson. This cartoon also pits the rabbit against one of his most formidable opponents, the hilariously terrifying Gruesome Gorilla (whose bear-trap grimace is the ultimate reflection of McKimson's fascination with teeth).

Like so many postwar couples, Gruesome and Mrs. Gorilla of Bingzi-Bangzi (the "land of ferocious apes," a helpful sign explains) long for a family. At least, Mrs. Gorilla does; Gruesome hates the idea. The ensuing grudge match between the roaring, angry would-be father and his recalcitrant, long-eared "baby," set to the raucously jazzy music of Carl Stalling and Raymond Scott, is prime Warner Bros. cartooning.

DUCK TWACY

The Great Piggy Bank Robbery

"NOTHING'S IMPOSSIBLE TO DUCK TWACY!"

TO GANGSTER HIDEOUT

THIS IS IT! ENTRANCE

Comic book maniac Daffy Duck receives the latest issue of Dick Tracy and pores over each exciting panel. Pretending to be like his hero, Daffy accidentally knocks himself out and dreams he is Duck Twacy. Investigating a wave of piggy bank thefts, he is led to the gangsters' hideout, where he encounters a plethora of villains inspired by Chester Gould's famous comic strip: Mouse Man, Snake Eyes, Pussycat Puss, Double Header, Jukebox Jaw, Rubber Head, the dreaded Neon Noodle, and an actual Dick Tracy villain, Flattop. The duck mows them down

with a machine gun and rescues his piggy bank—waking up from his dream, he finds himself kissing a sow in a muddy pigsty back home.

DIRECTOR: ROBERT CLAMPETT **STORY:** WARREN FOSTER **ANIMATION:** ROD SCRIBNER, MANNY GOULD, J. C. MELENDEZ, I. ELLIS **LAYOUTS AND BACKGROUNDS:** THOMAS MCKIMSON, PHILIP DEGUARD **VOICES:** MEL BLANC (DAFFY, NEON NOODLE, RUBBER HEAD, PIG) **MUSIC:** CARL STALLING

STEVE SCHNEIDER, animation historian This isn't just an appreciation of **THE GREAT PIGGY BANK ROBBERY**, it's a love letter to the late Bob Clampett, auteur of this loopiest of tunes, this marviest of melodies, this greatest of all short animations—that is to say, my favorite Warner Bros. cartoon. Banners and bouquets to the great Bob C. for this still-astonishing mélange of ultra-silliness and film noir. He creates a realm where stylizations feed into the fugue states so beloved of the director, where animation's capacity for compressing and distending time and space (and bodies!) is stunningly realized, where terror and

hilarity are shown to be natural bedmates, and where the whacked-out visions come so fast and thick that the thing seems to anticipate MTV by forty years.

Inspired but the nutcase characters featured in Chester Gould's Dick Tracy comic strip, Clampett created a one-of-a-kind trip that still leaves viewers slack-jawed ("What did those guys have in the cooler?" I heard just the other day). That this unhinged, yet seamlessly disciplined, fever dream was plunked out by the assembly line—just one of 37 cartoons released by Warner Bros. in its annus mirabilis of 1946—attests both to the genius of the system and the visionary genius of Bob Clampett, who overstepped constraints of genre and expectation to deliver something extraordinarily new. A tip of the Sherlockian hat to this master and all his crew, particularly the fantabulous animator Rod Scribner, who does things with Daffy Duck's body that you really shouldn't try at home. On every level, this masterpiece remains unbelieva—and I still don't say this lightly—ble.

A Gruesome Twosome

"COME WITH ME TO THE CASBAH—INCOGNITO! BABY, WE CAN'T MISS! YOU'D LIKE A PAIR OF NYLONS, HUH? THEN HOW ABOUT A KISS?"

It's wooing night in the back alley, with tomcats and tabbies canoodling along the fence tops. One feisty girl cat has two rival suitors: the Jimmy Durante–like Colonel and big, dumb Snooks. The girl doesn't want the pair to fight over her, so she says she'll date the first cat to bring her a bird. The two tomcats' rivalry leads to chaos in the ensuing hunt—and it doesn't help that their target is Tweety, who pounds the cats' paws with a mallet and tricks them into fighting in midair. Finally forced to team up, the cats try to catch Tweety unawares by disguising themselves as a horse. But the "naked genius" bird slips an angry bee and a giant bulldog inside the cats' costume with them. "I get rid of more puddy tats that way!" he says.

DIRECTOR: ROBERT CLAMPETT **STORY:** WARREN FOSTER **ANIMATION:** ROBERT MCKIMSON, MANNY GOULD, ROD SCRIBNER, BASIL DAVIDOVICH **LAYOUT AND BACKGROUNDS:** THOMAS MCKIMSON, MICHAEL SASANOFF **EFFECTS ANIMATION:** A. C. GAMER **VOICES:** MEL BLANC (TWEETY, DURANTE CAT, DUMB CAT), SARA BERNER (FEMALE CAT) **MUSIC:** CARL STALLING

MIKE BARRIER, animation scholar A GRUESOME TWOSOME is the third and last of Bob Clampett's cartoons with his baby bird, Tweety, and it rivals the first one, **A TALE OF TWO KITTIES** (1942), as Clampett's best with the character. Like the earlier cartoon, **A GRUESOME TWOSOME** pits Tweety against two cats, and Tweety is so overpowering that even two foes seem like far too few. There's scarcely a hint here of the cute yellow canary that Tweety would become when director Friz Freleng took the helm. Clampett's Tweety is not a baby bird anyone would want to encounter in a dark alley.

JERRY SAYS A GRUESOME TWOSOME's wooing kitties make pretty—well, arguably pretty—music to the classic 1919 song "Me-Ow" by Mel B. Kaufman and Harry D. Kerr. A favorite of house musician Carl Stalling, the melody enlivens many a Looney Tune.

Guided Muscle

"BEEP, BEEP!"

Wile E. Coyote (*Eatibus almost anythingus*) is stewing a delicious tin can for dinner but is revolted at the sight of himself sitting down to enjoy it. The Road Runner (*Velocitus delectiblus*) speeds by, giving the coyote some hope, but the bird proves to be too fast for him to catch by primitive methods. He launches himself from a bow (complete with an arrowhead screwed to his snout) just to smash into a cactus that topples off a cliff. A slingshot only succeeds in launching him into the ground—and even at that, a few seconds too late—and a cannon backfires Wile E. into a canyon wall. Wile E. so thoroughly coats the road in grease that he can't escape an oncoming truck; the bird is able to slide across it with ease anyway, leaving Coyote (in a great scene of frustration animated by Ken Harris) unable to extract himself from his slippery situation. The fuse of a dynamite stick dangled from a fishing rod fails to ignite the explosive, the fire instead continuing up the fishing rod it was dangling from, down the coyote's backside, and into a box of TNT. Wile E. consults **HOW TO TAR AND FEATHER**

A ROAD RUNNER (tenth printing) and makes a device that only manages to tar and feather the coyote. (The Road Runner reminds him with a sign: "Road runners already have feathers!") A final planted dynamite stick blows up the coyote, and he has finally had enough, putting up a sign: "Wanted—one gullible coyote—apply to manager of this theater." He ends the cartoon by dragging the "That's all, folks!" logo out.

> **DIRECTOR:** CHARLES M. JONES **STORY:** MICHAEL MALTESE **ANIMATION:** RICHARD THOMPSON, KEN HARRIS, BEN WASHAM, ABE LEVITOW **LAYOUT:** PHILLIP DEGUARD **BACKGROUNDS:** RICHARD H. THOMAS **VOICES:** PAUL JULIAN ("BEEP, BEEP!") **MUSIC:** CARL STALLING

JERRY BECK If I had to pick a "pure" Road Runner–Coyote film, this would be it. It's one of Chuck Jones's best chase films, produced at the peak of his artistic powers. By this time—this only being the sixth of twenty-three Road Runners that Jones would direct during the golden age—the characters are clearly defined, their motivations firmly established. The gag setups and payoffs are classic. Jones and his team make an art out of split-second timing and extreme facial reactions. **GUIDED MUSCLE** was also produced during the brief period when background-layout animator Maurice Noble was away from the studio (he was off designing industrial films for John Sutherland), and I prefer the more realistic—though still artistically stylized—backgrounds and layouts by Richard Thomas and Phillip DeGuard. They give the boulders more weight, the cliffs and jagged peaks more texture—and with those, more comic peril for the Coyote.

You'd never know from the classic comedy revealed here that at this time Jones considered the Road Runner cartoons to be throwaway, bread-and-butter pictures, simple gag reels that could be knocked off fast to allow him to extra time to work on a very special film—to wit, **ONE FROGGY EVENING**!

COYOTE
(Eatibus almost anythingus)

ROAD-RUNNER
(Velocitus Delectiblus)

TNT

WANTED
ONE GULLIBLE
COYOTE
APPLY TO
MANAGER
OF THIS
THEATER

Hair-Raising Hare

"MONSTERS LEAD SUCH IN-TERESTING LIVES!"

Bugs Bunny is getting ready for some shut-eye and can't help but think he's being watched. And indeed he is: A Peter Lorre–type scientist is watching him via television, planning on feeding Bugs to his pet monster. The scientist sends out a sexy female bunny windup decoy that immediately lures Bugs to the castle, where the scientist traps him inside. "Ya don't need to lock that door, Mac," Bugs coyly says. "I don't wanna leave!" Upon smooching the decoy, it becomes immediately dismantled. ("That's the trouble wit' some dames! Kiss 'em and they fly apart!" Bugs complains.) The scientist informs Bugs he has another little friend, but when he hears the monster's shrieking, Bugs sarcastically packs his luggage, indicating it's time he left ("Don't think it hasn't been a little slice of heaven—cause it hasn't!"). The monster, a big mound of red hair wearing tennis sneakers, is released, and chases Bugs around the castle.

DIRECTOR: CHARLES M. JONES **STORY:** TED PIERCE **ANIMATION:** BEN WASHAM, KEN HARRIS, BASIL DAVIDOVICH, LLOYD VAUGHAN **LAYOUT AND BACKGROUNDS:** ROBERT GRIBBROEK, EARL KLEIN **VOICES:** MEL BLANC (BUGS, SCIENTIST, MONSTER) **MUSIC:** CARL STALLING

Coming up against an open trapdoor, Bugs thinks fast, poses as an effeminate manicurist, and does the monster's nails ("I said to my girlfriend just the other day, *gee*, I'll bet monsters are interesting. . . ."), taking care to snap the beast's fingers in a few mousetraps. Bugs hears the monster sneaking on the other side of the wall and gets him to give away his position, allowing the rabbit to smack the monster unconscious (through the wall!) with a mallet. After having "disposed" of the monster, Bugs makes to take his leave, only to find the monster poised in a suit of armor, wielding an axe. Bugs fights back with an oversize horse and suit of armor, complete with a lance that socks the armored monster into the wall. Having "re-disposed of the monster," Bugs makes another attempt to leave, only to be caught by the beast. Bugs fools the fiend into getting frightened by something truly horrifying: the audience. "People!" the monster shrieks, as he runs through the walls in terror. As Bugs announces his "re-re-dispos[ing]" of the monster, the decoy returns. "Mechanical," Bugs says, before it plants a wet kiss on him. "Well . . . so it's mechanical!" he concludes, and follows off in a mock decoy walk.

J. J. SEDELMAIER, animation director, designer, and producer **HAIR-RAISING HARE** has always been a personal favorite of mine because I'm convinced it must have been one of the first Bugs cartoons I ever saw as a kid watching TV in the Chicago area. To this day, I can't hear "People!" without thinking of the safety-orange monster

screaming at the end. Also, whenever I've had to draw or design rubber gloves for a project, I immediately refer to the ones worn by the scientist at the opening of the story.

It's interesting to see how different Bugs's character is in this film, from, say, the cool and calm Bugs in **RABBIT SEASONING** (1952). He's much more the Groucho Marx type in this short; in fact,

I doubt you'll find another cartoon in which he does the Groucho walk more than here. The other unique aspect that has always grabbed me about this particular cartoon is the design of the monster. Where do his hands and arms go when we don't see them? Why the sneakers? It's this sort of stuff that reminds me why I love good cartoons: You don't *care* about this stuff. You just enjoy it.

JERRY SAYS This film's sequel, **WATER, WATER, EVERY HARE** (1952) actually named the red-haired monster "Rudolph," while in the later **DUCK DODGERS AND THE RETURN OF THE 24½TH CENTURY** (1980) Chuck Jones rechristened him "Gossamer." The latter has stuck as the "official" name.

A Ham in a Role

"CARTOONS! BAH! DEGRADING OCCUPATION. STOOGE FOR A CAT AND MOUSE!"

We begin at the ending of your typical Looney Tunes cartoon: A dog, standing on two legs, gets a pie in the face and runs a finger over his lips in the classic be-bee-dee-ba-bee-dee reaction. The Looney Tunes end-title card drops in front of him as a backdrop and the closing theme music plays.

Suddenly, we are behind the scenes. Indignant, the dog actor crawls out from under the backdrop, wipes himself off, knocks six pies out of his left ear, and reflects, "No longer shall I degrade myself in hammy slapstick. It is my destiny to become a great Shakespearean actor." He's in for it. Before he has even stepped one foot toward the door, he is subjected to a sublime succession of humiliating sight gags, of which he is completely unaware until the pen from his resignation letter to Mr. Warner clouds the tub of water that he's fallen into.

But we know from the credits that the stars of this cartoon are really the Goofy Gophers. And through their dainty ways, they will obliterate him and his high-falutin' words. Dog finds

DIRECTOR: ROBERT MCKIMSON **STORY:** SID MARCUS **ANIMATION:** CHARLES MCKIMSON, PHIL DELARA, J. C. MELENDEZ, EMERY HAWKINS **LAYOUT:** CORNETT WOOD **BACKGROUNDS:** RICHARD H. THOMAS **VOICES:** MEL BLANC (ACTOR, GOPHER #1, DIRECTOR), STAN FREBERG (GOPHER #2) **MUSIC:** CARL STALLING

our heroes fast asleep in the hollowed-out pages of his fat volume of the Bard's works as he tries on his best "To be or not to be." They must have read those pages as they cut them out, because as the dog perseveres through a series of characters and costume changes, the gophers cut him down with tricks that reflect the very words he is speaking. The ghost from HAMLET's "sulphurous and tormenting flames" has them giving him a hotfoot. They respond to Dog-as-Juliet's cry to drink by pouring a whole bathtub of water through a hole in the ceiling, and make sure her rose "by any other name would smell as sweet"...as the Limburger cheese they drop on his head. One of the gophers appears as Yorick,

who becomes a skeleton that dances in the dark. As Dog is clad in armor, a magnet makes him bounce painfully around his house. The ultimate and decisive blow comes as the dog wails, "A horse, a horse!" and they wheel a real horse toward him in a kicking stance. As Dog is jettisoned back to the studio, he cries, "Parting is such sweet sorrow."

Back in time for the next setup, the dog stands on his mark before the camera and declaims "To be or not to. . . ." as he gets a pie in the puss. The Looney Tunes end-title card drops in, and the theme music plays for real. He is literally put back in his place.

LIA ABBATE, artist and writer A HAM IN A ROLE certainly wins a place among the best of them for the sheer amount of highbrow entertainment and lowbrow slapstick it packs into its short length, and the brilliant way in which these opposing dynamics match up. In the cartoon's standard running time of six minutes, we are treated to a greatest hits of William Shakespeare with no less

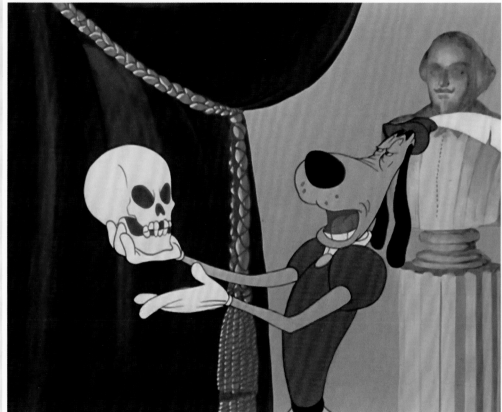

than ten of his best quotations. And for each spate of speechifying, there is an equal amount—more, really—of inspired physical gags. The genius of the cartoon is that each gag is a play upon the quotation itself, executed in such a crafty way that you never even see the culture coming at you, or much less care.

This Merrie Melodies short from director Robert McKimson was produced a year after the fall 1948 releases of Laurence Olivier's *Hamlet* and Orson Welles's *Macbeth*, when Hollywood was abuzz with the Bard. And so here we have the perennial scene of the bit actor who aspires to greatness.

You don't have to know a word of Shakespeare to enjoy all this great slapstick. Nevertheless, if you do, you'll be delighted to find that **A HAM IN A ROLE** truly is an appreciation of what we Shakespeare lovers cherish the most: his words.

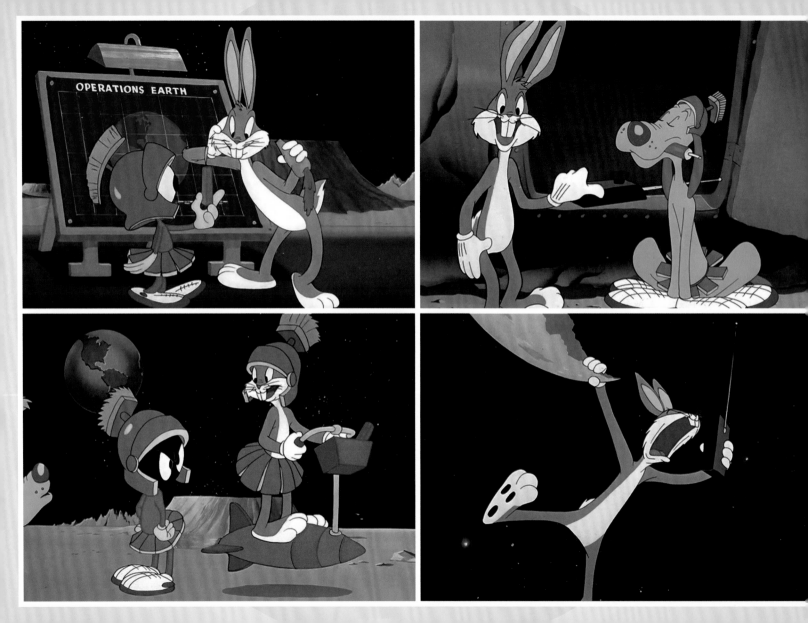

Haredevil Hare

"YOU MAKE ME VERY ANGRY! VERY ANGRY INDEED!"

As the cartoon opens, headlines announce, "Heroic Rabbit Volunteers as First Passenger" on a rocket to the moon. We see that it's Bugs Bunny, who (in a brilliant opening animated by Ken Harris) is being dragged kicking and screaming. "I've got a wife and kids! Millions of kids!" he hollers. But he's convinced to go when he sees a supply ship dropping a ton of carrots into the rocket. Bugs tries to leave via the escape hatch, but upon seeing Earth is now long gone, concludes that "only a coward would desoit his ship." The rocket makes a successful crash landing, causing Bugs to throw a series of fits (hilariously animated by Ben Washam). Bugs decides it's not so bad being the first living thing on the moon (passing by some "Kilroy was here" graffiti), until a rocket from Mars lands. A dinky man from Mars, sporting Roman war gear and tennis shoes, pops out of the rocket, and proceeds with his diabolical plans. He tells Bugs straight out that he's going to blow up the Earth with his invention. Bugs foils this plot by taking off with the incendiary device ("All the people I know are on the Earth!" he says). The Martian sends his faithful dog after Bugs and the Uranium Pew 36 Explosive Space Modulator.

After a failed attempt at contacting Earth (Bugs only receives a jingle: "Crumbly Crunchies are the best / Look delicious on your vest / Serve them to unwanted guests / Stuff the mattress with the rest!"), Bugs fools the dog into letting him keep the explosive. The dog realizes his error and charges Bugs, leaving the two in a comedic embrace. The Martian boots the dog for his foolishness while Bugs returns the explosive to them. This time it's rigged to a detonator, and Bugs sets it off, destroying most of the moon. Bugs gets through to the scientists, with a statement for the press: "GET ME OUT OF HERE!" We end with Bugs hanging onto the last bit of moon—with the Martian and his dog.

DIRECTOR: CHARLES M. JONES **STORY:** MICHAEL MALTESE **ANIMATION:** BEN WASHAM, LLOYD VAUGHAN, KEN HARRIS, PHILIP MONROE **LAYOUT:** ROBERT GRIBBROEK **BACKGROUNDS:** PETER ALVARADO **EFFECTS ANIMATION:** A. C. GAMER **VOICES:** MEL BLANC (BUGS, MARVIN MARTIAN, A.K.A. COMMANDER X-2) **MUSIC:** CARL STALLING

PAUL DINI, TV animation producer Before director Chuck Jones cast Bugs Bunny in the more or less permanent role of unflappable hero, the director and his animators seemed to delight in emotionally challenging their long-eared star. Nowhere is that more gleefully apparent than in 1948's **HAREDEVIL HARE**, wherein the reluctant space-going rabbit is called upon to display terror, greed, nonchalance, innocence, and frustration, with side trips to wise-guy confidence and doe-eyed flirtation. Ben Washam's brilliant animation of Bugs's extended post-crash jitters is reason enough to place this cartoon among the Warner Bros. greats.

But that wasn't enough for Jones. In **HAREDEVIL** he gives Bugs a new adversary: an alien commander of mild temperament and destructive intent. Later named Marvin the Martian, the persnickety little warrior is in stark contrast to the dimwitted Elmer Fudd, the mindlessly savage Tasmanian Devil, and the roarin' mad Yosemite Sam. Whereas those other enemies are just after the rabbit, the soft-spoken little Martian seeks nothing less than the complete annihilation of Earth. Marvin proved popular enough to bring back in four subsequent shorts, including the Daffy Duck vehicle **DUCK DODGERS IN THE 24½TH CENTURY** (1953), as well as numerous TV appearances and a full galaxy of licensed products.

A Hare Grows in Manhattan

"WELL, LOLLY, YOU KNOW HOW I HATE TO TALK ABOUT MYSELF, BUT... UH, LEAVE US TURN BACK THE CLOCK!"

At Bugs Bunny's palatial Hollywood rabbit hole, our star recounts his New York youth for gossip reporter Lola Beverly. We see baby Bugs's rabbit hole in a window box; we then join teen Bugs as he dances through town, singing "The Daughter of Rosie O'Grady." The seemingly naïve hare looks like an easy mark to bulldog bully Spike and his gang. But their "dog-pile on the rabbit" ends up with Bugs on top. Spike chases Bugs to an automat, where Bugs gives him a pie in the face, and then onto a rooftop, where Bugs tricks Spike into chasing a stick off the building's edge. The canine grabs a clothesline to arrest his fall. Bugs forces him to let go and thinks he's won. But Bugs has forgotten the rest of the mob, who menacingly surround our hero. Mounting a last stand, Bugs spies a bookstore's outdoor display and grabs a heavy tome to use as a weapon. But there's no need. When Spike and his gang see the title of the book, they all turn around and run: **A TREE GROWS IN BROOKLYN**. Being dogs, they want to go check it out.

> **DIRECTOR:** I. FRELENG **STORY:** MICHAEL MALTESE, TED PIERCE **ANIMATION:** VIRGIL ROSS, GERRY CHINIQUY, MANUEL PEREZ, KEN CHAMPIN **LAYOUT:** HAWLEY PRATT **BACKGROUNDS:** PHILIP DEGUARD **VOICES:** MEL BLANC (BUGS, BULLDOG), BEA BENADERET (LOLLY), TED PIERCE AND MICHAEL MALTESE (DOGS) **MUSIC:** CARL STALLING

LINDA SIMENSKY, vice president of children's programming, PBS There were several Bugs Bunny biography cartoons over the years. They didn't always match up, which I suppose is helpful in explaining the importance of character over backstory. In **A HARE GROWS IN MANHATTAN**, we get a glimpse of Bugs as he now lives as a Hollywood star, affecting movie-star diction and talking to the press. And then we get to see how Bugs started out a young innocent, up against the tough sweater-and-bowler-hat-wearing dogs of New York's Lower East Side.

Bugs begins as a bowtie-wearing rabbit tap-dancing down the street. Once he encounters the dogs, we have, in this cartoon, our first glimpse of Bugs as a winner. In the classic dog-pile scene, we think Bugs is at the bottom of the pile, but no, he's on the top, chanting the loudest. The line, "I'll murdalize you!" still gets a big laugh today, although I am not sure I can explain exactly how one gets murdalized.

One inspired bit of animation in this cartoon is the scene in which Bugs confuses the dog by dancing in a neon Egyptian-cigarette billboard. This scene today is edited for airing, given the shock viewers might experience seeing the word "cigarette" and the visual gags involving them.

JERRY SAYS Bugs Bunny's classic dog-fight saga also introduces Spike, who would be joined by his little buddy, Chester, for later battles with Sylvester. In **MANHATTAN**, Spike's voice starts out mean but gets increasingly oafish; in later shorts, the bulldog would be generally grimmer in tone.

The Hep Cat

"SOMETHING NEW HAS BEEN ADDED!"

Rosebud, a dog bearing a strong resemblance to one later called Willoughby, unsuccessfully chases after a cat every night. "You almost got him tonight," consoles an eavesdropping robin. All the cat really wants to do is to pitch some woo to the local gals, as he explains in an original rendition of "Java Jive" (primarily animated by Virgil Ross). Rosebud uses this addiction to his advantage, first with a failed love letter ("A ren-daze-vooze!" says the cat) and then with a female kitty puppet. This works well until the cat squeezes Rosebud's nose and kisses him full on the mouth. The cat is chased onto the clotheslines, where he gets Rosebud tangled up in baby clothing. The cat returns to his make-out session with the puppet, even after the robin informs him that she isn't real. "Well…I can dream, can't I?" he says.

EARL KRESS, comic book and animation writer This cartoon is one of director Bob Clampett's bat-out-of-hell-paced efforts. There's so much crammed into this short, I hardly know where to begin. It starts with the cat stepping along to the song "The Five o'Clock Whistle." This is two years before Red would sing the same song, with lyrics, in Friz Freleng's **LITTLE RED RIDING RABBIT**. A dog named Rosebud (a reference to the dying words uttered by Orson Welles's character in *Citizen Kane*) tears out of his doghouse after the cat. He misses his prey, and we find out this is a daily ritual.

> **DIRECTOR:** ROBERT CLAMPETT **STORY:** WARREN FOSTER **ANIMATION:** BOB MCKIMSON **VOICES:** MEL BLANC (CAT, DOG), SARA BERNER (BIRD), KENT ROGERS (DOG) **MUSIC:** CARL STALLING

The cat sings parody lyrics to the song "Java Jive" and compares his sex appeal to that of Victor Mature, as his head turns into an image of the movie idol. At various times, the cat also does impersonations of Charles Boyer, Lou Costello, and Jerry Colonna. The impersonations are all performed by Mel Blanc, who has claimed in some interviews he didn't do any impersonations. Wooing a female cat, the hero uses the line "a cup of coffee, a sandwich and you," which is actually a song title and a tune that musical director Carl Stalling would often use when there was food in a scene. The final set piece is the dog seducing the cat using a hand puppet, possibly foreshadowing Clampett's future career in puppetry with **TIME FOR BEANY** (1949–54) and, later, the animated series **BEANY AND CECIL**.

There's some really nice staging in this cartoon—for example, the scenes in which we only see shadows on a fence and the scene where the cat and dog race up a fire escape, shown at a steep down-angle from the top of a building. The staging, plus the outstanding script by Warren Foster, make this one of the greatest Looney Tunes.

> **JERRY SAYS** The first Looney Tune in color exemplifies Clampett at his most mischievous fun. An overabundance of blatant sexual humor proves that these cartoons were never squarely aimed at children.

High Diving Hare

"GIMME A TICKET! GIMME A WHOLE MESS OF 'EM! I'M A-SPLURGIN'!"

At a small-town opera house, ticket salesman Bugs announces a fifteen-act vaudeville show, including Frizby the Magician and the juggling team of Butterfingers and Clumsy. But pistol-packing patron Yosemite Sam only wants to see Fearless Freep, the high-diver, and when a storm delays Freep's arrival, Sam demands Bugs perform the dive in his place. But Bugs being Bugs, only Sam takes the plunge—again and again! Bugs first turns the diving board backwards, then converts it into a kind of seesaw. Things get silly as Bugs manipulates Sam's ego, first daring him to step "across this line" and off the board, then tricking him through a prop door that leads over the edge. Bugs even hoodwinks Sam with an American Indian guide disguise. In the end, Sam tries to saw the board off with a tied-up Bugs perched on top—but only the ladder and platform fall, while the board remains in midair, ignoring the law of gravity. "I never studied law," grins Bugs.

JEFF SMITH, cartoonist Friz Freleng was the funniest of the Warner Bros. cartoon directors.

DIRECTOR: I. FRELENG **STORY:** TED PIERCE **ANIMATION:** GERRY CHINIQUY, MANUEL PEREZ, KEN CHAMPIN, VIRGIL ROSS, PETE BURNESS **LAYOUT:** HAWLEY PRATT **BACKGROUNDS:** PAUL JULIAN **VOICES:** MEL BLANC (BUGS, SAM) **MUSIC:** CARL STALLING

You might think it was Tex Avery or Bob Clampett, and yes, Chuck Jones was amazing—his characters were better drawn, their movements more expressive—but pound for pound, Freleng's cartoons are laugh-out-loudier.

Yosemite Sam, a character created in 1944 by writer Michael Maltese as a parody of the short, volatile Friz Freleng, was Bugs Bunny's best nemesis. Years before Wile E. Coyote ever ordered a giant catapult from Acme, the sawed-off outlaw was getting laughs by being his own worst enemy.

Written by Ted Pierce, **HIGH DIVING HARE** is a one-gag cartoon. Seriously—there is only one joke in this cartoon. Yosemite Sam falls 500 feet into a barrel of water, over and over again. And it gets funnier and funnier with each whistling plunge. The setup involves a frontier town where Bugs Bunny is barking up a crowd, selling tickets to a vaudeville show featuring Fearless Freep, the world-famous high diver. There are a couple of nice touches in this opening scene: a beautiful evening sky with silvery moonlit clouds, courtesy of background painter Paul Julian; a huge poster behind Bugs's head that reads "Frizby"; and Bugs excusing himself in order to turn his back and take a quick nip of his carrot as if it were a flask.

When Fearless Freep is a no-show, Yosemite Sam leaps out of the audience and pulls his guns on Bugs, demanding, "I paid muh four bits ta see the high divin' act, an' I'm a-gonna SEE the high divin' act!" What follows is seven minutes of the two of them climbing up a ridiculously high ladder to the diving platform, and Sam going off instead of Bugs (the crazy ladder drawing, by layout man Hawley Pratt, will give you nosebleeds). Most, if not all, of the humor is provided by Sam's blustering temper, which blows every time the rabbit tricks him into stepping off the platform.

It's a rhythmic tour de force alternating percussive climbs and whistling falls. At the climax, we don't even see what Bugs does to Sam, we just wait about halfway up for Sam to come plunging back down. We know he's coming—the humor is in how fast it will happen.

Suddenly everything stops—all the frenetic energy, the hilarious Treg Brown sound effects—and the cartoon ends in a gravity-defying but cherished ending only Bugs Bunny could deliver.

The timing of Sam's high diving is all the more remarkable when you think about the fact that Warner's directors had no budget for editing after the film was finished. All the timing for action and gags was set in stone before a single frame was drawn. All Looney Tunes are fast, pared-down affairs that never waste a frame, but even by these standards, **HIGH DIVING HARE** is a precision masterpiece.

JERRY SAYS Freleng's brilliant series of variations on the high-diving theme include a period joke often missed today. "Open up that door," Sam shouts at Bugs—before adding "You notice I didn't say 'Richard'?" "Open the Door, Richard" was the number-one song on *Billboard's* 1947 hit list.

High Note

"HICCUP!"

I n a universe where musical notes are living beings, hundreds of them congregate to assemble the sheet music for Johann Strauss's "Blue Danube" waltz. But the "conductor" note in charge finds that one high note is AWOL. He's over in the adjacent sheet music for "Little Brown Jug"—and he's been drinking! The high note tipsily stumbles back to the "Blue Danube" sheet, but rather than take his place among the other notes on the score, he plays tricks like turning a sharp sign into a tic-tac-toe board and a rest

sign into a dog. The conductor pursues the high note around the score, but, clumsy as he might be, the conductor can't catch him at first. The chase moves to horseback, with the high note and the conductor riding eighth notes like steeds. High is at last caught with a treble-clef-turned-lasso and forcibly set where he belongs—but now dozens of *other* notes have run off to "Little Brown Jug" and have become soused themselves!

DIRECTOR: CHUCK JONES **STORY:** MICHAEL MALTESE **ANIMATION:** RICHARD THOMPSON, KEN HARRIS **LAYOUT:** MAURICE NOBLE **BACKGROUNDS:** PHILIP DEGUARD, WILLIAM BUTLER **FILM EDITOR:** TREG BROWN **VOICE:** MEL BLANC (HICCUPS) **MUSIC:** MILT FRANKLYN

DANIEL GOLDMARK, professor of musicology **HIGH NOTE** combines two of director Chuck Jones's favorite storytelling devices: pantomime and music. Having taken on opera, pompous conductors, self-absorbed singers, and classical-music war horses, Jones now turns his attention to the music itself, bringing to life the actual notes on the page. The notes cavort on the score, getting

ready for the performance. So we hear the notes themselves, plus Milt Franklyn's rearrangement of Johann Strauss's ubiquitous waltz.

JERRY SAYS In today's world, where vintage cartoons are typically mistaken for children's fare, masterpieces like **HIGH NOTE** set the record straight—with a healthy dose of classically adult booze humor.

Hillbilly Hare

"GRAB A FENCE POST, HOLD IT TIGHT, WHOMP YOUR PARTNER WITH ALL YOUR MIGHT!"

Vacationing in the Ozarks, Bugs Bunny encounters the Martin brothers, Curt and Punkinhead, who mistake the bunny for a Coy, the family with whom they are feuding. They chase Bugs into a dark powder house filled with explosives, where the rabbit offers them a match to see with. After they recover from the explosion, the Martins become smitten with a flirtatious hillbilly gal—Bugs in drag. They begin to square-dance with her thanks to a convenient jukebox, but are soon dancing with each other, doing whatever the caller (again, Bugs in disguise) instructs. The mountain men follow Bugs' malevolent instructions to a tee: pulling each other's beards, wallowing in a pigpen, being tied up by a hay baler, and finally being run off a cliff.

MIKE MALLORY, *animation historian* With **HILLBILLY HARE,** director Robert McKimson, story man Ted Pierce, and composer Carl Stalling

combined to create a comedic perfect storm: the picture without the soundtrack is funny; the soundtrack without the picture is funny; and the music by itself is funny. Even reading the

> **DIRECTOR:** ROBERT MCKIMSON **STORY:** TED PIERCE **ANIMATION:** ROD SCRIBNER, PHIL DELARA, JOHN CAREY, EMERY HAWKINS, CHARLES MCKIMSON **LAYOUT:** CORNETT WOOD **BACKGROUNDS:** RICHARD H. THOMAS **VOICES:** MEL BLANC (BUGS, CURT), JOHN T. SMITH (PUNKINHEAD, CALLER) **MUSIC:** CARL STALLING

song lyrics off the written page is funny! Just like Abbott and Costello's "Who's on First?" routine or Jack Benny and Mel Blanc's "Si-Sy-Sue" bit, the cartoon makes you laugh no matter how many times you've seen or heard it.

The cartoon's first half, in which Bugs repeatedly bests two dimwitted mountain men (who are identical except for the reverse coloration of their hats and beards), is conventionally funny, with good gags and two notable foils for Bugs. But what elevates **HILLBILLY HARE** to the top ranks of Looney Tune cartoons is its second half, a relentless, hilariously inane square dance called by Bugs (channeling the Western swing musician Bob Wills). The rabbit's instructions are religiously carried out by the hillbillies, who bludgeon each other senseless in the process. This three-minute crescendo of slapstick is one of the greatest sustained pieces of comedy ever drawn.

Hollywood Steps Out

CARY GRANT: "IF I EVER TOLD MY FAVORITE WIFE THE AWFUL TRUTH, I'D LAND RIGHT ON THE FRONT PAGE."

At a posh Hollywood nightclub, dozens of movie stars convene to dance and tell jokes. Edward G. Robinson welcomes Ann Sheridan, the "Oomph Girl." Cary Grant buys cigarettes from Greta Garbo. Johnny Weissmuller (Tarzan) dines in his leopard skin. James Cagney, Humphrey Bogart, and George Raft pitch pennies. Harpo Marx gives a hotfoot to Greta Garbo. And Bing Crosby leads the entertainment on stage. In the audience are Jimmy Stewart, Oliver Hardy, and the Three Stooges. Sally Rand does her famous bubble dance. Stone-faced actors Boris Karloff, Buster Keaton, Arthur Treacher, Mischa Auer, and Ned Sparks have no reaction. (And sitting in the reserve seats are caricatures of Looney Tunes executives Henry Binder and Leon Schlesinger.) All through the film, Clark Gable pursues a mysterious female who, in the end, turns out to be Groucho Marx!

DIRECTOR: FRED AVERY **VOICES:** KENT ROGERS (CARY GRANT, JAMES CAGNEY, BING CROSBY, EDWARD G. ROBINSON, MICKEY ROONEY, LEWIS STONE, JAMES STEWART, PETER LORRE, CLARK GABLE, NED SPARKS, HENRY ALDRICH, GROUCHO MARX), MEL BLANC (JERRY COLONNA), SARA BERNER (GRETA GARBO, ANN SHERIDAN, DOROTHY LAMOUR) **CHARACTER MODELING:** BEN SHENKMAN (UNCREDITED) **MUSIC:** CARL STALLING

KEITH SCOTT, cartoon voice actor Every few years, animated cartoon makers bite the hand that feeds them by good-naturedly dumping on the film industry. Schlesinger enjoyed success with the 1936 entry **THE COO-COO NUT GROVE**, while a then-recent example of the genre had been Disney's popular Silly Symphony **MOTHER GOOSE GOES HOLLYWOOD**. What makes director Tex Avery's cartoon unique is its mockumentary style: It's effectively a cartooned version of one of the many short films to feature movie stars "at play" and Hollywood "nightlife." Aside from a couple of purely gag-worthy characters (FBI boss J. Edgar Hoover, bandleader Kay Kyser), almost everyone we see, from Cary Grant to Groucho Marx, was then a movie megastar, representing all the film studios, not just Warner Bros.

There have been many twenty-first-century comments about how this cartoon's cultural references (like conga music) and its raft of celebrities are impenetrable to a contemporary audience. However, on its initial release, **HOLLYWOOD STEPS OUT** was hyped as a special event and given a publicity buildup in the *Los Angeles Times*. Audiences in 1941 would have greeted every caricature with instant recognition and hearty laughter.

Avery's cartoon had an unusually long gestation. It was in production some eighteen months before its release in the spring of 1941, and its path to completion included on-site research at the actual Ciro's nightspot (today the location of the Comedy Store on the Sunset Strip) and the hiring of Ben Shenkman, an accomplished caricaturist formerly with the Charles Mintz cartoon shop. Shenkman had recently done work on still another movie-star cartoon (**MOTHER GOOSE IN SWINGTIME**) released by Columbia for the Christmas of 1939—indeed, the Gable caricature is identical in looks and voice to his appearance in that film. Friz Freleng had first poached Shenkman for his 1940 celebrity sendup **MALIBU BEACH PARTY**, and, soon after, Avery grabbed him for **HOLLYWOOD STEPS OUT**. Shenkman did extensive character modeling for Avery and accompanied the director's background staff to Ciro's to ensure authenticity.

Kent Rogers performed most of the voice impressions with great skill, remarkable since Rogers was still in his teens! He had been doing fine celebrity sound-alikes for a popular radio program, *The Hedda Hopper Show*, and he made sure his name got to all the cartoon makers—in fact, Kent also did Clark Gable in the earlier **MOTHER GOOSE IN SWINGTIME**. Eventually Rogers became one of the early voices of Woody Woodpecker, and for Warner Bros. he voiced Willoughby, Horton, Henery Hawk, Beaky Buzzard, and the original voice of Junyer Bear. As Bob Clampett once remarked, had Rogers not been killed in 1944 during Air Force training, he would have been a much bigger name in cartoon history.

Honey's Money

"WHEN I GET MY HANDS ON THAT MONEY, I'LL BUY THE OLD LADIES' HOME AND KICK THE OLD LADIES OUT!"

Yosemite Sam reads about a local widow inheriting five million dollars. He dresses in his Sunday best and goes armed with candy and flowers to court her. However, she turns out to be a large, homely woman with an abnormally large, obnoxious child named Wentworth. Sam marries the widow with hopes of living in luxury, but instead ends up doing the housework and entertaining Wentworth. Forced to play "Horsie," Sam breaks his back. Forced to play catch, Sam is made to retrieve the ball in traffic. Forced to take the boy swimming, Sam fills the pool with alligators—who land on him after Wentworth cannonballs into the water. A highly stylized and rare solo Yosemite Sam cartoon, **HONEY'S MONEY** is actually a remake of an earlier cartoon, **HIS BITTER HALF** (1950), in which Daffy Duck plays the beleaguered stepfather role. It's a better fit with Sam's personality.

DIRECTOR: FRIZ FRELENG **STORY:** JOHN DUNN **ANIMATION:** GERRY CHINIQUY, VIRGIL ROSS, BOB MATZ, LEE HALPERN, ART LEONARDI **LAYOUT:** HAWLEY PRATT **BACKGROUNDS:** TOM O'LOUGHLIN **FILM EDITOR:** TREG BROWN **VOICES:** MEL BLANC (YOSEMITE SAM), JUNE FORAY (WIFE), BILLY BOOTH (WENTWORTH) **MUSIC:** MILT FRANKLYN

DAVID GERSTEIN, animation historian "A fanatic," in the words of the philosopher Santayana, "is someone who redoubles his effort when he has forgotten his aim." But fanatics aren't the only effort-redoublers out there. "Wherever [a heroine] went," ran an old song about stage melodramas, "she was never content / For the villain still pursued her." Professional bad guys pursue their goals—and girls—to an obsessive degree, too. What would happen when one such baddie actually realized he was bordering on fanatic behavior? How would he react?

In **HONEY'S MONEY**, this crisis comes to Yosemite Sam. For once starring without Bugs, the bandit marries a widow for her money—only to learn that she is a battle-axe and her son an innocently destructive giant. Sam's sensible side says it's not worth it, and that to stay in the relationship is fanaticism. But Sam's villainous greed says otherwise, and we get to watch the conflict play out.

Desperate to make married life endurable under the circumstances, Yosemite is driven to some of the darkest plots ever seen in a Looney Tune—efforts to murder his young stepson via alligators and speeding cars. Only Sam's sheer bombast and exaggerated evil make the material funny rather than tragic. Freleng takes an admirably successful risk. Sam's own risks aren't as successful...for him.

The Hypo-Chondri-Cat

BERTIE: "DID YOU EVER OPERATE ON A SICK CAT BEFORE, DOCTOR?"
HUBIE: "NAW, BUT I'LL TRY ANYTHING ONCE."

Seeking shelter from a rainy night, Hubie (the smart-guy gray mouse) and Bertie (his slow-witted, brown-furred companion) find a new dry place to call home. Once inside, they grab some cheese and are beginning to warm themselves at the fireplace when they meet Claude, the cat of the house. After a brief chase, it becomes obvious that Claude is a hypochondriac with a deep fear of catching cold. The mice quickly use the power of suggestion to make the cat feel (and look) worse. Claude turns green, purple, and plaid at the mere observation of his own pallor. The cat is soon begging for their medical help.

In response, the mice begin preparations for an operation, assembling an array of saws, knives, and sharp objects. The sight causes Claude to pass out on the operating table and have a surreal

DIRECTOR: CHARLES M. JONES **STORY:** MICHAEL MALTESE **ANIMATION:** BEN WASHAM, LLOYD VAUGHAN, KEN HARRIS, PHIL MONROE **LAYOUT:** ROBERT GRIBBROEK **BACKGROUNDS:** PHIL DEGARD **VOICES:** MEL BLANC (HUBIE, CLAUDE), STAN FREBERG (BERT) **MUSIC:** CARL STALLING

fever dream, after which he awakens in white gown (a flour sack) with wings (fastened by safety pins). He arises to witness Hubie and Bertie sobbing in the backyard, crying over Claude's grave site. The cat tries to tell them he's alive, but they supposedly cannot hear him. Hubie recalls that at exactly midnight, spirits appear. Moments later, they are startled by Claude's ghostly appearance. Once again, he begs the mice for help. Hubie and Bertie now lead him toward the edge

of a cliff and—despite his protests—push him off toward "cat heaven." Floating upwards thanks to a solitary helium balloon, Claude, now filled with an inner peace, bids the mice farewell and sails toward the moon.

HARRY MCCRACKEN, editor of *Animato!* Here's one cat-and-mouse cartoon where most of the violence is psychological—the botched "operation" and faked death that Hubie and Bertie put Claude through are practically Hitchcockian. The stages of grief that Claude goes through as he denies his own passing, gets panicky, and finally comes to accept it feature some of the best acting that Mel Blanc ever did.

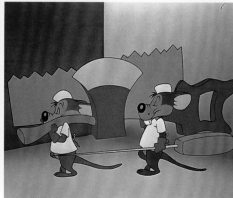

JERRY SAYS Director Chuck Jones had made psychology-driven cartoons before, most notably **HARE TONIC** (1945), in which Bugs Bunny convinces Elmer Fudd and the viewing audience that they have contracted "rabbititis," as well as earlier Hubie and Bertie mind games like **THE ARISTO-CAT** (1943) and

MOUSE WRECKERS (1949). Here, the formula reaches its apex as Jones hits his filmmaking stride. Jones is always exploring ways for us to see and feel what his characters are thinking. **THE HYPO-CHRONDRI-CAT** is the culmination of that process, combining Jones's superb comic timing and great character design with writer

Mike Maltese's story mechanics and with outstanding animation from his now-established crew. A particular standout here is the fever-dream sequence animated by Lloyd Vaughn.

I Love to Singa

"ENOUGH IS TOO MUCH! OUT OF MY HOUSE, YOU HOTCHA! YOU CROONER! YOU FALSETTO! YOU JAZZ SINGER! YOU…YOU…PHOOEY!"

A sign outside Professor Fritz Owl's home announces that he's a teacher of voice, piano, and violin, "But—No Jazz!" So the owl and his wife are confounded when their four eggs hatch. One owlet is a born opera tenor, another a violinist, and the third a flutist, but little Owl Jolson is a jazz singer and wants "to sing-a / About the moon-a and the June-a and the spring-a!" The parents hope nurture can trump nature: Mama teaches Jolson to sing "Drink to Me Only with Thine Eyes." But when baby owl reverts to his jazzy theme, Professor Owl throws him out of the house over Mama's objections. Alone, Owl Jolson scats his way to Radio Station G-O-N-G, where JACK BUNNY'S AMATEUR HOUR is in progress. Most of Bunny's goofy amateurs get the gong and drop out a trapdoor midperformance. But Owl Jolson enchants Bunny, enabling the owl to sing long enough for Mama Owl to hear on the radio. As Bunny prepares to give Jolson the evening's prize trophy, he sees his parents arrive outside the studio window and switches back to singing "Drink to Me Only." When a shocked Bunny starts to renege on the prize, Professor Owl decides to encourage his son's jazz singing after all—and even join in!

DIRECTOR: FRED AVERY **ANIMATION:** CHARLES JONES, VIRGIL ROSS **VOICES:** BILLY BLETCHER (PROFESSOR OWL, PAGLIACCI CONTESTANT), TOMMY BOND (OWL JOLSON), JACKIE MORROW (OWL JOLSON'S JAZZY SINGING), MARTHA WENTWORTH (MAMA OWL), BERNICE HANSEN (CONTESTANT), TED PIERCE (JACK BUNNY), LOU FULTON (STUTTERING CONTESTANT) **MUSICAL SCORE:** NORMAN SPENCER

DANIEL GOLDMARK, professor of musicology I LOVE TO SINGA may be one of the most instantly endearing cartoons Warner Bros. ever created. The story combines two themes that are as popular then as they are now—a child breaking away from his parents and contestants chasing the "rags-to-riches" promise of amateur shows (the lyrics to "I Love to Singa" specifically mention the preeminent amateur variety series of the time, *The Major Bowes Amateur Hour*). All of this is poured into the mold of Al Jolson's *The Jazz Singer* (1927), the talkie that changed the music industry when it appeared less than a decade earlier. The title song actually comes from another Jolson picture from 1936, *The Singing Kid*, showing how aware the animation division was of the music being produced in the feature film department.

JERRY SAYS While not as wacky as Tex Avery's later works, **I LOVE TO SINGA** is still the perfect metaphor for the changes this great director brought to the studio. Instead of following stuffy cartoon convention, Tex taught his peers to march to their own drummers.

An Itch in Time

"I BETTER CUT THIS OUT, I MAY GET TO LIKE IT!"

The backside of Elmer Fudd's dog becomes the new home of A. Flea, much to the displeasure of both man and dog. "Scwatching, scwatching, swatching! One more scwatch and I'll give you a bath!" warns Elmer. But keeping himself from scratching is next to impossible, given the all-out Armageddon the parasite has declared as he harvests the poor pooch's appetizing epidermis. Yet the dog still manages to relieve the itching without disturbing Fudd from his fireside reading of **LOONEY TUNES AND MERRIE MELODIES COMICS**—until the flea sets off explosives, causing the dog to finally break down and scoot across the floor on his rear end. ("I better cut this out, I may get to like it!" pants the dog, in a scene clearly intended for the Hays Office, which enforced the Motion Picture Production Code, to catch and snip. Alas, it's still here.) Elmer tries to make good on his threat, but the flea makes Fudd's hide his new home. The dog then tries to give his master a bath, but he slips on a bar of soap, and both dog and owner land in the tub. A. takes advantage of the situation. The flea hoists them onto his "blue plate special" and prepares for a feast. "Now I've seen everything!" exclaims the housecat upon witnessing this—and blows his brains out.

DIRECTOR: ROBERT CLAMPETT **STORY:** WARREN FOSTER **ANIMATION:** BOB MCKIMSON **VOICES:** ARTHUR Q. BRYAN (ELMER FUDD), SARA BERNERR (A. FLEA), MEL BLANC (CAT, DOG), TED PIERCE (HUBIE) **MUSIC:** CARL STALLING

MICHAEL SPORN, animator AN ITCH IN TIME is a cartoon from director Bob Clampett that centers around three characters: a dog, a blue hillbilly flea, and Elmer Fudd. In Bob McKimson's animation, the film is as funny as it is artful. McKimson remade the film a few years later in a half-hearted attempt called **A HORSEFLY FLEAS** (1947), adding a now controversial scene with American Indians; his direction wasn't nearly as good as Clampett's in the earlier film.

The cat's suicide is an odd stroke often cut from broadcasts. Some similarity also exists between **ITCH**'s unnamed dog and the dimwitted Willoughby, who debuted in Tex Avery's **OF FOX AND HOUNDS** (1940) as a takeoff on the characters in Steinbeck's *Of Mice and Men*. You know Willoughby: "Which way did he go, George? Which way did he go?"

JERRY SAYS Bob Clampett himself wrote "Food Around the Corner," the catchy little tune—so catchy it's hard to stop singing—that the flea sings in this cartoon. Its roots in "She'll Be Comin' 'Round the Mountain" are somewhat audible.

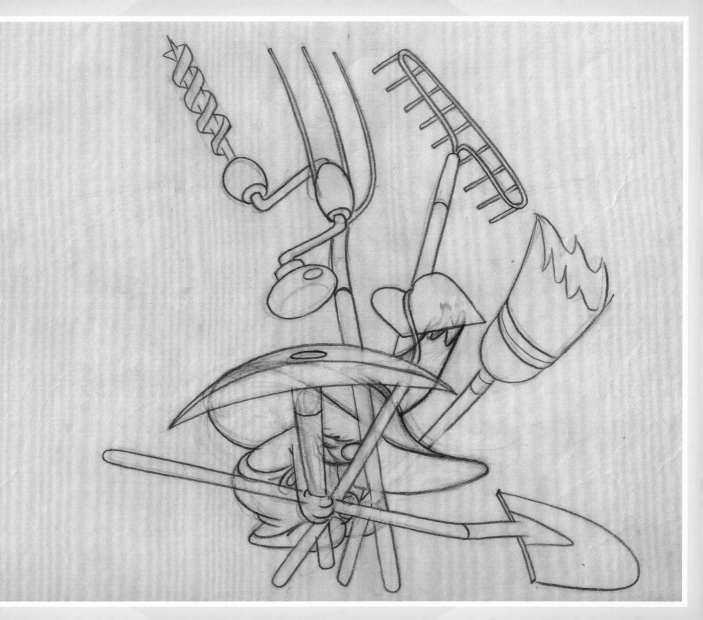

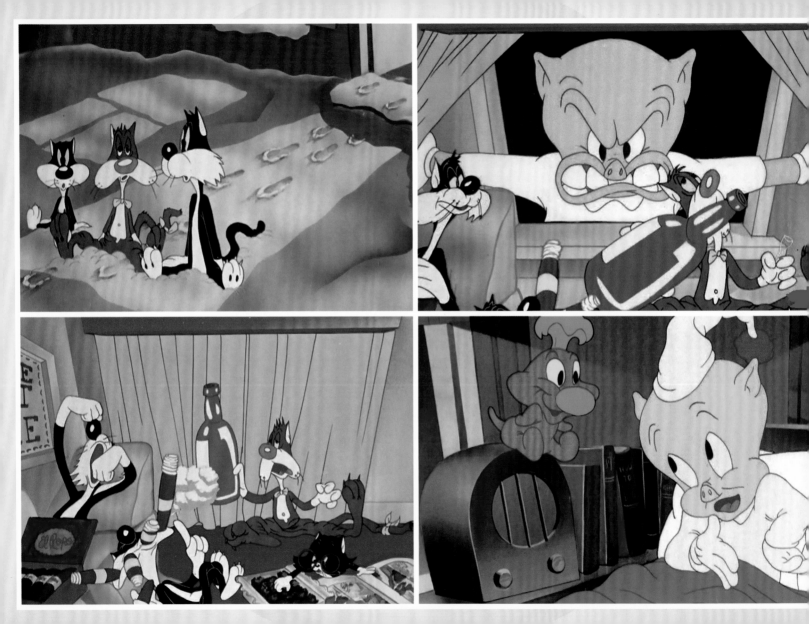

Kitty Kornered

"WE'VE BEEN SKIDDED OUT, SCOOTED OUT, BACKED OUT, AND BOOTED OUT!"

Porky Pig wants to put his four cats out for the night, but this gang of felines has other plans. A lengthy romp around the house ensues. A few of the highlights: the lanky, dopey cat squeezing himself into a fishbowl castle; Porky and a family of mice playing tug-of-war with Sylvester. Porky finally scares the cats off with his shadow-puppet dog "Leyuh-Leyuh-Lassie." Out in the cold, Sylvester gives a slobbering speech (hysterically animated by Manny Gould) to his feline comrades: "Are we men, or are we miiiiitth?" ("I like cheese!" retorts the kitten of the group.) So they strike back by disguising themselves as men from Mars, scaring Porky out of his wits and sending him straight for his musket. The cats are ready for him, dressed as Teddy Roosevelt's Rough Riders, and they "ch-a-r-r-r-r-ge" Porky right out the window! Embarrassed, Porky asks if anyone in the audience has a house to rent.

DIRECTOR: ROBERT CLAMPETT **ANIMATION:** MANNY GOULD, ROD SCRIBNER, J. C. MELENDEZ **LAYOUTS AND BACKGROUNDS:** THOMAS MCKIMSON, DORCY HOWARD **VOICES:** MEL BLANC (PORKY, SYLVESTER, NARRATOR) **MUSIC:** CARL STALLING

CRAIG YOE, comics historian In this uproariously funny film written by director Robert Clampett himself, everything and everyone is made of rubber. The last half has some of the most exhilarating action ever put on film.

Porky Pig—I love that guy! When YOE! Studio used to design a lot of products for the Warner Bros. stores back in the day, I'd always put in a good word for Porky. "No way," the suits squealed. "People don't like pigs." Well, I do, and I'm people! I got the same response when I worked for the Muppets and would suggest Miss Piggy products.

Pigs is pigs, and Porky is the greatest of the grunts. (Sorry, Miss Piggy!) I especially love how the Porker is pantless. Did the censors never notice how this swine was going around bare-ass naked?

De-pants-ed Porky *does* gets dumped on a lot. We all can relate. And in this cartoon he gets shat on by cats—or more properly, kitties. I like the title: **KITTY KORNERED**. Besides the obvious pun, I want to believe spelling "Kornered" with a K is a nod to *Krazy Kat*. And that komic-strip kat shared the surrealism and violence of this movie. Krazy Kat was the masochist, tortured by the brick-throwing hand of sadist Ignatz Mouse. In this round, it's kitties vs. pig, with the cats making sausage of Porky. But we love cartoon violence! In *Krazy Kat* the violence was poetic. In **KITTY KORNERED** it's just damn funny. So funny I remembered to laugh.

Little Red Riding Rabbit

"I'LL DO IT...BUT I'LL PROBABLY HATE MYSELF IN THE MORNING!"

Red Riding Hood is an obnoxious teenage bobbysoxer on her way to Grandma's house with a bunny rabbit (Bugs) in her picnic basket. The wolf disguises himself as Granny—who is off doing her part for the war effort, working the swing shift at Lockheed Aircraft—and kicks several other wolves out of the bed. Red arrives at the house and tries to ask Granny the traditional questions about her big snout, but the wolf, who's hungry for rabbit instead of teenage girls, just hurries Red out the door. Bugs escapes from the picnic basket and leads the wolf on a chase around the house, eluding him through a series of doorways. When the wolf disguises himself as a door, Bugs raps him on the forehead and yells, "Anybody home?"

Red reappears to ask the wolf, "Uh...what big ears you got?" This time, when the wolf throws Red out, Bugs is behind the pair and throws them both out. The wolf returns and corners Bugs, threatening him, each line mocked by Bugs. Soon enough,

Bugs has the distracted wolf singing "Put on Your Old Grey Bonnet," allowing Bugs to slip away. Bugs, now hiding in the wolf's nightgown, jabs him with a hot coal from the fireplace. The wolf jumps in pain and lands with his backside hanging over a pile of hot coals, his legs stretched between a table and a chair. Bugs piles heavy objects into the wolf's arms. Suddenly, Red makes yet another annoying appearance, and Bugs decides to place *her* in the wolf's situation over the coals. He and the wolf end up pals.

> **DIRECTOR:** I. FRELENG **STORY:** MICHAEL MALTESE **ANIMATION:** MANUEL PEREZ **VOICES:** MEL BLANC (BUGS), BEA BENADERET (RED RIDING HOOD), BILLY BLETCHER (WOLF) **MUSIC:** CARL STALLING

ANDREW FARAGO, curator, Cartoon Art Museum
LITTLE RED RIDING RABBIT is, hands down, my favorite Friz Freleng cartoon. The direction's

great, the animation is top-notch, the patter is snappy...but what makes this cartoon stand head and shoulders above the 300-plus others Freleng directed is the music.

Carl Stalling kicks things off with "The Lady in Red" playing over the opening credits, which is fun and all, but when Red first appears onscreen, belting out her unforgettable rendition of Cole Porter's "The Five o'Clock Whistle," you know you're in for something special. Bea Benadaret nails her performance, and within a few ear-splitting notes, you know everything you'll ever need to know about Red.

What kills me, every single time, is the duet between Bugs and the Big Bad Wolf on "Put on Your Old Gray Bonnet (With the Blue Ribbon on It)." How did Carl Stalling know that would be the funniest possible song for a cross-dressing wolf chasing a rabbit while avoiding a meddlesome bobbysoxer?

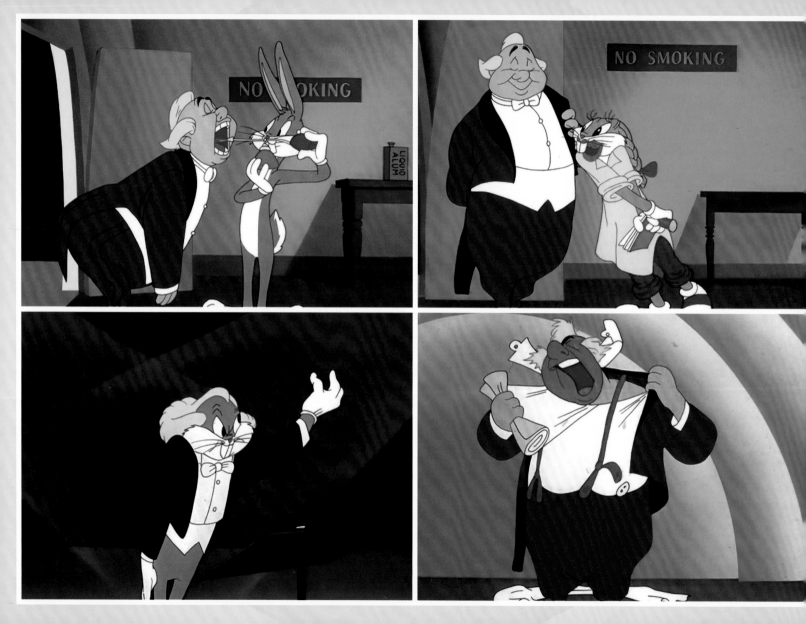

Long-Haired Hare

Bugs enlivens the woods with an impromptu performance of movie and minstrel songs. But Bugs's noisy music is a distraction for opera singer Giovanni Jones, just then practicing at his nearby estate. When Jones destroys Bugs's banjo—and then his harp, and then his tuba—"Of course," says Bugs, "you know this means war!" Soon Bugs has invaded Jones's next Hollywood Bowl concert, where he causes the stage to shake around the singer, asks for an autograph with an exploding dynamite "pen," and finally costumes himself as conductor Leopold Stokowski, forcing Jones to hold a high note till the theater facade crumbles around him.

MIKE BARRIER, animation scholar If there can be such a thing as the perfect Bugs Bunny cartoon, **LONG-HAIRED HARE** may be it. At the least, it's the perfect expression of Bugs as he emerged in the partnership of director Chuck Jones and his longtime writer, Michael Maltese. In the

"OH, MR. JONES! FRANKIE [SINATRA] AND PERRY [COMO] JUST AREN'T IN IT! YOU'RE MY SWOONER DREAMBOAT LOVER BOY!"

DIRECTOR: CHARLES M. JONES **STORY:** MICHAEL MALTESE **ANIMATION:** PHIL MONROE, BEN WASHAM, LLOYD VAUGHAN, KEN HARRIS **LAYOUT:** ROBERT GRIBBROEK **BACKGROUNDS:** PETER ALVARADO **VOICES:** MEL BLANC (BUGS, GIOVANNI TALKING, MUSICIANS), NICOLAI SHUTOREV (GIOVANNI SINGING) **MUSIC:** CARL STALLING

Jones-Maltese collaborations, Bugs is not the mischief-maker of earlier cartoons but instead a sort of counterrevolutionary. The rabbit just wants to be left alone, but when other characters try to impose on him, he responds powerfully. His adversary in **LONG-HAIRED HARE** is Giovanni Jones, an arrogant, short-tempered opera singer who attacks Bugs (and cuts short the rabbit's music-making) three times, setting up a delicious confrontation at the Hollywood Bowl—a confrontation that builds until the Bowl itself collapses onto the feckless singer's head.

JERRY SAYS When the orchestra offers Bugs-as-Leopold a baton but the rabbit breaks it and throws it away, it's a reference to the real-life Stokowski's usual refusal to conduct with a baton.

Mexicali Schmoes

"WHERE WE GET THESE BRAINS, JOSE?"

After singing a slow ballad containing every hackneyed Spanish phrase imaginable, two lazy, clueless pussycats named Jose and Manuel decide to pursue Speedy Gonzales, the fastest mouse in all Mexico. They lure Speedy to their fiesta, but the mouse soon clobbers them. Inspired by a cartoon starring "the gringo, Bugs Bunny," the cats tempt Speedy with cheese bait threaded onto a fishhook. But the mouse grabs the bait and pulls Jose on a one-way express trip to Los Angeles. Later, the cats plant a minefield,

DIRECTOR: FRIZ FRELENG **STORY:** WARREN FOSTER **ANIMATION:** VIRGIL ROSS, GERRY CHINIQUY, ART DAVIS **LAYOUT:** HAWLEY PRATT **BACKGROUNDS:** TOM O'LOUGHLIN **FILM EDITOR:** TREG BROWN **VOICES:** MEL BLANC (SPEEDY, JOSE), TOM HOLLAND (MANUEL) **MUSIC:** MILT FRANKLYN

and Speedy maneuvers the schmoes into the middle of it. Calling it quits, they decide instead to pursue Slowpoke Rodriguez, the slowest mouse in Mexico. But Manuel forgets to tell Jose one important fact about Slowpoke Rodriquez: "He packs a gun."

DAVID GERSTEIN, animation historian The straight man–funny man pair is a comedy trope as old as the hills: Pair a sensible, earnest character with a goony eccentric, then let one guy drive the plot while the other makes trouble. Alas, while a very common trope, it's also one infrequently used to best advantage. Dozens of cartoons from dozens of studios focus so completely on the funny man that the straight man becomes a bore. Yet there

is a better way to handle this dynamic. In live action, Laurel and Hardy set the trend: While Ollie (Hardy) was the "straight man" insofar as his character attempted to earnestly, sensibly accomplish a goal, he was never boring. His relative seriousness simply made his reactions funnier when "funny man" Stan (Laurel) hindered him. Hardy proved that a straight man could be funny, too.

Such was also the case when the Looney Tunes crew took on this pairing. In **MEXICALI SCHMOES**, stocky Jose is more serious and calculating than geeky Manuel, but in their attempts to catch Speedy Gonzales, both cats provide equal hilarity. The treatment easily transcends the characters' feline nature and Mexican culture: Rocky and Mugsy (**BUGS AND THUGS**) and Henry Bear and Junyer (**A BEAR FOR PUNISHMENT**) follow flawlessly in the same tradition. It's amazing how, outside of Warner Bros., so many cartoon studios' straight man–funny man pairings flopped.

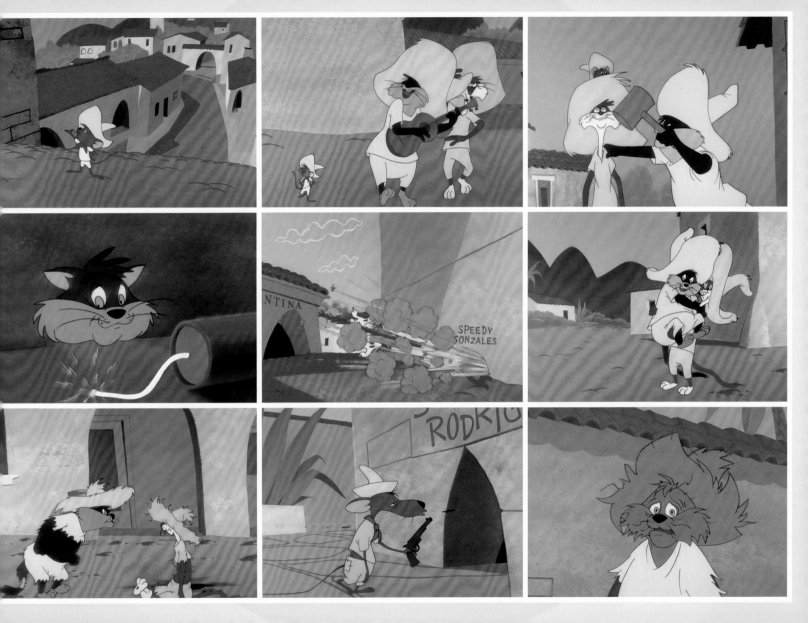

Much Ado About Nutting

A squirrel comes across a nut shop and goes straight for the peanuts. He soon realizes that he can have any nut in the market and, after considering walnuts and Brazil nuts, decides to crack the biggest nut he can find: a coconut. It's not as easy as he thinks, however. He maneuvers the heavy nut into the park and begins to try various ways to open it: throwing it off a tree, sawing it in half, using an axe, blowing it up with dynamite, and even using a pneumatic drill. He rolls the coconut up to the top of the Empire State Building and drops it off the roof—but the nut doesn't crack, the street does. The squirrel returns the nut to the shop, where it falls from its display—and cracks open to reveal another coconut inside! With this, the squirrel faints.

JOHN CANEMAKER, animator and animation historian **MUCH ADO ABOUT NUTTING**, one of director Chuck Jones's great one-off shorts,

DIRECTOR: CHARLES M. JONES **STORY:** MICHAEL MALTESE **ANIMATION:** LLOYD VAUGHAN, KEN HARRIS, BEN WASHAM **LAYOUT:** MAURICE NOBLE **BACKGROUNDS:** PHILIP DEGUARD **MUSIC SCORE:** CARL STALLING **ORCHESTRATIONS:** MILT FRANKLYN

balances keen observations of real squirrel behavior (nervous tail and whisker twitches alternated with one-frame head turns and changes in direction) against a magical little-man-in-a-squirrel-suit anthropomorphism reminiscent of Felix the Cat. The determined squirrel's pantomime and timing are superbly sharp. His Wile E. Coyote–like hunger for the taste of coconut meat drives him to progressively desperate efforts to open the stubborn fruit's hard shell.

I love one scene in particular that showcases Jones's ability to express so much in a single pose with minimal movement: After the squirrel has pushed the coconut up the nearly 2,000 steps of the Empire State Building's 103 floors (such great perspective layout!), the effort it takes him to raise his feet and take two painful steps eloquently scream "exhaustion." There is a similar defeated walk toward the end of **ONE FROGGY EVENING** (1955) in which the poor schlub who has tried to cash in on a singing froggy and has failed miserably walks two zombie steps, a cartoon Willy Loman. I love that tiny walk, too, for the physical and psychological insight it succinctly offers into a broken man and his shattered dream.

Nasty Quacks

"I LIKE HIM! HE'S SILLY!"

A doting father gives his daughter a cute little duckling for a pet. It grows into Daffy Duck, who only exists to make the father's existence a living hell. After having to listen to Daffy's loud recollections of his wild parties at one disastrous breakfast ("One guy was swinging from a chandelier, you'd have thought he was a monkey! Come to think of it, he *was* a monkey!"), Father decides that today is the day the duck must die, despite his daughter's protests.

DIRECTOR: FRANK TASHLIN **STORY:** WARREN FOSTER **ANIMATION:** ART DAVIS, I. ELLIS, RICHARD BICKENBACH **LAYOUT AND BACKGROUNDS:** RICHARD H. THOMAS **VOICES:** MEL BLANC (DAFFY, FATHER, BABY), SARA BERNER (AGNES), ROBERT C. BRUCE (NARRATOR) **MUSIC:** CARL STALLING

A knife duel results in Daffy kicking the father down the stairs, and an attempt to slip the duck a mickey goes awry. The father then decides to give his daughter a *new* fluffy duckling so she'll forget about Daffy. The plan works, and Daffy is kicked out of the house, taking most of the roof with him. He vows revenge on the duckling. Daffy can't murder the little guy, so he feeds the baby duck Vitamin B_1 to make it grow to his size. His plans change the moment he sees that the duckling has become a voluptuous female duck. Father merrily skips down to breakfast, thinking his house is finally a Daffy-free zone, only to find the table is now occupied by Daffy and his entire obnoxious family.

GREG FORD, animation historian The last of director Frank Tashlin's five-film winning streak starring Daffy Duck, **NASTY QUACKS** casts the addled, ring-necked hysteric as a kindergartener's coddled mascot. It seems that the once-adorable duckling Daffy, given by a doting dad to his daughter Agnes, has become the bane of the father's existence. A semi-abstract growth chart in the picture's prologue shows Daffy maturing into adulthood so precipitously that he bumps his head on the cartoon's upper frame line.

A comparison might be made to the plot of the hit play *The Man Who Came to Dinner*, in which an insufferable dinner guest becomes incapacitated and overstays his welcome for endless, grueling months. Daffy, as Warner Bros.' blue-collar answer to George S. Kauffman and Moss Hart's patrician wordsmith Sheridan Whiteside, terrorizes the household not with acerbic putdowns but exuberant, palsy-walsy camaraderie.

To little Agnes's delight and her daddy's chagrin, Daffy coarsely blabbers on at the table while slapping mounds of butter on his toast. His last monologue culminates in an impromptu sword-fight (using breakfast silverware) between the nasty-quacker and the master of the house. The father's later attempts to oust the duck, which include spraying "Eau de la Duck" perfume and honking a duck mating call, occasion action scenes that display Tashlin's artist's flair for angular, geometric character poses.

One of the cartoon's funniest bits finds the borderline bratty Agnes swooshing in to Daffy's defense before her father does the duck corporeal harm. While other animation directors showed an antsy reluctance to caricature females, Tashlin distinguished himself as an equal-opportunity exaggerator. What with the outsized bow in her hair and the wholeheartedness with which she flings her moppet body into harm's way, yammering a torrent of almost indecipherable pleas that end with a clearly audible "'cause you know I love him," Agnes earns admission to the pantheon of excellent cartoon females created by Frank Tashlin. Others include Hatta Mari from **PLANE DAFFY** (1944), the egg-obsessed mother duck from **BOOBY HATCHED** (1944), the Rosie the Riveter–like single mom from **BROTHER BRAT** (1944), the molested hen from **STUPID CUPID** (1944), and, lest we forget, Petunia Pig.

JERRY SAYS Director Frank Tashlin turned **NASTY QUACKS** into a stylization experiment by designing the characters around angular shapes rather than the usual pears and spheres, with the bulk of the footage expertly animated by Art Davis and Izzy Ellis. It's a laugh-provoking masterpiece of sustained exaggeration from Tashlin.

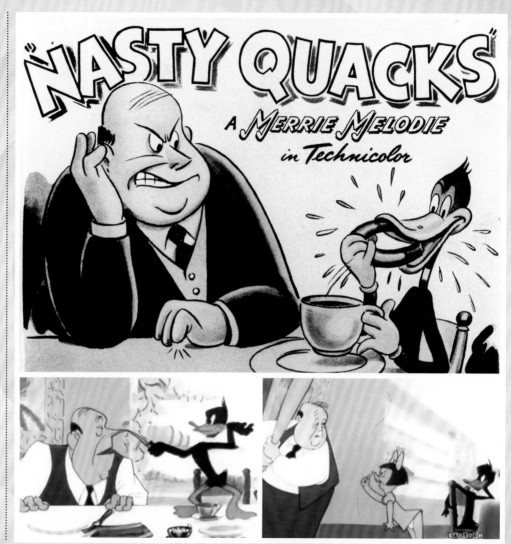

Old Glory

"I DON'T SEE WHY I HAVE TO LEARN THE OLD PLEDGE OF ALLEGIANCE, ANYWAY!"

Little Porky Pig, struggling to learn the Pledge of Allegiance, is visited by the spirit of Uncle Sam, who explains the history of the American Revolution, the founding of the United States, and the country's western expansion. A rare departure for the studio, this unique cartoon contains a number of significant firsts. For one, it's a straight, dramatically told history lesson and a wonderfully patriotic reminder of highlights in U.S. history. It is also the first Porky Pig cartoon in color (not counting his brief debut in 1935's **I HAVEN'T GOT A HAT**), as well as the first time Chuck Jones directed the character. Considering how Jones would refine Porky's character in later cartoons, it's interesting to note his characterization of the pig as an innocent schoolboy in this film.

TOM SITO, animator and director No Hollywood studio had a closer relationship with the Franklin D. Roosevelt administration than Warner Bros. It was lauded by friends and vilified by enemies as the public-relations arm of the New Deal. In the summer of 1939, the American people watched with alarm the growing crisis in Europe and Asia. Franco was winning in Spain, the Japanese militarists were winning in China, and the German Reich did not seem satisfied with just annexing Austria and Czechoslovakia. Within the United States, American Fascist, Nazi, and Communist societies declared that our democratic system was outmoded. Washington responded with a call for more patriotic films extolling the virtues of Americanism. Warner Bros. asked producer Leon Schlesinger to create a cartoon short to complement a series of patriotic live-action shorts they

> **DIRECTOR:** CHARLES M. JONES **STORY:** RICHARD HOGAN, DAVE MONAHAN, ROBERT GIVENS **ANIMATION:** ROBERT MCKIMSON **VOICES:** MEL BLANC (PORKY), JOHN DEERING (UNCLE SAM), JOHN LITEL (PATRICK HENRY), TED PIERCE (PAUL REVERE), PAUL TAYLOR'S SPORTSMEN **MUSIC:** CARL STALLING

were creating. In turn, Schlesinger turned to Chuck Jones, his newest director.

OLD GLORY is one of the few serious Warner Bros. cartoons (another is 1940's **TOM THUMB IN TROUBLE**). Porky Pig, representing an everyman…er, everychild…er, everypig…doesn't know why he has to learn the Pledge of Allegiance. So an accommodatingly grave Uncle Sam, straight out of the James Montgomery Flagg posters, sits Porky on his knee and explains the founding of America to him. With Lincoln-like patience, Uncle Sam describes the heroism of Paul Revere and the Minutemen, the writing of the Constitution, and the opening of the West. (Incidentally, trivia fans like to note that when Porky, filled with patriotic verve, proudly recites his Pledge of Allegiance, the line "one nation, under God" is not heard—the line was not officially added until 1954.)

The scene showing the simple American colonists uniting to fight, symbolized by a close-up of their marching feet slowly growing in number, was a thinly veiled reminder to a 1939 audience

PLEDGE to the FLAG   GEO

"I pledge allegiance to the Flag of the United States of America and to the Republic for which it stands, one Nation indivisible with liberty and justice for all."

that they too might soon be called upon to unite against Hitler and Tojo. The American-themed iconography builds in an explosion of waving Stars and Stripes, cannon fire, a ringing Liberty Bell, and blaring trumpets, all backed by the thundering Warner Bros. orchestra under a masterful arrangement by Carl Stalling and his orchestrator, Milt Franklyn.

At this point in his career, Chuck Jones was very influenced by the realistic, high-budget feature films of the Walt Disney Studios. Whenever a new Disney film was released, he would grab his tuxedo and his wife and attend the premiere. His first shorts of the character Sniffles the Mouse had a definite Disney look to them. Now, with this assignment, Chuck was free to flex his directorial muscles. He employed realistic human design and a lot of dramatic angles and cutting not normally suited for comedy. He used numerous rotoscoped human figures with cast shadows and ground-plane shadows on the figures, which were done with multiple exposures under the camera. The footage of Patrick Henry declaring "Give me liberty or give me death!" was traced over live-

action footage of actor John Litel recycled from a 1936 Oscar-winning Warner short, **GIVE ME LIBERTY**. In addition to the unusual, intricately shaded rendering of Porky, Jones also put in a white highlight to the shine on the pig's cheeks that was "self-line," meaning hand-inked in color, rather than the normal black outlines.

All these expensive, painstaking techniques were usually avoided in the regular Looney Tunes of the time. Looney Tunes director Bob Clampett once told me you had to argue with Schlesinger just to get him to approve the shooting of an occasional pencil test. Looney Tunes were rarely longer than six minutes because Leon refused to budget or schedule for anything more. By contrast, **OLD GLORY** was much longer than a normal Merry Melodies short—almost nine minutes. The fact that the normally frugal producer allowed his young director to go Frank Capra crazy must have meant that, for once, money was no object to the main studio. The boys in Washington had to be kept happy.

A lot of the animation was done by future director Bob McKimson, acknowledged by his peers as being one of the best draftsman in the studio at the time. Ben Washam once told me Bob was a "toe-to-toe draftsman," meaning he could start drawing a figure from the left toe and go completely around the top down to the right toe, all without a preliminary rough sketch. McKimson worked without the live-action reference (the rotoscope) and animated the Uncle Sam and Porky scenes by hand-drawing all the "key" (most important) frames himself, creating the essential reference for the in-betweeners. The gentle facial expressions the animator gave Sam do look more realistic than the figures that had been rotoscoped. While good for fast physical action, those figures all have a pasted-on, flat, neutral facial expression. The close-up shot of Paul Revere and

his horse is drawn from an upper-three-fourths angle, a particularly difficult angle for any artist to draw, much less animate.

Bob McKimson's scene in which Uncle Sam leads Porky by the hand over to his seat is particularly beautiful. You can see the stumbling awkwardness of a young child trying to keep up with the long, slow strides of a large adult. These are two distinctly different people, moving at their own individual tempi, probably animated all on one level—that is to say, drawn on one piece of paper, as was the custom of the time. McKimson also had to plan out the moving background under the characters and "compensate the pan" when Sam starts walking and then stops to pick up a discarded American history book. Compensating the pan meant calculating, in hundredths of an inch, the reduction in increments the background is moved while the animation slowed the characters to a stop. Remember, this was all done without computers, calculated manually on a nonmotorized animation camera. A camera move so tightly in synch with the animation could only be done by the animator himself. Many times, the most difficult scenes are the most mundane, since they attract our notice only if they are done incorrectly. It takes great complexity aforethought to achieve real simplicity.

OLD GLORY opened at the Cathay Circle Theatre in Los Angeles just in time for the Fourth of July holiday. It was very well received. In the 1950s and '60s it had a second life on children's TV and was very popular during the counterculture heyday. The cartoon was projected on the walls of rock clubs like the Fillmore East, where the sight of the American flag being saluted by a pig, the then-current symbol of police authority, was considered ironically funny to most patrons.

The Old Grey Hare

"SMELLEVISION REPLACES TELEVISION! CARL STALLING SEZ IT'LL NEVER WORK!"

DIRECTOR: ROBERT CLAMPETT **STORY:** MICHAEL SASANOFF **ANIMATION:** ROBERT MCKIMSON, ROD SCRIBNER **VOICES:** MEL BLANC (BUGS), ARTHUR Q. BRYAN (ELMER FUDD) **MUSIC:** CARL STALLING

The voice of God tells a weeping Elmer Fudd that, yes, he eventually will catch that "wabbit," and takes him far into the future. Elmer, now a wrinkly old coot, finds that much has changed over the years and that his gun has been replaced with a Buck Wodgers Wightning-Quick Wabbit-Killer. He meets up with Bugs, now also an old fogey with lumbago, and finally does succeed in shooting him! Dying, Bugs gives Elmer his photo album, and we witness a flashback of baby Elmer's first encounter with little Bugsy Bunny. Other than Bugs suckling on a bottle of carrot juice, Elmer wielding a pop gun, and their stopping the chase to have an afternoon nap, not much has changed over the years. Back in the future, Bugs digs his own grave while Elmer mourns for him. Naturally, Bugs pulls a fast one and tips Elmer into the plot, burying the hunter alive. Bugs burrows underground to plant one last kiss on Elmer's wrinkly face and give him a parting gift: a huge stick of TNT, which explodes after the iris-out, shaking the end title card.

GREG FORD, animation historian In the last two or three years before Robert Clampett abruptly left the Warner Bros. cartoon studio in the mid-1940s, the renegade director surrendered an unwieldy bunch of late-blooming, oddly self-reflexive masterworks. Clampett's craving for summation reaches epochal proportions in **THE OLD GREY HARE,** as Elmer is fast-forwarded all the way to the year 2000 (gasp!). So comically premature is Clampett's yen for retrospection that he essays a cradle-to-grave biopic of Bugs Bunny and Elmer Fudd, reminiscing over their long-standing relationship, even though the pair had only existed onscreen for about four years at the time. Daringly, **GREY HARE** never depicts Bugs in his audience-friendly prime but portrays him either as a decrepit septuagenarian or a wide-eyed toddler.

The infantile fracases of baby Bugs and Elmer, fortified with stop-and-start timing that permits breaks for nap time, cram more sharp slapstick into their three minutes than was fitted into the whole run of the **TINY TOON ADVENTURES** series. The childhood flashbacks also validate Clampett's

As for the senile shenanigans of the arthritic characters in the cartoon's other half, the contributions of two star animators from Clampett's unit, Rod Scribner and Robert McKimson, rise to the surface. Eruptions of Scribner's elastic, taboo-flouting work begin almost immediately: No sooner does that old codger Bugs Bunny unearth himself and utter the fateful greeting "Eh…what's up, Prune Face?" than he lunges forward, wraps his hands around his old buddy's throat, and murderously strangles him. The

...nt Bugs re-
...m **HARE-UM**
...first appear-
...crystallized

figures then regroup almost instantaneously and the narrative proceeds apace, the alleged perpetration entirely forgotten. Given the unnaturally rubberized exaggeration of the neck-wringing and the "Did I really see that?" rapidity with which the action reverts back to normalcy, the net effect is less a justification of homicide than a cathartic shock.

Where Scribner's animation was expected to go off on expressionistic tangents of stretchable-bendableness, McKimson's awesome task was to restore some degree of anatomical correctness. In **GREY HARE**, McKimson reprises Bugs's uproarious deathbed soliloquy and "dying" histrionics, which the animator had first executed for **A WILD HARE**. Only this time, McKimson dutifully

renders them with the participants caked in "old age" makeup.

To the tune of a gurglingly warbled "Memories" (the Kahn–Van Alstyne classic), Bugs pulls an inevitable last-ditch switcheroo, and the rabbit frenziedly cackles, "So long, Methuselah!" Just as the bomb he thrusts into Fudd's mitts detonates after the cartoon ends and rattles the "That's all Folks!" sign, Clampett correctly surmises that the comedy would outlast even his regrettably early exit from the Warner animation scene.

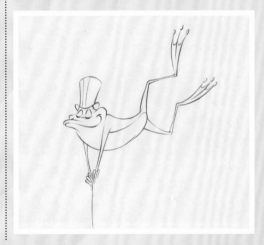

One Froggy Evening

"HELLO, MA BABY! / HELLO, MA HONEY! / HELLO, MA RAGTIME GAL!"

In the cornerstone of the J. C. Wilber Building—"Built 1892," reads its inscription—lies an ordinary-looking tin box. And in that box lives Michigan J. Frog, an ordinary-looking frog with extraordinary 1892-style singing and dancing skills (voiced by the singer and bandleader Bill Roberts). When the building is wrecked, a workman finds this freak of nature and greedily plans to profit from it. But by accident or design, the frog will only perform when the man is alone with him. In front of audiences at talent agencies and theaters, the frog is just a floppy, ordinary frog. After a series of such failures drives the man to poverty and jail, he hides the frog in a new building's cornerstone...where, a century later, another greedy workman finds him. Uh-oh.

MIKE BARRIER, animation and comics scholar
"Elegance" is not a word that usually comes to mind in connection with a cartoon, but director

DIRECTOR: CHARLES M. JONES **STORY:** MICHAEL MALTESE **ANIMATION:** ABE LEVITOW, RICHARD THOMPSON, KEN HARRIS, BEN WASHAM **LAYOUT:** ROBERT GRIBBROEK **BACKGROUNDS:** PHILIP DEGUARD **VOICE:** BILL ROBERTS (FROG) **MUSIC:** MILT FRANKLYN

Chuck Jones's **ONE FROGGY EVENING** deserves that label. Everything in it is in perfect balance. Its star is a mysterious frog that sings and dances—but only in the presence of the construction worker who uncovered him. So Jones arranges for the frog's voice to be the only one that we in the audience ever hear. Likewise, the frog dances and gestures with great freedom and exuberance as it sings, but otherwise there's striking economy of movement—the calculating squint of an eye is all that's needed to reveal a state of mind. It's the perfect way to tell a story that, like many of writer Michael Maltese's best stories for Jones, might

have seemed a little too cruel and cynical were Jones's direction not so deft.

Operation: Rabbit

Running from his cave hideout, Wile E. Coyote stops in front of the rabbit-hole home of Bugs Bunny, sets up a portable door, and knocks on it. When a puzzled Bugs answers the door, Coyote tells him, in no uncertain terms, that the predator is going to eat him for supper. Before Bugs can get out another word, the coyote informs him of his superior intellect and strength and gives the rabbit the "customary two minutes to say your prayers." Bugs yawns, slams the door on him, and retreats into his home. Wile E. sighs, "Why do they always want to do it the hard way?" The first plan of OPERATION: RABBIT involves an electric pressure cooker placed over the rabbit hole. Bugs tricks the coyote into looking under the cooker—and trapping him under it. A second attempt involves rigging a cannon with extra pipe to direct a cannonball into Bugs's hole. Bugs detours the cannonball with even more pipe, sending the explosive ball back to Wile E.'s cave. While working on a third plan, Wile E. receives a visitor: Bugs Bunny, willing to give himself up! He's prepared a will and needs Wile E. to sign it as a witness. Unfortunately for the coyote, he's handed a TNT fountain pen.

"ALLOW ME TO INTRODUCE MYSELF. MY NAME IS WILE E. COYOTE, GENIUS."

Back at the drawing board, Coyote works up the plans for an explosive rabbit decoy disguised as a female bunny. Before he can send it to Bugs, Wile E. gets another knock at the door—this time it's an explosive coyote femme fatale. Both decoys blow up in his face. Plan four is a flying saucer programmed to blast a rabbit. Bugs confounds the saucer by using a chicken mask—and sabotages the controls to go after Coyote, blowing his cave headquarters to bits. Next, we find Wile E. working in a explosives house, filling a set of carrots with nitroglycerin. Admiring his handiwork, he is oblivious to Bugs hauling his house onto the path of an oncoming train. The ensuing explosion leaves the coyote dazed and clinging to a mountain perch. The next day, the battered coyote sets up his door in front of the rabbit hole. He introduces himself, "My name is Mud!" and collapses. Bugs reminds us that "Mud spelled backwards is Dum!"

DIRECTOR: CHARLES M. JONES **STORY:** MICHAEL MALTESE **ANIMATION:** LLOYD VAUGHAN, BEN WASHAM, KEN HARRIS, PHIL MONROE **LAYOUT:** ROBERT GRIBBROEK **BACKGROUNDS:** PHILIP DEGUARD **VOICES:** MEL BLANC (BUGS, WILE E. COYOTE) **MUSIC:** CARL STALLING

STEPHEN PASTIS, cartoonist I had no idea Wile E. Coyote ever talked. Nor that he had the voice of a teetotaling gentleman. But what is most intriguing to me about Wile E. Coyote's appearance in **OPERATION: RABBIT** is that he terms himself a "genius." Unfortunately, this adds fuel to an ugly ongoing argument my eleven-year-old son, Tom, and I have had for the past three years. Tom has always maintained that Wile E. Coyote is

brilliant. His failures, according to Tom, are not due to any lack of cerebral power but rather to an extraordinary streak of bad luck.

To my dismay, Tom's argument is factually supported here by (a) Wile E.'s business card, which does in fact say "Genius"; (b) Wile E.'s neat, uncluttered workspace, which can be an indicator of a well-organized, sharp mind; and (c) Wile E.'s vaguely British accent, which, unfairly or not, gives the appearance of a more sophisticated intellect.

I, however, maintain that Wile E. is no genius at all. Witness his turning his back on Bugs to look down a hole (a rookie maneuver), his failure to notice the dynamite stick lit on both ends, and his unforgivable blindness to the fact that the structure he is working in is being dragged by a tractor onto train tracks. That's not bad luck: It's idiocy. (I will, however. excuse his failure to see the hot female coyote for the incendiary device she is. Lust has blinded some of history's greatest minds.)

The debate goes on.

JERRY SAYS This is the second appearance of director Chuck Jones's Coyote character (following **FAST AND FURRY-OUS** by two and a half years and preceding the second Road Runner film, **BEEP BEEP**, by four months). Here Jones gives Coyote a voice and personality—brought brilliantly to life by Mel Blanc. This pairing of Bugs versus a pompous "genius" was so successful Coyote was brought back several other times as a recurring foil for Bugs. Here, Jones dubbed him "Wile E. Coyote" for the first time. The name would stick, even though up to this point it had never been used in a Road Runner cartoon.

Page Miss Glory

"BOY, DO I SLAY 'EM!"

Hicksville is a boring Podunk, so it's a big day when celebrity Miss Glory comes to town. At Hicksville's one hotel, bellhop Abner practices his manners. But as time marches on and Miss Glory doesn't show, Abner dozes off, dreaming that his hotel is a vast, big-city tower with hundreds of high-roller guests, all musically asking Abner to page Miss Glory. Trying to find her, Abner steps on an old lady's skirt, pulling it off and turning her into a fan dancer. Glamorous Miss Glory (a caricature of Marion Davies, who had recently starred in a movie with the same title as this cartoon) arrives at the rooftop garden.

Everyone rushes there to meet and serenade her. Abner tries to get there, too, but when he finally catches an elevator, the operator goes on break! Ignorant Abner pushes buttons at random, sending himself everywhere but the garden. In the end, the elevator pops out of the roof, with Abner thrown earthward. He lands in the path of a jangling streetcar—but it's really Abner's Hicksville hotel boss, ringing the bell for the actual Miss Glory's arrival. Alas, the swanky star they'd expected is just a lollipop-licking, Shirley Temple–like little kid!

WILL FRIEDWALD, author and music critic PAGE MISS GLORY marks a rare instance when the two meanings of the word "cartoon" come into conflict—as audiences understood it in 1935–36, the term could mean an animated one-reeler

DIRECTOR: FRED AVERY **MODERNE ART:** CONCEIVED AND DESIGNED BY LEADORA CONGDON **WORDS AND MUSIC:** HARRY WARREN AND AL DUBIN **VOICES:** BERNICE HANSEN (MISS GLORY), JACKIE MORROW (ABNER), FRED AVERY (CUSTOMER), THE VARSITY THREE (VOCAL GROUP)

screened at the local movie house or the non-animated but nonetheless lively cartoons found in magazines like *Esquire* and the *New Yorker*. **MISS GLORY** looks like the drawings of legendary 1930s *New Yorker* cartoonists Peter Arno or John Held Jr. come to life.

In 1936, the Hollywood cartoon was a family medium rather than, in the parlance of the day, a "kid draw," while magazine cartoons were usually aimed at a distinctly adult readership. **PAGE MISS GLORY** is one of the most adult-oriented animated efforts of its day. There's almost nothing in it that a kid would find entertaining. Even considering that the story takes place in two very different locales—a hick town contrasted with an über-glamorous Art Deco hotel (a place so modern that they spell it *moderne*)—what humor there is mainly revolves about the conspicuous consumption of alcohol. Almost as much is guzzled here as in a *Thin Man* movie! The other major comic sequence involves a stern matron accidentally deprived of her clothing and thus her dignity, which prompts her to launch into a spontaneous fan dance that reveals an embarrassing patch on her tuchus.

MISS GLORY further draws on the discrepancy between the small town, where the streets are populated with as many barnyard animals as people, and the imagined Deco wonderland. Seen today, the most pronounced contrast is between the present and the past—to our contemporary sensibilities, even the title seems antiquated.

Although director Tex Avery made an attempt to inject some kind of humor in the piece (the booze and indecent-exposure jokes are funnier than an extended bit involving uncooperative elevators), **MISS GLORY** is remembered more for its musical sequences. The Merrie Melodies series of cartoons started as a vehicle for Warner Bros. to plug its music-publishing holdings, but, as film critic Leonard Maltin has pointed out, by the mid-1930s, entries like **GOIN' TO HEAVEN ON A MULE** seemed like weak-sister imitations of the live-action films that inspired them. Not so with

MISS GLORY—in fact, there's nothing in the live-action feature to compete with the cartoon. One even feels that Busby Berkeley missed his calling. When he would position dozens and dozens of identical-looking girls—all wearing the exact same costume, makeup, and wigs—in elaborate dance routines, he was trying for an effect that could have been better achieved through animation. **MISS GLORY** boasts several animated dance sequences that, in this respect, could be described as out-Buzz-ing Berkeley; the key sequences look like someone took the sketches from the fashion designer of one of the Fred Astaire–Ginger Rogers classics and animated them.

There were barely even a handful of comparable efforts, namely, animator Ub Iwerks's **MERRY MANNEQUINS** (1937) and Disney's Silly Symphony **COCK OF THE WALK** (1935). Even among this trio, **PAGE MISS GLORY** stands out.

In its visual opulence, made acceptable by setting everything—choreography as well as gags—on a steady beat, Avery found a copasetic middle ground between Buzz Berkeley and abstract animator Oskar Fischinger.

> **JERRY SAYS** This early Tex Avery vehicle is famous for its Art Deco design and Busby Berkeley–like choreography, but a few classic Avery gags creep in. Miss Glory's admirers include a top-hatted slicker who rushes from a steam cabinet and a chef who drops his cake through the floor. A fat hotel diner orders a huge pile of food—only to eat half an olive and depart!

A Pest in the House

SHOUTED: "IF THERE'S ANYTHING WE'VE GOT PLENTY OF, IT'S GOOD OL' PEACE AND QUIET!"

The labor shortage has Elmer Fudd resorting to hiring Daffy Duck as a bellhop in his hotel. Unfortunately, a burly businessman (Arthur Q. Bryan, speaking in his real voice) threatens to clobber Elmer if his rest is disturbed at any time during his visit. Daffy means well in seeing that his boss doesn't suffer the punishment, but he only earns Elmer a few beatings by being helplessly obnoxious to the guest: Daffy silences a singing drunk by getting drunk himself, then scratches the window clean, and (in a superbly staged, posed, and animated scene by Ken Harris) gets the guest out of bed to tell a joke about a traveling salesman, only to forget what the punch line is—"But it was a *riot*!" Daffy concludes. Later, when Daffy attempts to get the furnace working by banging it with a wrench, Elmer races to muffle the sound, only to be berated by Daffy for causing the furnace valve to whistle. Finally, Elmer attempts to avoid another noise-caused beating by appointing Daffy manager, but it doesn't fool the guest, and Fudd receives one last pop in the nose.

> **DIRECTOR:** CHARLES M. JONES **STORY:** TED PIERCE, MICHAEL MALTESE **ANIMATION:** BEN WASHAM, KEN HARRIS, BASIL DAVIDOVICH, LLOYD VAUGHAN **LAYOUT AND BACKGROUNDS:** RICHARD MORLEY **VOICES:** MEL BLANC (DAFFY, NARRATOR), ARTHUR Q. BRYAN (ELMER, TIRED GUEST) **MUSIC:** CARL STALLING

DAVID BOWERS, animator and director **A PEST IN THE HOUSE** is a great cartoon featuring a terrific performance from Daffy Duck. Although it's directed by Chuck Jones, he hadn't yet developed Daffy into the selfish, greedy, ill-tempered foil to Bugs Bunny that he would become. For me, the cartoon is the best of two worlds: the wonderful drawings, poses, and comic timing of Jones's direction coupled with the much funnier Daffy of directors Bob Clampett and Frank Tashlin.

The premise of the cartoon is simple. A tired, tired man wants peace and quiet in his hotel room so he can grab some shuteye, but bellhop Daffy keeps him awake—by trying to help him sleep. My favorite gag is when Daffy promises to silence a singing drunk in the next room. Offscreen, we hear Daffy enter the drunk's room, a cork is popped, and then Daffy noisily joins the drunk in a horrible rendition of "How Dry I Am." The whole bit plays over a beautifully posed and animated scene of the guest as he tries to sleep. We see him get more and more restless until he sits up to close in on the camera, his red eyes blazing with rage and frustration. Daffy was rarely more obnoxious—or funnier.

Pigs in a Polka

"TONIGHT IT GIVES ME EXTREME PLEASURE TO PRESENT OUR INTERPRETA…INTERPRET…INTER…INTOIPRETATION OF A FAMILIAR FAIRY TALE ENTITLED 'THE BIG BAD WOLF (ANDTHETHREELITTLEPIGS).'"

A wolf conductor loftily introduces an enactment of the story of the three little pigs and the big bad wolf, all timed to Brahms's Hungarian Dances. The first pig builds his straw house over a prefab wire structure; the second pig builds his out of matchsticks. The third pig lays bricks the hard way. His lazy brothers mock him, and mock the wolf, too, when he shows up in gypsy drag. The wolf burns up the straw house, collapses the matchstick house, and tries to break the brick house, but only manages to bust in one side and out the other. Later, the wolf fools the lazy pigs with a peasant woman costume, but the third pig tricks the wolf into dancing till his disguise falls off. In the ensuing chase, the pigs take an elevator to safety in the basement, while the wolf travels down the shaft the hard way. Ouch!

DIRECTOR: I. FRELENG **VOICES:** MEL BLANC (WOLF, PIG #3), SARA BERNER (PIGS #1 & #2) **MUSIC:** CARL STALLING

GREG FORD, animation historian Friz Freleng invaded Disney territory with **PIGS IN A POLKA**, an irreverent reworking of Disney's breakthrough short subject **THE THREE LITTLE PIGS** (1933), here reimagined and propelled in its entirety by Brahms's Hungarian Dances. From the obligatory scene-setting rigmarole of the three pigs slapping together their three separate houses of straw, matchsticks, and bricks, it's abundantly clear that Friz means to reapply the same tweaked synchronization of classical music to animated action that he achieved in the Franz Liszt–driven

RHAPSODY IN RIVETS (1941). The music-action symbiosis is, if anything, more accentuated than before. Even the cartoon's concluding iris-out first zeros in, then briefly bulges out again on the half beat, and lastly telescopes back to black in a concentrated one-to-one bond with the last three notes of Brahms's final musical flourish.

Where **PIGS IN A POLKA** noticeably breaks new ground is in its prolonged passages of ballet-like choreography mixed with rude pratfalls. The wolf bursts upon the scene, Cossack-stepping down a path (and law-abidingly signaling for a left turn as he rounds the corner), and is next spotted skulking from behind one tree to behind another in perfect rhythm.

At times, gags in **PIGS IN A POLKA** kiddingly call into question the very nature of the musical

synchronization on which the film is founded. During a heartrending violin solo, for instance, the wolf, in disguise as a poor old babushka, fakes playing a sympathy-inducing violin in a storm of phony snow (talcum powder liberally dispensed from a contraption mounted on his back). But once the wolf is let inside, Pig #3 divines the actual source of the weepy violin riff, uncovering an old-time phonograph player hidden underneath the wolf's dress. Pig #3 need only turn the record over to the flip side, which treats us to a selection sampled earlier in the film, and the wolf can't help but break into an encore Cossack dance, shaking off his old lady's garments in the process and revealing his identity.

In the final chase scenes of **PIGS IN A POLKA**, the relationship of music to image seems to be determined more organically—by comic feel—and less literally. The prolonged, swelling orchestration at the film's finish finds its unlikely visual analogy in an extended pan shot of the unsuspecting wolf as he falls down an interminable elevator shaft. At this point, sound and image are so well conjoined that one almost doesn't stop to ask how a twenty-five-floor elevator possibly could fit inside the pigs' rustic two-story brick hangout.

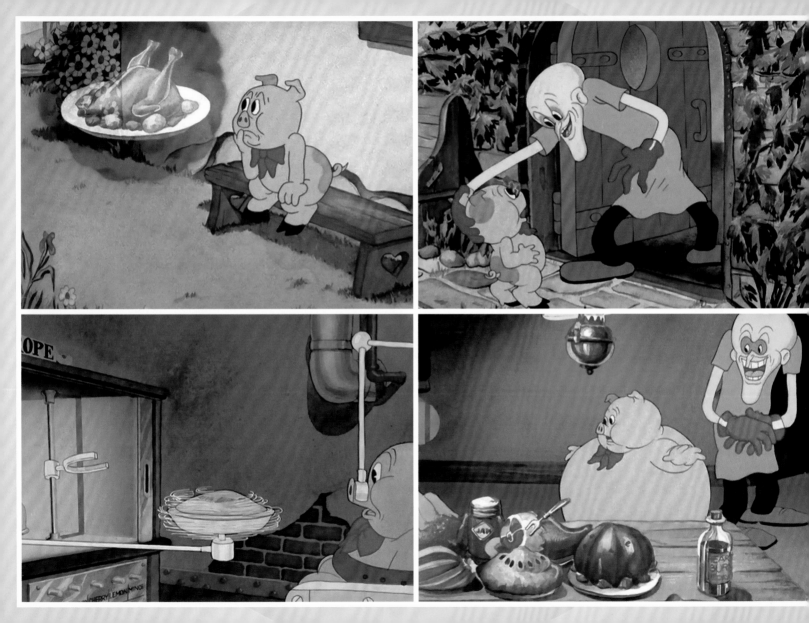

Pigs Is Pigs

"YOU LIKE PIES?"

This cute amorality play is best known for its unforgettable, elaborate nightmare sequence. One little pig, in a family of piglets, would rather obsess over food than play. When Mama puts a hot pie on the windowsill to cool, Piggy quickly eats it. At dinner time, Piggy ties all the spaghetti together while the family says grace, and slurps up the family meal in one breath. That night he dreams of visiting a strange house, where he is presented with a table filled with his favorite foods. The mystery man of the house is a strange, yellow-skinned, red-gloved, hiccupping mad scientist who straps the pig into a chair and force-feeds him everything from bananas to ice cream. A mechanized sandwich maker piles the ingredients on high, allowing director Friz Freleng to pull the subsequently oft-used "Hold the onions!" gag for the first time. The piggy is released from this torture as a massive blob. On his way out the door, he grabs a turkey leg for the road, takes a bite and explodes. He wakes up from his nightmare and runs downstairs—to eat his breakfast.

YVETTE KAPLAN, director, writer, and animator
It's Friz Freleng's fault I'm not thinner. I used to think it was my own fault for not having any willpower. But nope, after watching this short again

DIRECTOR: I. FRELENG **ANIMATION:** BOB MCKIMSON, PAUL SMITH **VOICES:** BILLY BLETCHER (MAN IN DREAM), MARTHA WENTWORTH (MAMA PIG) **MUSIC:** CARL STALLING

for the first time since I was a kid, I know for sure. It's Freleng's fault.

PIGS IS PIGS was one of my favorite cartoons when I was young. It was wild, scary, surreal. And it was a redemption story! And boy, did I love those. I was a huge fan of Max Fleischer's **COLOR CLASSICS**, which were all about kids getting punished for one thing or another. A little squirt wants to be a big shot? No prob! Let's scare the pants off of him! A mere tot wants to drive a train? Fine! But let's see him do it without any brakes! Sure, the kids were terrified. But they learned their lessons, and I loved that. In my memory, **PIGS IS PIGS** was the same thing. A kid—a piggy little piggy—ate too much and got punished for it. Horribly, cruelly, disgustingly: powerless and strapped to a chair, his mouth held open by a vise, robotic arms shoveling in enough food to choke a herd of horses. Weight Watchers has nothing on this technique—this poor little pig would never eat again!

Or so you'd think. And that's how I remembered it. But no, watching it again, I was shocked to see that's not what happened at all. Instead, immediately after the pig's torture, his once plump little body now engorged, disfigured, and barely recognizable, he waddles to escape out the front door. But wait—is that a bowl of mush on the table? Yes. Poor pig. Does he scream? No. Does he faint? No. Does he vomit? No! He grabs it and eats it all.

And it all became clear: Some kids never learn. Or else, like me, they learn too well. Take the **COLOR CLASSICS**, for instance. From them I learned to not be a tough guy, to always play safe, and to not be like greedy Humpty Dumpty. Thanks to **PIGS IS PIGS**, I learned a lesson, too: Food is too good to say no to. So I won't. Bring on the chips. Cheeseburger please, with fries. And a nice big slice of cherry pie. With ice cream! Like I said, willpower has nothing to do with it, because it's all Friz Freleng's fault.

JERRY SAYS Apart from the same title, **PIGS IS PIGS** has no relation to the 1954 Disney cartoon nor to the short story by Ellis Parker Butler.

Plane Daffy

"THE LITTLE LIGHT—IT STAYS ON!"

The carrier pigeon flight station is losing all of its men to Hatta Mari, a Nazi femme fatale who slips her victims "Mickeyblitz Finnkriegs" to get them to spill military secrets. We see this happen to Pigeon 13, who blows his brains out in shame after his treachery (missing the first time). Daffy Duck, "the squadron woman-hater," is recruited to take the next military secret through, but he is just as easily taken in by Hatta. The gal gives him an electrifying kiss, but Daffy returns the favor by shocking her in return (brilliantly animated by Art Davis). Daffy is then chased around her love nest, and after hiding in the icebox, he reveals that "the little light—it stays on!" Finally cornered with a musket lodged in his throat (the whole thing, mind you), Daffy refuses to hand over the document and swallows it. Hatta straps Daffy to an X-ray machine and broadcasts the results to Hitler and his minions. "Hitler is a stinker," it reveals. "That's no military secret!" cries Hitler.

"Ja, everybody knows that," reply Goering and Goebbels before blowing their brains out for their error.

"They lose more darn Nutzis that way," woo-hoos Daffy.

DIRECTOR: FRANK TASHLIN **STORY:** WARREN FOSTER **ANIMATION:** CAL DALTON **VOICES:** MEL BLANC (DAFFY, HITLER, GOERING), SARA BERNER (HATTA MARI), ROBERT C. BRUCE (NARRATOR) **MUSIC:** CARL STALLING

MARTIN GOODMAN, animation historian In many ways, Frank Tashlin's **PLANE DAFFY** resembles other wartime cartoons directed by Warner Bros. personnel. The femme fatale Hatta Mari, the transmutation of Homer Pigeon into a jackass after spilling secrets to the Nazi temptress, and the swastikas that adorn Hatta Mari's earrings, garter tops, and shoes are all echoed in the contemporaneous Private Snafu cartoons directed by Bob Clampett and Chuck Jones. Even Homer's Mortimer Snerd voice was used by Clampett for Beaky Buzzard in 1942, and Daffy's manic behaviors and plastic anatomy seem to align more with Clampett's style than Tashlin's. What sets this short apart is the burgeoning sense that Tashlin was beginning to incorporate cinematic structure and technique to his animated cartoons. The short opens with grim narration superimposed over a down shot of stoic military carrier pigeons poring over a map; the lighting effects are dramatic, and

clouds of cigarette smoke rise steadily above the birds. Later in the film, Daffy opens a sequence of doors trying to escape Hatta Mari. She is behind every one, holding an increasingly large weapon, and each time the perspective is different as Tashlin experiments with camera angles.

The frank sexuality of this cartoon is evident, and even Hatta Mari's photograph sways its hips seductively. Sexual excitement, release, and even post-coital bliss are suggestively portrayed. Tashlin takes risks that only a very adult filmmaker would attempt, and it's amazing that this short got by the censors. The combination of imaginative approach, aggressive sexuality, and wartime élan make **PLANE DAFFY** one of Warner's best wartime efforts.

GREG FORD, animation historian Remarking on the abundance of cartoon-like contortion in Tashlin's live-action 1950s laughfests, film critic Andrew Sarris, in *The American Cinema*, tenders a salient if somewhat condescending observation: "The suspicion persists that if Tashlin had not had Jerry Lewis and Jayne Mansfield, he would have invented their equivalents." That suspicion is confirmed by a certain shapely knockout in

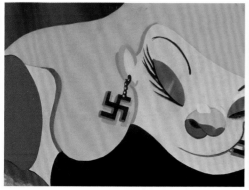

rockets Daffy to Hatta's hideaway like a moth to a flame.

The duck-pigeon encounter brings us to the subject of Daffy Duck's sex life, always fertile fodder for yucks. Daffy's dalliance with Hatta Mari is funnier than Daffy Duck in squaw drag pitching woo to a burly Indian brave in **THE DAFFY DUCKAROO** (1942), funnier than sleuth Daffy's flirtatious interrogation of a sultry murder suspect in **THE SUPER SNOOPER** (1952), and funnier even than Daffy's courtship of milady Melissa in **THE SCARLET PUMPERNICKEL** (1950). It's exceptional for its body language (amid a romantic clinch, Daffy's neck stretches to giraffe-like lengths to avoid Hatta's lethal smooch), its unrelenting hyperbole (Hatta's osculations administer electric shocks before liquefying Daffy into a puddle of goop), and its judicious placement of one-liners (Daffy cribs comedian Jerry Colonna's catchphrase, "Something NEW has been added!" after his retaliatory kiss ignites fireworks of its own).

PLANE DAFFY. On a visual level, the animated Hatta Mari unmistakably qualifies as a Jayne Mansfield progenitor. The curvaceous design of this top-heavy Nazi se-duck-tress is a before-the-fact approximation of the Mansfield physique that Tashlin parlayed a dozen years later in **THE GIRL CAN'T HELP IT** (1956).

With a true movie freak's penchant for stylistic pilferage, Tashlin opens **PLANE DAFFY** by citing a classic live-action war picture: a montage of World War II carrier pigeons "stiff-upper-lipping it" in the manner of the World War I aces from Howard Hawks's *Dawn Patrol* (1930). Just as Hawks's (human) flyboys stoically chalked out the names of each downed pilot, so Tashlin's carrier pigeons cancel out the names of every confrere to have been "torched" by wicked Hatta Mari. Tashlin spoofs the solemnity of the pigeons' predicament by overdoing it through the soberness of the film's mock-heroic narration and the sternness of the pigeons' near-frozen visages; their he-manly reticence is finally undercut when their leader unfurls an undulating Hatta Mari pinup and the entire unit keels over in a swoon like a pack of screaming bobbysoxers.

To continue with the cartoon's voiced-over verse, neatly structured in quatrains with recherché rhymes by story man Warren Foster, "In this moment of crisis / From out of the ruck / Steps the squadron woman-hater / Daffy Duck." A bad excuse for a woman-hater right from the get-go, courier Daffy braves onslaughts of wind, hail, sleet, and rain—but one mere peek at a female gam, strategically displayed in a doorway,

Porky in Wackyland

"IT CAN HAPPEN HERE!"

This cartoon begins with a newspaper head-line informing us that "Porky Hunts Rare Do-Do Bird Worth $4000,000,000,000!! P.S. 000,000,000." Cut to aviator Porky Pig flying past Dark Africa and Darker Africa to land squarely in Darkest Africa, directly in front of a border marker reading "Welcome to Wackyland / 'It Can Happen Here' / Population: 100 nuts and a squirrel." Porky's plane tiptoes into the territory and is immediately greeted by a roaring beast—who turns effeminate and politely says "Boo!" before dancing off gaily into the nighttime forest. The landscape Porky encounters can only be described as surreal; as he explores deeper, he watches a rising totem pole of zany characters lift the sun into its proper position to begin a new day. A loony character arises from a flower, playing the "William Tell Overture" on his nose, then goes into a wild drum solo that brings forth all the screwball citizens of Wackyland.

Porky tries to spot the Do-Do but gets distracted by a "Cat-Dog," a duck screaming "Mammy!" and a three-headed Stooge creature whose "Mama was scared by a pawnbroker sign." Porky is led to a castle, in which the Do-Do finally appears—via motor boat—to confirm he's really the last of the

Do-Dos ("Vo-doe-dee-o-doe!"). The pig chases the bird all over the landscape, as the feathered freak flies through walls, up invisible elevators, and even on the back of the Warner Bros. shield to escape. Porky finally outsmarts the bird when he dresses as a Wackyland newspaper boy, sells the bird a bogus newspaper, and bops him on the head. "Yes, I'm really the last of the Do-Dos," says the bird, "Ain't I, fellas?"—as hundreds of Do-Dos now descend on Porky yelling, "Yeah, man!"

DIRECTOR: ROBERT CLAMPETT **ANIMATION:** NORMAN MCCABE, I. ELLIS **VOICES:** MEL BLANC (PORKY, DO-DO), DAVE WEBER ("LEMME OUTTA HERE!"), TED PIERCE (MYSTERIOUS VOICE), BOB CLAMPETT (VOCAL EFFECTS) **MUSIC:** CARL STALLING

STEVE SCHNEIDER, animation historian No mere Looney Tune, **PORKY IN WACKYLAND** was Warner Bros.' Emancipation Proclamation. Building on the creaky liberties inaugurated by director Tex Avery, here Bob Clampett scoffs and shreds the conventions—realism, literalism, infantilism, cutesiness, and worse—that, with the ascendancy of Disney, had come to caramelize cartooning. By reminding us of animation's horizons—namely, none at

all—this anything-goes film illustrates Sigmund Freud's notion that humor arises from breaking taboos. And breaking taboos is something that animation, with its limitless freedom, is uniquely gifted to do.

Sure, Clampett set his inspirited nonsense way off in no-man's-land—here masquerading as Africa—but with the Do-Do let out of the bag, he could drop his cover and turn his sharp, satirical eye on things back home. And that's when things really get good and crazy. When "It can happen here!" points to your own backyard, the most incisive of humor can happen. Which it did, gloriously, at Warner Bros. for the next twenty or so years.

JERRY SAYS This is one of director Bob Clampett's signature films and certainly one of his wildest. Clampett said it was based on a newspaper article that he read about an actual expedition to Africa to hunt for a rare bird. It's Clampett's homage to Salvador Dalí, comic-strip artist Milt Gross, and Lewis Carroll, with a touch of Dr. Seuss and the director's own, unadulterated id thrown in the mix.

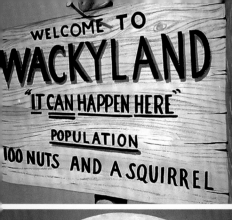

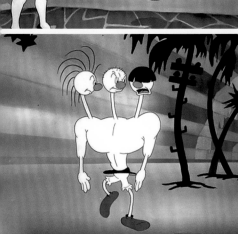

HOTEL BILL
ROOM $62.50
BREAKAGE   29.60
REPAIR DOORS   30.00
ELEVATOR   97.
PIPES   46.20
DOOR KNOBS   35.40
GLASS   120.18
RUGS   69.80
FIX LIGHTS   26.30
NEW DESKS   90.22
LOVE SPOTS   11.86
TOTAL   500.62

Porky Pig's Feat

"ANY SIMILARITY BETWEEN THIS HOTEL AND OTHER HOTELS, LIVING OR DEAD, IS PURELY COINCIDENTAL."

Porky Pig and Daffy Duck unsuccessfully attempt to slip past the corpulent manager of the Broken Arms Hotel after Daffy has gambled away all their money. They are kept prisoner in their room. To escape, they try, among other things, pushing the manager down a circular staircase, tying sheets together to climb to the sidewalk, and using a rope to swing across to another hotel. In the end, after months of effort, they decide to call their hero, Bugs Bunny, for advice. The only problem is that Bugs, too, is trapped in the hotel—in the next room.

DIRECTOR: FRANK TASHLIN **STORY:** MELVIN MILLAR **ANIMATION:** PHIL MONROE **VOICES:** MEL BLANC (DAFFY, PORKY, HOTEL MANAGER) **MUSIC:** CARL STALLING

MARK MAYERSON, animator Frank Tashlin had a very personal style of cartoon direction. He chose unusual camera angles and was never afraid to cut shots quickly for humorous effect. His characters were often posed in "extreme" (exaggerated) positions, and those poses were held far longer than other directors would dare.

Tashlin's direction is so flamboyant that it is as entertaining to watch as the characters. **PORKY PIG'S FEAT** is fairly standard from a story standpoint, typical of Warner Bros. cartoons that pit characters against each other. It's how Tashlin tells this story that makes it so memorable.

JERRY SAYS **PORKY PIG'S FEAT** was the first film Frank Tashlin directed upon his return to Leon Schlesinger's studio after three and a half years away (two and a half at Disney and one at Columbia/Screen Gems). It's also his first film with Daffy Duck.

Rabbit Fire

"RABBITS AU GRATIN DU JOUR UNDER TUBED LEATHER, DROOL, DROOL."

DIRECTOR: CHARLES M. JONES **STORY:** MICHAEL MALTESE **ANIMATION:** LLOYD VAUGHAN, KEN HARRIS, PHIL MONROE, BEN WASHAM **LAYOUT:** ROBERT GRIBBROEK **BACKGROUNDS:** PHILIP DEGUARD **VOICES:** MEL BLANC (BUGS, DAFFY, ELEPHANT), ARTHUR Q. BRYAN (ELMER) **MUSIC:** CARL STALLING

Elmer Fudd is following Bugs Bunny's tracks in the woods. He's actually tracking Daffy Duck, wearing bunny shoes, who is leading Elmer to Bugs, only wanting to liven up things with his tomfoolery. Held at gunpoint, Bugs confides to Elmer that it's really duck season. What follows is a legendary sequence (animated by Lloyd Vaughan) of Daffy and Bugs arguing over which season it really is, with every bit ending in Daffy getting his head blasted in some new way.

Bugs nails up a "Duck Season Open" sign, so to complicate things, Daffy disguises as Bugs. Bugs disguises as Daffy, and replaces the sign with "Rabbit Season Open," getting the real Daffy blasted once again. Bugs and Daffy try to tantalize Elmer with various rabbit and duck recipes, but Elmer reveals that he's a vegetarian and only hunts for the sport of it. After both the duck and the rabbit hide out in Bugs's hole, Bugs pops up to scold Elmer for hunting rabbits with an elephant gun, telling Fudd that he should be hunting elephants with it. "You do, and I'll give ya such a pinch!" says an elephant (his sissy voice a caricature of comedian Joe Besser), who appears out of nowhere to administer a beating to Elmer. Bugs then disguises himself as sweater-wearing hunting gal, and Daffy as "her" hunting hound, but that ruse doesn't work, either. The tables turn when Bugs and Daffy find a sign announcing that it's really "Elmer Season." We end with Bugs and Daffy, donned in Fudd-type clothing, tracking their victim. "Be vewy, vewy quiet! We're hunting Elmers! Huh-huh-huh!"

Elmer eventually runs out of ammunition ("No more buwwets!"), but Daffy needs to see for himself and gets one last one through his scalp.

TOM SITO, animator and director **RABBIT FIRE** is the first of director Chuck Jones's Bugs-Daffy-Elmer cycle of shorts, now called the "Hunting Trilogy," the other two being **RABBIT SEASONING** (1952) and **DUCK! RABBIT, DUCK!** (1953). Chuck had Bugs Bunny making a cameo in a Daffy short the previous year, but this was the first time Bugs and Daffy shared top billing together.

In **RABBIT FIRE** we see Jones refine his efforts to redefine the personalities of the key Warner characters as he saw them. In Bob Clampett and Tex Avery cartoons, Daffy Duck was a crazy, surreal anarchist. Here, Jones turned him into Bugs Bunny's long-suffering sidekick, the id-driven

Bob Hope to Bugs's unflappable Bing Crosby. Elmer Fudd is not so much of an antagonist as a force of nature, the occupational hazard of being a woodland creature. Instead, the rivalry between Bugs and Daffy is the central conflict of this cartoon. The more Bugs remains in control, the more Daffy flies off the handle, providing Bugs psychological victory.

This is the first cartoon in which writer Mike Maltese gives us a version of the old vaudeville routine of flipping someone's meaning via rapid repetition:

Daffy: "It's rabbit season!"
Bugs: "Duck season!"
Daffy: "Rabbit season!"
Bugs: "Rabbit season!"
Daffy: "Duck season!"
Bugs: "Rabbit season!"
Daffy: "I say it's duck season, and I say, FIRE!"

These routines and their variations were very popular on the radio, acted out by duos like Abbott and Costello. We worked it into **WHO FRAMED ROGER RABBIT** (1988) when detective Eddie Valiant tricks Roger into drinking a strong whiskey. " I don't want one." "Oh, but you do." "No I don't." "But you do." "I don't." "You don't." "But I do!"

The cartoon is really a tour de force from voice actor Mel Blanc. He not only does all the rapid back-and-forth banter between Bugs and Daffy, at one point he does Daffy imitating Bugs's voice, Bugs imitating a woman's voice, and both of them imitating Elmer's trademark lisp. You have to keep reminding yourself that this was all done by one person. (The only other actor is Arthur Q. Bryan, who voices Elmer.)

The animation—by Chuck's crew Ken Harris, Lloyd Vaughan, Phil Monroe, and Ben Washam— was particularly well done. Ben Washam told me

that the animators were challenging one another to see how long they could hold a pose for comedic effect and still have it seem believable. When Daffy's threshold of frustration had been reached, having been shot in the face for the umpteenth time, he walks over to Bugs and glares at him. Ben said he tried to hold that still pose for as long as he could before Daffy said "You're despicable!" Here, it lasted more than two seconds. The comedic pause is an art Jack Benny and Oliver Hardy were particularly good at. It's easy to get a laugh by hitting someone or blowing something up. But to get laughter from nothing more than a look— that takes exceptional timing.

Chuck has said, "When Daffy is on his own in a cartoon, he is definitely the dominant star" (for instance, in 1950's **THE SCARLET PUMPERNICKEL**). But the director liked this interplay between the two leads, especially because it made Daffy's vulnerability and frustration more empathetic. Audiences felt for Daffy as his efforts to get back at Bugs were frustrated, over and over again. Chuck once confessed, "People ask me which character I most identified with. I'd like to think that I was Bugs, but, upon reflection, I fear I am really Daffy."

SHOE SHINE

Rabbit of Seville

"THERE, YOU'RE NICE AND CLEAN / THOUGH YOUR FACE LOOKS LIKE IT MIGHT HAVE GONE THROUGH A MACHINE."

An outdoor theater is presenting the opera *The Barber of Seville* when hunter Elmer chases Bugs from the nearby woods onto the stage. Instantly a part of the performance, barber Bugs hustles Elmer into his shop and gives him a wild shave. Furious, Elmer grabs his gun, but Bugs costumes himself as a femme fatale and woos Elmer back into place. Again a barber, Bugs builds a Carmen Miranda hat on Elmer's head; as a snake charmer, Bugs charms an electric razor to menace the hunter. The two chase each other in rising barber's chairs. Next, Bugs uses fertilizer to grow flowers on the hunter's bald pate. Soon, Bugs and Elmer are facing off with weapons—and then flowers and candy, leading to a musical marriage and Elmer's plunge into a huge wedding cake. "Next!" says barber Bugs. Bugs has done many a drag scene, but **RABBIT OF SEVILLE** provides a rare example of payback, with a dazed Elmer later dressed up as the bunny's blushing bride.

DIRECTOR: CHARLES M. JONES **STORY:** MICHAEL MALTESE **ANIMATION:** PHILIP MONROE, BEN WASHAM, LLOYD VAUGHAN, KEN HARRIS, EMERY HAWKINS **LAYOUT:** ROBERT GRIBBROEK **BACKGROUNDS:** PHILIP DEGUARD **VOICES:** MEL BLANC (BUGS), ARTHUR Q. BRYAN (ELMER) **MUSIC:** CARL STALLING

GREG FORD, animation historian Chuck Jones's two most beloved operatic extravaganzas starring Bugs Bunny, **WHAT'S OPERA, DOC?** (1957) and **RABBIT OF SEVILLE**, veer down somewhat different paths stylistically. **WHAT'S OPERA, DOC?** relies on a more removed, high-concept graphic sense and the shock effect of Maurice Noble's splendidly expressionistic set design. The humor of **RABBIT OF SEVILLE**, staged against Robert Gribbroek's straightforward backgrounds, depends more exclusively on the cartoon's intense synchronization whereby every bit of slapstick action, mini-movement by mini-movement, links to the accompanying Rossini score. In **SEVILLE**, Jones was really harking back to an older Warner Bros. legacy: director Friz Freleng's **RHAPSODY IN RIVETS** (1941) and **PIGS IN A POLKA** (1943), perhaps the two most insistently "Mickey Moused" (perfectly synched) musical cartoons ever made.

Interestingly, the younger Jones wrote admiringly of these two Freleng pictures in an essay for an obscure film journal from the mid-1940s. The essay clearly points the way toward **RABBIT OF SEVILLE**: "The music was not used as a background," Jones wrote, "but as the dictating factor in the actions of the characters. Thus, when the musical pace was *allegro* their actions became quick and lively: If the music moved to *prestissimo* they became frantic in their endeavor to keep up with it. It moved from there to *mysterioso*, *grave*, or *pianissimo*; in any case, the characters were dragged inexorably with it."

Jones's maverick film scholarship informed other aspects of **RABBIT OF SEVILLE**. Several of

Bugs's facial expressions as he slops various forms of goop on Elmer's scalp are derived from Charlie Chaplin's sympathetic barber character in *The Great Dictator* (1940). So, too, are certain of the cartoon's tonsorial props, namely, the barber chairs that are cranked upward and upward into the theater rafters.

So dexterous was the comic timing of Jones and his crew at their peak during the early 1950s that they could conjure great jokes in the most incidental of actions. When Bugs Bunny sprinkles Figaro Fertilizer on Elmer's scalp instead of more orthodox lotions, Elmer's noggin briefly seems to sprout real hair. Fudd lights up at this, of course, and only then do red wildflowers bloom on the fertilized stems, to the victim's shocked dismay. What's telltale, though, are those six or seven microseconds of sheer elation when Elmer believes that he's grown actual hair. It's this brief uplift that makes his final letdown funny.

Furthermore, it gives the tip-off that Elmer's baldness may have been bothering him for all these years—that it may be yet another source of the inferiority feelings that drive Fudd to hunt the little gray rabbit.

Rabbit Seasoning

"PRONOUN TROUBLE!"

"If you're looking for fun / You don't need a reason / All you need is a gun / It's rabbit season!" read just a few of the signs Daffy Duck has plastered the forest with to cover up the fact that it's really duck season. Elmer Fudd meets up with Bugs Bunny and tells Bugs he still hasn't "seen a wabbit yet." Daffy, dumbfounded by his stupidity, solves this dilemma and orders him to shoot Bugs immediately.

"Would you like to shoot me now, or wait till you get home?" Bugs asks.

"Shoot him now!" Daffy screams.

"You keep out of this; he doesn't have to shoot you now!" Bugs retorts, but Daffy is adamant ("He does so have to shoot me now!"), and demands that Elmer shoot him. Blam!

Daffy asks to run through it again and halts Bugs at the switch, but is so eager for gunfire that Daffy gets himself shot again. Elmer gets fed up with waiting and shoots at both of them, chasing them into Bugs's burrow. Daffy takes a peek to make sure the coast is clear and gets shot again. Bugs suggests Daffy act as a decoy and lure him away, but Daffy has

DIRECTOR: CHARLES M. JONES **STORY:** MICHAEL MALTESE **ANIMATION:** BEN WASHAM, LLOYD VAUGHAN, KEN HARRIS **LAYOUT:** MAURICE NOBLE **BACKGROUNDS:** PHILIP DEGUARD **VOICES:** MEL BLANC (BUGS, DAFFY), ARTHUR Q. BRYAN (ELMER) **MUSIC:** CARL STALLING

had enough. "No more for me, thanks!" he says. "I'm drivin'!"

Next, Bugs dresses as a Southern belle who's hankering for a duck dinner; Elmer (and his erectile hunting hat) immediately falls for the belle, much to Daffy's disgust. Daffy pulls off the disguise, and Bugs pulls the "here or home" shtick again. But Daffy is too smart this time: He tells Elmer to wait until he gets home to shoot. And Elmer does, going home with the duck by his side. Daffy soon returns to Bugs, his beak backwards and smoking. "You're desthpicable," the duck scowls.

J. J. SEDELMEIER, animation director, designer, and producer Of director Chuck Jones's three "Shoot 'im now!" cartoons (the others being 1951's **RABBIT FIRE** and 1953's **DUCK! RABBIT, DUCK!**),

RABBIT SEASONING has always been my favorite. Bugs, Daffy, and Elmer are so tightly defined as the characters we all know and love that they're almost parodies of themselves. Even though this short is the second of the series, it's still fresh and tight. What's also amazing is how it doesn't feel like a cartoon that's almost sixty years old. The timing of the cuts—Daffy's expression when Elmer says to Bugs that he "hasn't even seen a wabbit yet"—and the miscellaneous, eccentric W. C. Fields–like sound effects that seem to ooze out of Daffy are still cool today.

Rhapsody in Rivets

Franz Liszt's "Second Hungarian Rhapsody" soars to new heights—literally—as the foreman of a construction crew, a cigar-smoking lion, conducts his workers through the musical building of a skyscraper. Rivet guns and hammers become xylophone sticks; a saw, a cello bow. Steam shovels, picks, and a cocktail-shaker-like cement mixer swing to the melody. Big and little workers harmonize with inversely sized mallets; a bricklayer frenziedly lays bricks to the rhythm. Even the foreman's blueprints simulate sheet music, with the skyscraper's floors labeled like new parts of the score. Minor calamities arrive when a sleepy little worker fails to hit a high nail just right and when men knock nails into one another's backsides. But most of the trouble is due to a deadpan little basset hound. First seen hustling back from lunch, he spaces out on the job, unwittingly hammers a coworker on the nose, and almost gets smacked by a passing elevator. In the end, the skyscraper is built at tremendous speed, rushing upwards and even sideways through the sky. But when basset hound slams the entry door shut, the entire building crumbles to the ground.

DIRECTOR: I. FRELENG **STORY:** MELVIN MILLAR **ANIMATION:** GIL TURNER **VOICE:** MEL BLANC (BRICKLAYER) **MUSIC:** CARL STALLING

DANIEL GOLDMARK, professor of musicology While almost every studio in Hollywood took on Liszt's "Second Hungarian Rhapsody" at one time or another, Warner Bros. did it twice—both times with Friz Freleng directing (**RHAPSODY RABBIT**, 1946, was the other). What sets this version apart from all the others is that, while it keeps the spirit of a concert or performance, the execution is different. Freleng's central metaphor—comparing the skills and coordination of a construction crew to those of an orchestra—works remarkably well, giving a new twist to what had already become a cliché by then, a well-known classical work being played (or murdered) by a motley group of musicians. And because the "Rhapsody" was also a classical standard, bordering on a pop hit, Freleng could easily use just the best-known parts of the work to drive the several dozen gags.

JERRY SAYS When George Gershwin wrote his "Second Rhapsody" in 1931, he initially subtitled it "Rhapsody in Rivets." One can even hear a rivet-gun motif in Gershwin's melody. One has to wonder whether Gershwin's subtitle inspired Freleng's Oscar-nominated cartoon ten years later, even if Liszt instead of Gershwin was the musical source material.

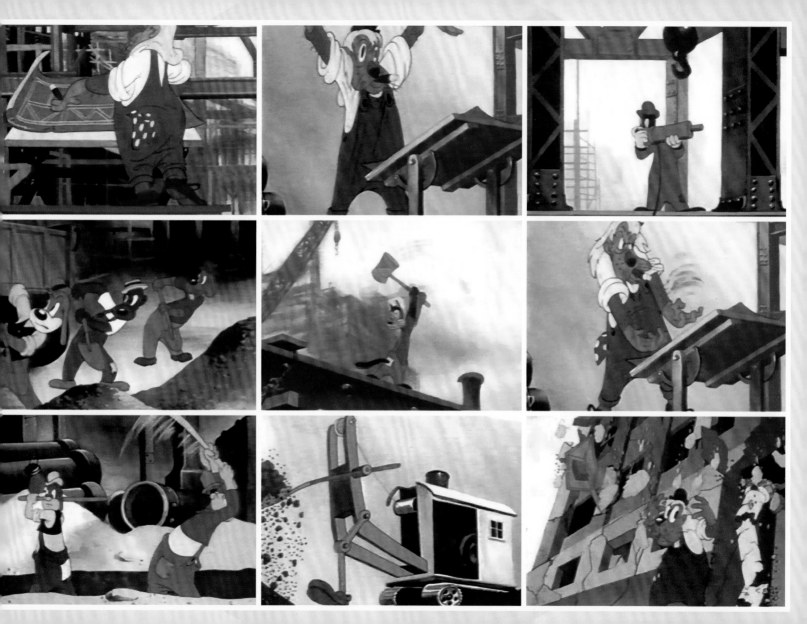

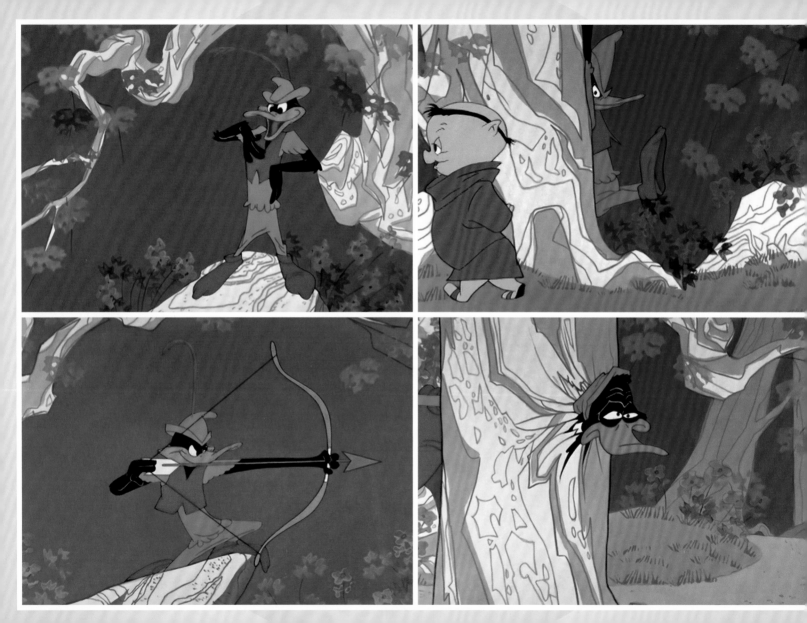

Robin Hood Daffy

"YOIKS AND AWAY!"

DIRECTOR: CHUCK JONES **STORY:** MICHAEL MALTESE **ANIMATION:** ABE LEVITOW, RICHARD THOMPSON, KEN HARRIS **LAYOUT:** MAURICE NOBLE **BACKGROUNDS:** PHILIP DEGUARD **FILM EDITOR:** TREG BROWN **VOICES:** MEL BLANC (DAFFY, PORKY) **MUSIC:** MILT FRANKLYN

Robin Hood (Daffy Duck) is traipsing through Sherwood Forest, surrounded by wanted posters displaying his picture. Daffy merrily plays his lute and sings of the legendary bandit—until he trips up and lands in the lake. His fall is witnessed by a fat friar (played by a skeptical Porky Pig), who can only laugh at the soggy duck. Daffy challenges Porky to a duel with his "buck-and-a-quarter" staff but winds up injuring his beak—and ends up back in the lake. Porky is seeking Robin Hood to join up with his merry band. When Daffy announces that he is, indeed, the one and only Robin Hood, the pig refuses to believe him. To prove his identity, Daffy then attempts to rob a wealthy traveler, but each attempt ends in failure. Swinging from tree limb to tree limb only gets him pummeled by numerous trunks in the way. Clearing the trees, Daffy swings again, only to slam into a boulder. In classic Wile E. Coyote style, the duck attempts to use catapults, giant crossbows, and wrecking balls to stop his oblivious victim. Each try backfires and only serves to punish the duck. When Porky still refuses to believe, Daffy himself gives up, changing his name and attire to become Friar Duck.

LINDA SIMENSKY, vice president of children's programming, PBS My son took up fencing two years ago, and I immediately began doing the "Guard! Turn! Parry! Dodge! Spin! Hah! Thrust!" gag. It got a big laugh, but it wasn't until I showed him Chuck Jones's **ROBIN HOOD DAFFY** that he understood why I had any clue about fencing. Daffy Duck does some fancy work with a quarterstaff—until he hits himself in the bill, providing the cartoon with a running gag.

ROBIN HOOD DAFFY is a visual delight abounding with physical gags, bold colors—bright green against a yellow sky—and layouts and backgrounds that complement a leotard-wearing duck swinging through the trees on a rope. Daffy gets some classic moments, including a lute song and some arrow gags, but by the end he is fairly unsuccessful as a Robin Hood and gives it all up. As Daffy himself notes, "Ha ha. It is to laugh."

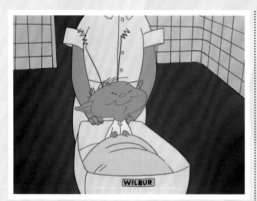

Rocket-bye Baby

"I'M SO WORRIED ABOUT THE BABY. HE'S DOING YOUR INCOME TAX!"

When a cosmic force is disturbed, a Martian baby is delivered to Earth and vice versa. Joseph Wilbur is greeted in the hospital by an elf-eared, green, antenna-sporting baby. His wife, Martha, is ashamed that Joseph is embarrassed to take their son out for a stroll just because he's communicating with bees and terrifying old ladies. But she begins to see her husband's point about their baby being a bit odd when he does their taxes, spells "E=MC²" on his toy blocks, and predicts hurricanes thirty years out. Joseph decides the *Captain Shmideo*

television program will straighten the lad out. It does inspire the baby to take up a hobby: building a toy flying saucer.

Meanwhile, the couple receives a message from Mars informing them of the mix-up; the Martians tell the Wilburs they will be exchanging the Earthling baby, "Yob," for the Martian baby, "Mot." But Mot takes off in his flying saucer, halting the possibility of any exchange, and heads for the city. Joseph follows closely behind. There, a windbag is making a speech scoffing at the idea of green men in flying saucers; at the sight of Mot he is immediately reduced to hysteria. Mot is taken aboard the Martian space cruiser, leaving Joseph falling to his doom without his Yob. The father awakens, finding he is still in the waiting room with a copy of *Science and Research* in hand. He goes to meet his real baby, and is relieved that

it's a healthy normal boy—with a wristband that reads "Yob."

SHAENON K. GARRITY, webcomics author
Produced in 1956, midway between the classics **ONE FROGGY EVENING** and **WHAT'S OPERA, DOC?**, **ROCKET-BYE BABY** finds Chuck Jones pushing away from the Warner Bros. house style and toward his own modernist sense of design, influenced in part by the UPA animation studio. His characters are both cute (no one animates more adorable babies) and crisply stylized, with simplified figures and dots for eyes. The backgrounds by Philip DeGuard, who would later paint the backgrounds for **WHAT'S OPERA, DOC?** from Maurice Noble's designs, add a cockeyed, angular flair. If the gentle gags lack the breakneck comedy of some of Jones's other work from this, his greatest period, **ROCKET-BYE BABY** is still one of his best-looking shorts, a beautiful piece of animation and design. It also features some of the director's funniest reaction shots, including a little old lady who pauses to tune her voice on a pitch pipe before screaming.

Beneath its cute premise, **ROCKET-BYE BABY** is a 1950s alien-invasion movie, and it reflects the basic anxiety of all such movies: fear of an

DIRECTOR: CHUCK JONES **STORY:** MICHAEL MALTESE **ANIMATION:** KEN HARRIS, ABE LEVITOW, BEN WASHAM **LAYOUT:** ERNIE NORDLI **BACKGROUNDS:** PHILIP DEGUARD **EFFECTS ANIMATION:** HARRY LOVE **FILM EDITOR:** TREG BROWN **VOICES:** DAWS BUTLER (NARRATOR, JOSEPH WILBUR, CAPTAIN SCHMIDEO), JUNE FORAY (MARTHA, NURSE) **MUSIC:** MILT FRANKLYN

outsider disrupting suburban American conformity. There's nothing wrong with Mot, the Wilburs' Martian baby—if anything, he's exceptional. But he's different. He freaks out the neighbors. His mint-green skin glows in startling contrast to the muted, earthy colors of the rest of his cartoon world. Joseph Wilbur doesn't want an exceptional child, he wants a child like everyone else has. When Mot's Martian parents come calling,

Joseph leaps at the opportunity to trade the baby he's been raising for his "real" son.

The trouble is that Mot is so adorable, it's hard to sympathize with his human father's efforts to get rid of him. He's got squinty black eyes with little Chuck Jones eyelashes, for heaven's sake! Maybe Joseph Wilbur's problems are just the problems many men in the 1950s had relating to their infants (check out that hospital waiting

room in the opening scene, packed with haggard, helpless dads-to-be). Either way, the snazzy-looking science fiction fable ends without resolving this underlying tension, and maybe that's what makes **ROCKET-BYE BABY** so fascinating.

Russian Rhapsody

"PUMPERNICKEL VIT DER SAUERKRAUTEN FROM DER DELIKATESSIN VIT LIVERWURST, UND HASSENPFEFFER UND DER CHATTANOOGA CHOO CHOO!"

It's "once upon a time, way back in 1941," and all of Germany's warplanes headed for Moscow are disappearing. "Could It Be Gremlins?" read the headlines. ("H-m-m-m-m, Could Be!" reads another paper.) Regardless, Hitler is furious, and rants to his people about the situation. He will be sending the "greatest superman of all time" to bomb Moscow: himself. Shortly after taking off, Hitler is hijacked by gremlins that look an awful lot like the staff of the Termite Terrace (the nickname Warner Bros. animation team gave to themselves), who sing about themselves with a ditty titled "Gremlins from the Kremlin." One gremlin uses a "termiteski" to eat away the wing of the plane, one replaces Hitler's C-ration card with an A card, and a tubby one finally succeeds in stabbing Hitler in the rear with his thumbtack cap. After the gremlins attach a socket to the Führer's nose and electrocute him, he chases them around the plane. They scare him senseless with a Stalin mask, saw the floor out from underneath him, and send the plane after him, crushing him and

forming his final resting place. A gremlin sings the song once more. Hitler pops out to do a final impression of comedian Lew Lehr ("Nutzis is de cwaziest peoples!") before being clobbered back into the earth for keeps.

DIRECTOR: ROBERT CLAMPETT **STORY:** LOU LILLY **ANIMATION:** ROD SCRIBNER, BOB MCKIMSON **VOICES:** MEL BLANC (HITLER, NARRATION, GERMANS), ROBERT C. BRUCE (NEWS VOICE), SHERRY ALLEN GROUP **MUSIC:** CARL STALLING

MARK KAUSLER, animator RUSSIAN RHAPSODY is a funny musical cartoon about a man who was certainly the antithesis of comedy. The breadth and depth of Hitler's hatred of Jews and crimes against humanity were not fully known in 1944, when this cartoon was released. Director Bob Clampett, as usual, cast his animators well, giving Bob McKimson a showcase for his exceptional performing and drawing ability in the extended animated close-up of Hitler addressing the Nazi

Party faithful. McKimson makes Hitler a monster with huge shoulders and huge hands that reach out toward the camera in sweeping gestures. The range of emotions that Hitler goes through in his speech—from slobbering hatred as he rolls his r's, to teary resignation as he recalls the "Irish" General Tim O'Schenko (Russian Marshal Timoshenko), to his "Who else?" quip at the end, an impression of Yiddish comedian Artie Auerbach—are not just funny but also among the sharpest political observations created in the golden age of animation.

McKimson also animated the scene on board the plane in which Hitler screams as the gremlins hold up a mask of Stalin, which was solidly drawn and sharply observed. Did Joe McCarthy consider hauling Clampett up before HUAC in the Army-McCarthy hearings after the war? He might have been tempted after seeing this cartoon, one of the most solidly pro-Russian of the war years.

Bob Clampett really was the hare that outraced the Disney tortoise to be the first to put

animated gremlins on the screen. He made two gremlin cartoons before Leon Schlesinger got a cease-and-desist letter from Roy O. Disney, who was developing a gremlin feature at the time. That's why **RUSSIAN RHAPSODY** has such a generic title; originally it was called **GREMLINS FROM THE KREMLIN** after the song the gremlins sing in the cartoon. The title was changed to placate Disney.

Gremlin characters, being the rascally underminers that they are, were a good fit for the bad-boy comedy of the 1940s Warner Bros. cartoons.

We really don't have to know which gremlins were caricatures of which cartoonists to laugh at the humor of the goony little guys as they take Hitler's plane to pieces. They are all Russians, so the designer (Gene Hazelton?) made the

caricatures of Warner animators Rod Scribner, Ray Katz, Mike Sasanoff, Bobe Cannon, and their crew look Slavic to boot!

Satan's Waitin'

"DON'T BE CHICKEN, CAT: YOU'VE GOT EIGHT LIVES LEFT!"

Sylvester is chasing Tweety to the top of a building, but accidentally skids off and plummets. He's managed to procure a few of Tweety's tail feathers and tries to save himself, but Tweety takes them back, thanking the putty tat for returning them. Sylvester hits the pavement and dies. However, the escalator up to heaven is roped off, leaving the escalator to hell as the only option. In the fiery bowels, Sylvester meets the devil (expertly acted in animation by Virgil Ross). Things don't look good for our hero, and he is told to wait on a stone sofa for his other eight lives to come to meet him. "You won't have long to wait," cackles Satan, "I'll hurry 'em along!"

Back on earth, Sylvester vows to give up chasing Tweety, but he gives in to the devil's temptation, and the chase is back on. Sylvester is almost immediately crushed by a steamroller, sending down life number two. He then goes after the bird in an amusement park, where life number three is literally scared out of him by a monstrous bulldog head. As the hunt continues, Sylvester is then shot multiple times on a shooting gallery, clearing lives four through seven, and loses his eighth life due to standing up in a roller coaster. With one life left, Sylvester decides to shut himself off from society by locking himself (with food and water) in a vault at the Last National Bank. Unfortunately, that very night he loses his last life due to some bungling burglars mishandling nitroglycerine, dooming all of them to eternal damnation. "Ya used too much, Muggsy," one says. "Now he tells 'im!" says Sylvester.

> **DIRECTOR:** I. FRELENG **STORY:** WARREN FOSTER **ANIMATION:** VIRGIL ROSS, ARTHUR DAVIS, MANUEL PEREZ, KEN CHAMPIN **LAYOUT:** HAWLEY PRATT **BACKGROUNDS:** IRV WYNER **VOICES:** MEL BLANC (TWEETY, SYLVESTER, SATAN, MUGGSY) **MUSIC:** CARL STALLING

YVETTE KAPLAN, director, writer, and animator
Why hasn't Hollywood made a feature version of **SATAN'S WAITIN'**? The premise is perfect! Cat dies while trying to catch cute but psychopathic Tweety Bird. Is sent to hell for sentencing. When it is discovered (due to technical error) that cat still has eight other lives to go, he is returned to Earth for another chance to catch Tweety—and eight more rounds of torment. Is that a recipe for a blockbuster or what?

But please, no casting Ben Stiller and Jim Carey in this one. Unh-unh, no way. The movie would have to star Sylvester the Cat and Tweety Pie themselves, as there is no other duo I'd pay to see reliving their hysterically dysfunctional patterns over and over again. Nine times in this cartoon alone! Of course, I'd love to see Sylvester chomp on that evil little bird at least once. . . .

Which reminds me: What's with Tweety getting top billing? Sure, maybe he's a star, but come on, he practically has a cameo here! That bird just phones it in. Nope, this is Sylvester's spotlight. What does a cat have to do to get some good representation in this town? Thanks to that little no-talent twerp, the poor cat falls off a roof, gets flattened by a steam roller, is literally scared to death, is shot not once but four whole times, smashes into a stone wall, and is blown to bits in

a bank heist. Come on! Well, this is *my* pitch, and in my dream feature, the clown gets top billing. Got it, Hollywood?

The other thing I'd change is this: You know that held shot of Tweety and Sylvester passing in and out of frame in the shooting gallery? Well, I'd make it twice as long—maybe even three or four times as long. That would make it four times as hysterical, and I'd be in absolute heaven...oh, sorry, wrong location. That would be another movie altogether, wouldn't it? Hey, that's a great idea. **HEAVEN'S WAITIN'.** The sequel! Sylvester has nine lives, and in every single one he gets to eat Tweety Pie. Baked, broiled, ground, and flambéed! **HEAVEN'S WAITIN'**—and so am I! Don't worry, Sylvester, I have a good feeling about this one. But just in case, how do you feel about Ben Stiller?

Scaredy Cat

"AND JUST WHAT WERE YOU GOING TO DO WITH THAT ANVIL?"

One stormy night, Porky Pig enters his creepy new home with his neurotic cat, Sylvester. Though told to stay in the kitchen, Sylvester clutches to an oblivious Porky and stays on his backside until Porky is in his bedclothes and under the covers. The pig throws Sylvester back downstairs, where he finds mice performing a death-row march for a prisoner cat, with a masked executioner following. Mortified, Sylvester runs back into the bedroom, where he tries to pantomime what is going on. Porky doesn't believe his story, so Sylvester threatens to shoot himself, forcing the pig to agree to let him sleep with him. The mice push the bed out the window, but Porky is saved by a flagpole that flings a Sylvester-less bed back into the room. Sylvester returns just in time to prevent an anvil from being dropped on Porky, though it only makes Porky suspect the cat is guilty.

When the mice roll a bowling ball down the banister at Porky's head, Sylvester saves the pig again, but Porky is convinced that the cat shoved him. Placed unconscious in a laundry basket, Sylvester is taken down below by the mice, where he is subjected to unknown torture and returns white as a sheet. Porky believes that Sylvester is

DIRECTOR: CHARLES M. JONES **STORY:** MICHAEL MALTESE **ANIMATION:** LLOYD VAUGHAN, KEN HARRIS, PHIL MONROE, BEN WASHAM **LAYOUT:** ROBERT GRIBBROEK **BACKGROUNDS:** PETER ALVARADO **VOICE:** MEL BLANC (PORKY) **MUSIC:** CARL STALLING

playacting, and tries to prove what a coward the cat is by entering the kitchen alone. Sylvester peers in and witnesses another death-row march. This time Porky is the victim, so Sylvester flees to save himself. His conscience gets the best of him and points out a startling fact: Cats are bigger than mice. So Sylvester returns, with a whole tree as his weapon, and rids the house of every last rodent. Porky thanks Sylvester for his heroism, while the executioner pops out of the cuckoo clock to knock Sylvester cold with a mallet. The mouse then takes off his mask to say, in an impression of comedian Lew Lehr, "Pussycats is the cwaziest peoples!"

YVETTE KAPLAN, director, writer, and animator
The enormously amusing **SCAREDY CAT**, from director Chuck Jones and writer Mike Maltese, is a near perfect cartoon. Porky and Sylvester are a clown-and-straight-man duo on par with

any you can think of. And though it's Porky, the straight man, who gets top billing in the opening title card, the wordless clown, Sylvester, steals the show—and my heart. "Welcome to our new home, Sylvester!" stutters Porky cheerfully as they enter through the door of an old, creepy, shadow-filled house, complete with ominous soundtrack. Sylvester is scared out of his wits from the first frame of his entrance—trembling, teeth shattering, and holding so tightly to Porky as to need surgical removal. But does Porky notice? Nah, he's just pissed that the darn cat is acting so weird.

The more obvious Sylvester's torment, in fact, the more oblivious Porky becomes—and the funnier the gags. In a brilliantly staged and choreographed bit of business that brings me to tears, both from laughter and from awe, Sylvester silently shadows Porky so closely he ends up in his pajamas. But Porky doesn't even notice until he sleepily fluffs his pillow, which he vaguely notices looks like Sylvester. Only in animation! And that is the key. The wordless scene is animated physical comedy at its best. Forget Porky—I'll protect you, Sylvester. I know just what you're trying to say.

The Scarlet Pumpernickel

"IT'S GETTING SO YOU HAVE TO KILL YOURSELF TO SELL A STORY AROUND HERE."

Tired of comedy roles, Daffy begs unseen studio honcho J. L. to cast him in an epic drama. In old England, the Scarlet Pumpernickel (Daffy) is a daring highwayman who always escapes the Lord High Chamberlain's men. The chamberlain (Porky) is furious, but Milady Melissa loves the handsome outlaw. So Porky hatches a plan: He'll arrange for Melissa to wed the grand duke (Sylvester). Pumpernickel will crash the wedding—and meet his end. Or will he? Disguised as a gentleman, the Pumpernickel infiltrates the castle to learn the details. Then he sneaks into the wedding the back way, spiriting Melissa to the inn where he hides out. When the wronged duke finds her there, Scarlet engages him in a dramatic swordfight. But J. L. keeps expecting more drama, so screenwriter Daffy obliges with escalating side effects such as dams bursting, cavalries charging, and volcanoes erupting. They aren't enough for the studio exec. In the end, the beaten Scarlet Pumpernickel "blow[s] his brains out"—and so does Daffy, right on J. L.'s office floor.

DIRECTOR: CHARLES M. JONES **STORY:** MICHAEL MALTESE **ANIMATION:** PHIL MONROE, BEN WASHAM, LLOYD VAUGHAN, KEN HARRIS **LAYOUT:** ROBERT GRIBBROEK **BACKGROUNDS:** PETER ALVARADO **VOICES:** MEL BLANC (DAFFY, PORKY, SYLVESTER, ELMER, J. L.), MARIAN RICHMAN (MELISSA) **MUSIC:** CARL STALLING

GREG FORD, animation historian While genre parodies are common in animation today, **THE SCARLET PUMPERNICKEL** was something of an anomaly in 1950. Still, **PUMPERNICKEL** does a more than efficient job in spoofing all the lushly exaggerated live-action costume epics on which it's based: There's the grandiose set decoration, the use of chiaroscuro lightning and shadow à la Michael Curtiz (director of *Captain Blood* and *The Adventures of Robin Hood*) during the big swordfight, the all-star cast, the ridiculously episodic pacing of the grand finale, and so forth. Director Chuck Jones's character poses have never been sharper, and writer Michael Maltese's dialogue and Mel Blanc's line readings never more extraordinary. (For instance, in an unforgettable set piece, a dashingly outfitted Grand Duke Sylvester gallantly soliloquizes, "Firtht, I am happy. For I am to wed the fair Melith-tha!")

Maltese's keen ear for mangled grandiloquence never lets down—this is definitely the only Looney Tunes cartoon to get a laugh from a slipped-in archaic word like *mayhap*. Similarly unflagging is the writer's acute sensitivity to the desperate hyperbole of a frazzled, frantic pitchman like Daffy Duck as he piles on one voiced-over, cooked-up

crescendo after another—a heap of Sturm und Drang that only results in the inspired bathos of an overpriced kreplach.

It's the "real life" Daffy, though, as seen in the cartoon's wraparound plot of the studio script meeting, that best clues us in to what separates this film from the spate of animated genre parodies currently being churned out. Most modern-day satires trade on anachronism, and the hero and the audience end up complicit in their smug superiority to the antiquated vehicle. But what's funny about **THE SCARLET PUMPERNICKEL** is the tremendous investment its hero puts into his costumed character, and the vast chasm that yawns between Daffy's inflated perception of himself and the highly flawed little black duck that he really is. **PUMPERNICKEL** fixed the pattern for many Jones-directed Daffy Duck cartoons to follow. The director cast the angst-ridden duck in a series of larger-than-life roles he would prove hopelessly unequal to: a would-be dashing swashbuckler (**ROBIN HOOD DAFFY,** 1958), a Holmesian detective (**DEDUCE, YOU SAY,** 1956), a futuristic space ace (**DUCK DODGERS,** 1953; **ROCKET SQUAD,** 1956), a gunslinging cowboy (**DRIP-ALONG DAFFY,** 1951; **MY LITTLE DUCKAROO,** 1954). Every time, Daffy was hopelessly alienated from his surroundings, a low-comic schlemiel in highly romanticized settings that called for superheroism. This schizophrenic split between actor and role found ultimate expression in Jones' **DUCK AMUCK** (1953)—a genre parody of the animation medium itself.

JERRY SAYS This all-star epic includes so many Looney Tunes character cameos that a few are peripheral to the plot, including Ma Bear as lady-in-waiting and Elmer Fudd as owner of the King's Nostril Inn.

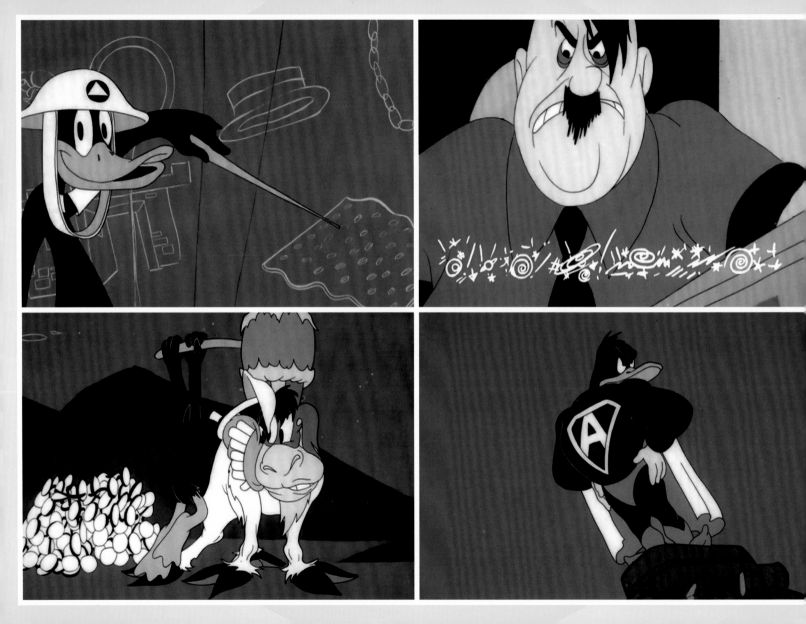

Scrap Happy Daffy

"WE'RE IN TO WIN!"

The film opens on salvage warden Daffy Duck's scrap pile, where signs urge citizens to "Get that lead out!" The duck sings how "We're in to Win," stopping to whistle at a bathing-suit-clad lass while listing what can be salvaged for victory, and finishes by addressing a horse's ass as "Schicklgruber" (Adolph Hitler's true family name), which cross-dissolves to the real Führer! Hitler is furious over how successful the non-Aryan duck's scrap pile is, so he orders it to be destroyed. A Nazi submarine launches a torpedo at it, containing the Germans' secret weapon: a scrap-eating billy goat. After a few too many tin cans, though, "William" gets the hiccups. Daffy attempts to cure them with a seltzer concoction until he notices the innocuous-looking goat is wearing a swastika. "This tin termite is a Nazi!" Daffy shouts. Things don't look good when Daffy is unable to subdue the goat. Defeated, he sighs, "What I'd give for a can of spinach now!"

But the spirits of Daffy's mallard forefathers remind him that "Americans don't give up," filling Daffy with enough pride to become "Super-American." Now in superhero garb with a set of muscles, Daffy clobbers the goat and sends it running back to the U-boat, where Daffy dismantles the cannon the Nazis are firing at him. Just as he's mangling the periscope of the retreating submarine, Daffy is awakened by the faucet he's really mangling. But it wasn't quite a dream—the Nazis call out from their salvaged sub at the top of the scrap pile: "Next time you dream, include us out!"

DIRECTOR: FRANK TASHLIN **STORY:** DON CHRISTENSEN **ANIMATION:** ART DAVIS **VOICES:** MEL BLANC (DAFFY, HITLER, LINCOLN), DOROTHY LLOYD (WHISTLE) **MUSIC:** CARL STALLING

ERIC GOLDBERG, animator and director You won't be seeing this Frank Tashlin classic anytime soon on your local TV station or Boomerang for two reasons: Not only is the cartoon in black and white, it's blatant World War II propaganda. Granted, it isn't as rabid as many other propaganda cartoons of the time (See **BUGS BUNNY NIPS THE NIPS**; **TOKYO JOKIO**; **YOU'RE A SAP, MR. JAP**; **THE DUCKTATORS**…gosh, the list is endless). But long gone are the days when cartoons like these would be blithely shuffled into the mix of afternoon children's shows. In **SCRAP HAPPY DAFFY,** Tashlin's screwball version of Daffy Duck extols the virtues of donating scrap metal and rubber to the war effort (the scraps were recycled into tanks, guns, ammunition, and anything else required by the U.S. military at the time). He sings an extended rhyming song while pointing out, on a graffiti-illustrated fence, all the types of items that can be donated. He imitates, in three mirrors, "freedom's foes"—Hitler, Mussolini, and Tojo—and stockpiles such an enormous collection of scrap that even Adolf Hitler gets wind of it.

Despite the film's jingoistic nature, it still boasts all the hallmarks of a great Tashlin cartoon: Dynamic, stylized poses in the animation. Graphically styled layouts and backgrounds. And outrageous humor—we dissolve from the back end of a horse with a black tail to the forelock on Adolf's face; the goat is capable of doing a four-footed military goose step. **SCRAP HAPPY DAFFY** is one of the classic World War II propaganda cartoons.

Show Biz Bugs

"THERE CAN ONLY BE ONE EXPLANATION FOR WHITE TILE IN A DRESSING ROOM...AND THAT'S IT!"

Vaudeville star Daffy Duck arrives at the Bijou to find himself outclassed by Bugs Bunny, his performing partner. Bugs's name dwarfs Daffy's on the marquee; Daffy's dressing room is a repurposed bathroom. And when Daffy and Bugs dance together on stage, only Bugs wins the cheers. The rabbit's seconds-long encore brings the house down again, while Daffy's frenetic "Jeepers Creepers" tap dance has the theater so quiet we can hear crickets chirp. Defiant Daffy tries a trained pigeon act, but after he has set up a fancy assortment of props, his pigeons fly straight out the window. Magician Bugs is next on the bill; Daffy tries to prove that the rabbit's sawing-in-half routine is a fake, but finds himself actually sawed in half. Next, awaiting Bugs's xylophone solo, Daffy arms the xylophone with dynamite. But when Bugs plays "Those Endearing Young Charms," he misses the note that's the trigger for the TNT—prompting frustrated Daffy to correct him and get blasted. In the end, Daffy says he's "forced...to use the act I've held back for a special occasion." The duck swallows various flammable substances, swallows a lit match, and blows himself up. At last, the audience loves him! Now a ghost, Daffy rues that he "can only do [the act] once."

DIRECTOR: FRIZ FRELENG **STORY:** WARREN FOSTER **ANIMATION:** GERRY CHINIQUY, ART DAVIS, VIRGIL ROSS **LAYOUT:** HAWLEY PRATT **BACKGROUNDS:** BORIS GORELICK **FILM EDITOR:** TREG BROWN **VOICES:** MEL BLANC (BUGS, DAFFY) **MUSIC:** MILT FRANKLYN

MARK EVANIER, comic book writer By 1957 there wasn't much about Daffy Duck that was daffy. He'd morphed into a greedy, self-obsessed rival to Bugs...and maybe the most psychotic property in the rarely stable Warner Bros. canon. **SHOW BIZ BUGS** is enormously funny, though, as we watch him match Wile E. Coyote in his self-inflicted destruction of both ego and body. A couple of the jokes are familiar. The explosive ending to a performance of "Those Endearing Young Charms" came straight out of **BALLOT BOX BUNNY** (1951), and the studio used it before that in a Private Snafu cartoon. (People sometimes ask if cartoons can be educational. Absolutely. As a small lad, I learned never to play "Those Endearing Young Charms" on any piano I had not personally inspected.) The suicidal ending, which has been sliced and diced a dozen different ways by TV Standards and Practices censors over the last few decades, was previously seen in a 1949 Porky Pig vehicle called **CURTAIN RAZOR**, which has also been chopped to pieces in the ensuing years.

The comedy works so well that in the 1960s, when Friz Freleng and Chuck Jones were cobbling together the **BUGS BUNNY SHOW** for television, **SHOW BIZ BUGS** provided the template and theme: Bugs was the star, and all of Daffy's attempts to upstage him and grab the spotlight came to naught. You'd think the characters would learn. When was the last time anyone bested the rabbit at anything? **TORTOISE BEATS HARE**?

JERRY SAYS Friz Freleng's classic stage spoof tries hard to justify Daffy's frustration. Still, the duck's adoption of a Yosemite Sam attack method—the TNT-rigged musical instrument—illustrates Daffy's ongoing evolution into a more low-down character.

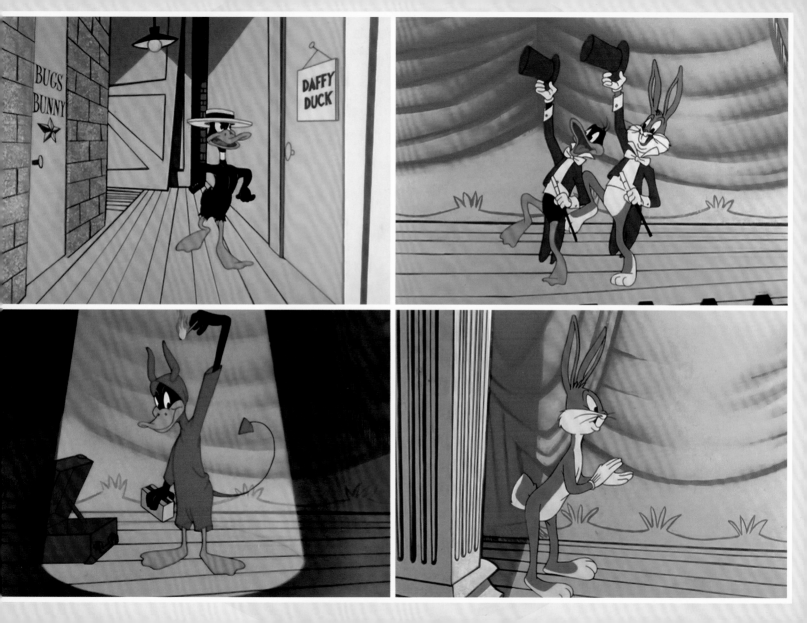

Slick Hare

"IF HE WANTS ME, ALL HE HAS TO DO IS WHISTLE."

All the stars in Hollywood are having a night on the town at the Mocrumbo: Leopold Stokowski conducts a jukebox, Gregory Peck uses a razor to cut his steak, Ray Milland pays for his booze with his typewriter (and gets mini-typewriters as change), and Frank Sinatra gets sucked into his soda straw. Humphrey Bogart beckons waiter Elmer Fudd over to request fried rabbit, but Fudd can't find one anywhere. Bugs Bunny just happens to be in the shipment of carrots, and is delighted to find out Bogart wants to have him for dinner—until he finds out what's on the menu. Bugs escapes the kitchen and dresses as Groucho Marx, only to find Elmer beside him dressed as Harpo. After crashing into Sidney Greenstreet's stomach, Bugs hides in Carmen Miranda's fruit hat while she performs. As Elmer chases the rabbit back onstage, Bugs performs a rumba dance for the audience (wonderfully and hilariously animated by Gerry Chiniquy).

Back in the kitchen, Bugs poses as a waiter himself, giving Elmer the dessert orders to prepare and immediately returning to throw the food in Elmer's face. Fudd gets wise and tries to hit Bugs, but he misses and hits Bogart ("Why did you hit me in the face with a coconut custard pie with whipped cream?" the actor asks), who tells him he's got five minutes left to come up with that rabbit. They immediately pass by, and Elmer pleads for mercy, fearing the worst. Bogart concedes that "Baby [his pet name for his wife, Lauren Bacall] will just have to have a ham sandwich instead." Upon hearing this, Bugs decides to be the main course for the beautiful blonde. "If it's rabbit Baby wants," he says, "rabbit Baby gets!"

DIRECTOR: I. FRELENG **STORY:** TED PIERCE, MICHAEL MALTESE **ANIMATION:** VIRGIL ROSS, GERRY CHINIQUY, MANUEL PEREZ, KEN CHAMPIN **LAYOUT:** HAWLEY PRATT **BACKGROUNDS:** PAUL JULIAN **VOICES:** MEL BLANC (BUGS, WAITER, RAY MILLAND), ARTHUR Q. BRYAN (ELMER), DAVE BARRY (HUMPHREY BOGART) **MUSIC:** CARL STALLING

KEITH SCOTT, cartoon voice actor One of the last of Warner Bros.' topical caricature cartoons, **SLICK HARE** is much more accessible to a modern audience than some other entries in the movie-star parody genre. This is because Bugs Bunny and Elmer Fudd carry the comedy. With these two strong personalities in the foreground, the throwaway movie-star gags are more like the icing on a cake. This makes **SLICK HARE** somewhat different than cartoons like **THE WOODS ARE FULL OF CUCKOOS** (1937) and **HOLLYWOOD STEPS OUT**, in which the caricatures make the film.

Bugs Bunny aside, however, some topical references in **SLICK HARE** will be confusing to younger viewers. It's important to realize that Humphrey Bogart and his wife Lauren Bacall were then the hottest screen team in Hollywood. When this cartoon was made in 1947, they had recently been seen together in *The Big Sleep* (1946) and later that same year in Warner Bros.' comedy *Two Guys from Milwaukee*, the latter a perfect warm-up to **SLICK HARE**.

Certain other jokes were fresh when the **SLICK HARE** storyboard was finished in February 1946—namely, Gregory Peck and Ray Milland mocking their famous roles in 1945's *Spellbound* and *The Lost Weekend*, respectively—although even those gags had faded a tad by the time the cartoon was released in November 1947. No matter: Bogart and Bacall, as well as the bulky character actor Sidney Greenstreet, were still highly prominent in big-budget Warner Bros. features, and the cartoon worked well as topical comedy. It also benefited

from director Friz Freleng's customary pinpoint timing in sequences like the pie routine.

Music director Carl Stalling needed a Latin-themed soundtrack for the Mocrumbo (a play on the actual Mocambo nightclub). For this cartoon he deferred to a specialist, hiring Alfonso Sanchez to arrange the score. A month or so into production it was decided to use the song "Sambaiana" for both the Carmen Miranda parody and Bugs Bunny's marvelous dance sequence (worked out by Freleng and top animator Gerry Chiniquy). The Warner music department had to pay a fee of $400 to bandleader-composer Humberto Herrera for

the use of his song in this cartoon. It is unknown whether Herrera's original recording was used or if Stalling conducted the number afresh, but the vocalist who sings for Ms. Miranda was not listed in the Warner archives when I did research there; perhaps it is Carmen herself.

The fine comic impressionist Dave Barry did the Bogart imitation. Earlier, Barry had done his excellent Bogie in Bob Clampett's **BACALL TO ARMS** (1946). Actually, Freleng had first used Barry as the Great Gildersleeve–like voice emanating from a radio in **LIFE WITH FEATHERS** (1945), and the mimic had gone on to do several

other cartoons when specialty voices outside the domain of Mel Blanc were needed. Barry, Blanc, and Arthur Q. Bryan recorded their dialogue in separate sessions on March 2, 1946, when the cartoon was still known by its working title "The Time, the Chase, and the Rabbit" (a pun on a recently released Warner feature about a night-club, **THE TIME, THE PLACE, AND THE GIRL**).

Steal Wool

"MORNIN', RALPH!" "MORNIN', SAM!"

DIRECTOR: CHUCK JONES **STORY:** MICHAEL MALTESE **ANIMATION:** RICHARD THOMPSON, KEN HARRIS, ABE LEVITOW **LAYOUT:** MAURICE NOBLE **BACKGROUNDS:** PHILIP DEGUARD **FILM EDITOR:** TREG BROWN **VOICES:** MEL BLANC (SAM, RALPH) **MUSIC:** MILT FRANKLYN

Sam Sheepdog gets up promptly at six o'clock in the morning to start his workday, which begins by walking to work with his good friend and neighbor, Ralph Wolf. They punch the time clock and exchange pleasantries, then go their separate ways—Sam perches on a cliff to keep guard on the flock of sheep in the meadow, while Ralph crawls down below, as his job is to steal the sheep. When caught, Sam exacts violent punishment on the desperate wolf, their off-the-job friendship notwithstanding. None of the attempts Ralph makes—using a lasso, building a bridge made of dynamite sticks, wedging a lever

under Sam's backside, firing an enormous cannon, and snapping a giant elastic band—get the wolf any closer to a sheep. When they punch out at the end of the day, Sam tells Ralph he's been working too hard. "Why don't you take tomorrow off?" the sheepdog says. "I can handle both jobs." The poor pummeled Ralph thanks his buddy as they slowly walk home.

GREG FORD, animation historian Much of the mythic resonance of Wile E. Coyote's all-consuming, Sisyphean scrambles after the Road Runner would seem to stem from the lunar emptiness of the desert and the absence of any more civilized environment. Yet when Chuck Jones deposited the coyote in a more "human," workaday context and set his struggles against a verdant, ironically bucolic backdrop, his plight registers as even more absurdist. For Coyote (graced with a red nose and recast as Ralph Wolf) had an alternative

life as half of an adversarial pairing with an affable sheepdog named Sam. Unluckily for the wolf, Sam's sight-obscuring mop top hides an ability to see everything, materialize everywhere, and ubiquitously mete out swift, draconian justice.

Jones's wolf and sheepdog characters weren't natural foes at all, it seems, but were just filling out their professional posts as everybody does in a well-ordered capitalist society. They'd greet each other chummily on the way to their respective daily grinds. Only after punching their time-cards and listening for the starting whistle would the two operate with the bash-or-be-bashed, survivalist instincts governing warring cartoon

characters, with the coyote (a.k.a. Ralph J. Wolf) bearing the brunt of the conflict.

STEAL WOOL provides a few extra peeks at Sam and Ralph's preparations prior to the beginning of the work day: Sam strides atop a ridge and snaps himself into a vigilant pose as the stalwart guardian of a dumb flock of sheep, while Ralph matter-of-factly readjusts his facial features, pressing down his eyebrows with his fingers to approximate a mean-looking furrowed brow and manually realigning his upper lip to bare his fangs. Thus, when the day's activities begin, Ralph can seamlessly transition into a serpentine, four-footed tiptoe over the grassy knolls and make his first stab at sheep thievery. The omnipresent Sam can then catch him unawares and administer the day's first sock in the snoot. Periscopes, lassoes, and a footbridge constructed out of lit sticks of dynamite figure prominently in the ensuing string of spot gags. As with Jones's ritualistic Road-Runner-go-round, what happens is a foregone conclusion. Instead, the comedy comes from *how* it happens.

The later **SHEEP IN THE DEEP** (1962) saw a slight amelioration in working conditions for the wolf and the sheepdog with the addition of a lunch break. **STEAL WOOL**, on the other hand, represents an especially rough day at the office for Ralph. His underestimation of the slingshot properties of a giant rubber band in the film's apocalyptic final gag (whose running time clocks in at more than a full minute) brings forth a juggernaut of dislodged boulders and uprooted oaks that leaves the weary beastie a trifle the worse for wear. Which begets the question: Where's universal health care when you really need it?

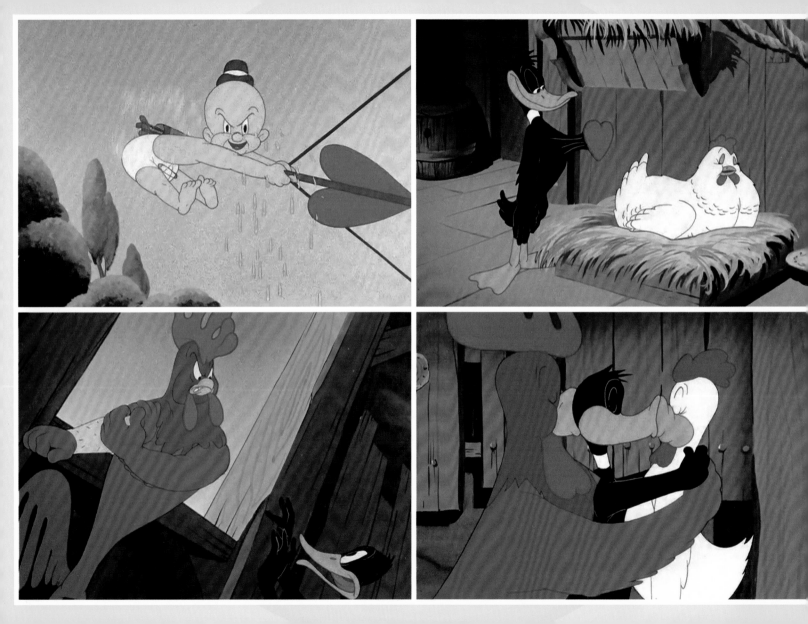

The Stupid Cupid

"NOW I'VE SEEN EVERYTHING!"

Spring is here, and Elmer Fudd is Cupid, making soul mates of birds, horses, even cats and dogs. ("Now I've seen everything!" says a cat right before shooting all nine of his lives out at the sight of a bulldog trying to woo him.) Next on Elmer's list is Daffy Duck, who's bathing in a trough, singing "Don't Sweetheart Me." But Daffy is fed up with the "barebacked bandit's" meddling arrows. In a hilarious rant animated by Art Davis, Daffy shows Cupid the results of his shenanigans last spring: a photo album filled with pictures of a shotgun wedding and hordes of ugly ducklings. Daffy sends Elmer on his way, but Elmer sends a king-size arrow back at the duck, knocking Daffy through several barns. Daffy immediately gets aroused at the sight of a plump hen and attempts to have his way with her. The hen's husband, a burly rooster, finds the two embraced. The rooster attempts to clobber Daffy, but the duck comes out of his trance and clears up that it was the fault of that "stupid Cupid." The rooster decides to let bygones be bygones, and Daffy goes on his merry way—until Elmer shoots him *again*, and Daffy returns for more amour, butting in between the rooster and hen's own embrace!

DIRECTOR: FRANK TASHLIN **STORY:** WARREN FOSTER **ANIMATION:** ART DAVIS **VOICES:** MEL BLANC (DAFFY, HORSE, DOG, CAT, ROOSTER), FRANK GRAHAM (ELMER FUDD LAUGHS) **MUSIC:** CARL STALLING

MARTIN GOODMAN, animation historian Though this farcical short contains some shoddy animation, Frank Tashlin's imaginative direction and Warren Foster's hilarious dialogue lift **THE STUPID CUPID** above its shortcomings and into the realm of unforgettable comedy. As usual, Tashlin approaches his cartoon as a cinematic tableau in which wildly distorted characters experience exaggerated emotions: When Daffy confronts a giggly Cupid about the misery he caused the duck in the previous year, Daffy's beak becomes a elongated platter that flattens the sprite's lower jaw. As Daffy savagely berates Cupid, his suddenly serpentine body clings to Elmer's shape like a dark outline. When Cupid exacts his revenge on the duck with an arrow the size of a redwood, the shot is lined up in deep perspective from Elmer's point of view. Daffy's pursuit of hapless Emily Hen utilizes multiple camera angles, and rapid-fire gags (such as the appearance of Daffy's family in a jalopy right on cue) enliven the short.

Tashlin signifies lust through the use of blurring speed, and since there is so much of it in this short, the cartoon moves at a supersonic pace. Foster's hysterical script hits one peak with Daffy's rant against Cupid and another as Daffy desperately begs forgiveness from Emily's husband. Frenzied apologies gush from Daffy's beak until the duck, in utter abjection, frantically kisses the rooster's feet in order to avoid a beating. Outstanding timing, gags, and dialogue dominate the entire short. And do look for Daffy's two-headed son.

The Stupor Salesman

"I'M NOT LEAVING TILL I SELL YOU SOMETHING!"

DIRECTOR: ARTHUR DAVIS **STORY:** LLOYD TURNER **ANIMATION:** J. C. MELENDEZ, DON WILLIAMS, EMERY HAWKINS, BASIL DAVIDOVICH **LAYOUT:** DON SMITH **BACKGROUNDS:** PHILIP DEGUARD **VOICES:** MEL BLANC (DAFFY, SLUG, MCSLUG) **MUSIC:** CARL STALLING

Daffy Duck, ace door-to-door salesman for the Excelsior Appliance Company, tries to sell the current occupant of an abandoned country house something from his case. Hiding out in the house is Slug McSlug, a notorious bank robber, who has just escaped a police dragnet but can't escape a certain determined duck. Daffy offers McSlug "Sure-Shot Shootin' Iron Polish" for his gun, plus a pair of brass knuckles and a bullet-proof vest ("Guaranteed to get your money back if it fails to work!" Daffy tells him). The duck, trying to demonstrate his Sure-Shot lighter by attempting to ignite the kitchen stove, is thrown out of the house. With gas continuing to seep throughout the house, McSlug tries to spark the lighter himself—and he does, blowing the house to bits. The explosion gives Daffy the idea to sell McSlug a new house that will go with the only remaining piece of the old one: the doorknob!

MIKE MALLORY, *animation historian* There is not a wasted cel in **THE STUPOR SALESMAN**. At first glance, the story of a bank robber who cannot escape the diabolical persistence of door-to-door salesman Daffy Duck (at his stream-of-consciousness best) sounds like a conventional pest-vs.-threat cartoon, but it is not. The short zooms by with the insistent pacing of the early Warner Bros. gangster films it aggressively parodies. Rarely, if ever, has one seven-minute cartoon burst its seams so thoroughly with inventive sight gags, throwaway jokes, and visual details. **THE STUPOR SALESMAN** is perhaps the ultimate showcase for the talents of Arthur Davis, whose tenure as director for Warner Bros. was relatively brief but who brought to the job a startling cinematic style. He staged the action within the camera's depth of field, moved characters to and from the lens rather than having them run past it, and used Dutch angles, spin transitions, and action dissolves—all unique and sometimes breathtaking.

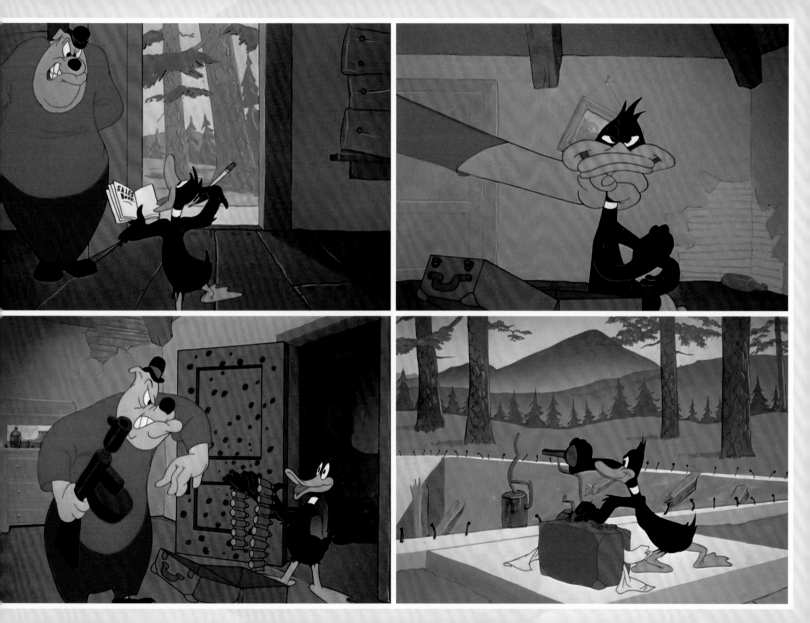

Swooner Crooner

"LOOK-A HERE, PORKY, OLD MAN. LET THE OL' GROANER TAKE A WHIRL AT THOSE SLICK CHICKS."

Porky Pig's Flockheed Eggcraft Factory is 100 percent devoted to war work. Hens line up, hens punch in, hens lay eggs on assembly-line belts. Farmer Porky boxes up eggs to send to the Allies—until the eggs run out, that is. A rooster who sings like Frank Sinatra is in town, and Porky's hens go AWOL to watch the crooner and swoon. Desperate to lure them back, panicked Porky auditions Nelson Eddy, Al Jolson, Jimmy Durante, and Cab Calloway birds. But it's super-cool Bing Crosby who grabs the chicks with "When My Dreamboat Comes Home." Indeed, come home they do: The hens are still horny, but now they're laying instead of lolling. Jealous "Frankie" begins to compete with Bing, and a singing battle begins—with Porky the ultimate winner. In the end, with eggs heaped under the moon, our pig asks the roosters how they did it. "It's very simple, Porky," they reply, and do a little scatting—which gets Porky laying, too.

WILL FRIEDWALD, author and music critic
SWOONER CROONER pivots around caricatures of

DIRECTOR: FRANK TASHLIN **STORY:** WARREN FOSTER **ANIMATION:** GEORGE CANNATA **VOICES:** MEL BLANC (PORKY), DICK BICKENBACH (BING CROSBY, FRANK SINATRA), SAM GLASSER (AL JOLSON, JIMMY DURANTE, CAB CALLOWAY, NELSON EDDY), SARA BERNER AND BEA BENADERET (SWOONING CHICKS) **MUSIC:** CARL STALLING

popular male singers of the wartime era, reimagined as barnyard poultry. The MacGuffin (central device) of the plot is that one such crooning rooster, patterned after Frank Sinatra, has caused all the hens to stop laying eggs. At the time, the real-life Sinatra, the most notable new star of the period, was inspiring teenage girls to cut classes and flock (forgive the term) to hear him at New York's Paramount Theater. The depiction of chickens (shown wearing bobby socks) going crazy over "The Voice" is no more outrageous than the real-life riots that were taking place, most famously in Times Square on Columbus Day 1944.

However, once Porky establishes that a crooning rooster can get the hens to stop laying, he presumes another might start them laying again. Tashlin's imaginative sequence showing the hens' reaction to Sinatra (which Tex Avery would later try to top in 1948's **LITTLE 'TINKER**) is surpassed by the scenes of Porky auditioning a string of radio and film baritones in chicken drag, all of whom are singing Warner Bros.' published musical repertoire: Nelson Eddy performs "Shortnin' Bread,"

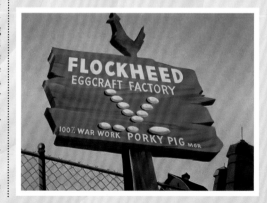

Crosby and Sinatra. In fact, without the visual reference points, one probably couldn't even tell the chicken was trying to do Sinatra. (The vocalist actually sounds to me more like he's trying to mimic Ink Spots tenor Bill Kenny.) It wouldn't do to caricature Crosby with a lot of animated movement, so instead Tashlin and his crew compensated with details like Crosby clicking his pipe between notes.

SWOONER CROONER plays on the rivalry between Sinatra and Crosby at the time—it's a battle of Hawaiian shirt vs. bow tie. As in real life, the two iconic crooners become pals at the end, uniting in the cause of helping Porky stimulate egg production and, one assumes, win the war.

In my favorite of Frank Tashlin's mature feature films, *The Girl Can't Help It* (1956), the director deftly interweaves broad comedy with toe-tapping musical sequences, showing that the proper use of rhythm is what makes both mediums work. But twelve years earlier, in **SWOONER CROONER**, the director showed comedy and music are brilliantly used in support of each other. He could have called it **THE HENS CAN'T HELP IT**.

> **JERRY SAYS** The take-away images from this Tashlin classic are the horny hens' wolfish reactions, but incidental gags shouldn't be overlooked. Frankie rooster is thinner than his microphone stand, and the Flockheed water pump has an office water cooler inside. Let's not even ask why the assembly-line belt carries the chickens and their nests—but not their eggs.

hitting a note so high it causes his neck to stretch and his tail feathers to pop off. Al Jolson tackles "September in the Rain" down on one knee, with outstretched arms and white gloves: the chicken equivalent, one imagines, of blackface. Jimmy Durante sings "Lullaby of Broadway," twisting his piano stool to shoot himself into the air, then popping out of his upright. And Cab Calloway belts out "Blues in the Night," spinning and flashing his baton (actually, Tashlin's portrayal of

the singing bandleader is somewhat tamer than real life).

When none of the above crooners proves satisfactory, Porky then places his faith in a Bing Crosby–inspired fowl who refers to himself as "the Old Groaner." The rooster adroitly mimics Crosby's well-known alliteration, snappy rhymes, and fancy verbiage. Interestingly, the aural imitations of the four singers who fail their tryouts are on the money, but not so the approximations of

A Tale of Two Kitties

"I TAWT I TAW A PUTTY TAT!"

Two hungry cats named Catstello and Babbitt are hunting for a bite to eat. At first, the plump Catstello (who seems to begin every sentence with "Hey, B-a-a-a-abitt!") is reluctant to catch a bird. But when he learns that this is a "poor little dinky-winky, itsy-bitsy, defenseless boid," the dumpy cat is suddenly raring to go. Catstello gets "height-tro-phobia" easily, though, and needs convincing—in the form of a needle to the rear—to go up the ladder and get the bird. He loses his balance and shatters the ladder ("Look, stilts!" he yells down), but Babbitt easily saves him. For the cats' next attempt, Babbitt shoves Catstello into a jack-in-the-box with springs on his feet, launching him up to the bird's nest. Here is where newborn Tweety utters his first words: "I tawt I taw a putty tat!"

Tweety administers several beatings to Catstello's head as it springs up, topping the abuse off with a dynamite stick. Later in the evening, Babbitt sets off a powder keg under a disgraced Catstello, launching him skyward and missing the nest by a mile. He ends up hanging onto a wire by one foot, but Tweety decides to do his legendary "dis widdle piddy" routine for the first time on the cat's toes. As Catstello plunges, Tweety throws the feline a rope—attached to anvil, which crushes Catstello, and (in a fantastically rubbery scene by Rod Scribner) brings so much of the earth down the crater with him that the impact drags Babbitt, watering his victory garden, to him! At night, Babbitt attaches wings to Catstello and launches the fat cat into the sky ("I'm a spitfire! P'tooey!" he calls out excitedly), but Tweety slaps on his air-raid warden hat and calls the "Fourt' Interceptor Tommand" to shoot the unidentified flying object out of the sky. Catstello lands safely on Babbitt. As Tweety, still wearing his warden's helmet, initiates a blackout, the cats make one last attempt at an attack. Tweety shouts them down: "Turn out those lights!" And they do.

DIRECTOR: ROBERT CLAMPETT **STORY:** WARREN FOSTER **ANIMATION:** ROD SCRIBNER **VOICES:** MEL BLANC (TWEETY, CATSTELLO), TED PIERCE (BABBIT) **MUSIC:** CARL STALLING

FRANK CONNIFF, writer and actor **A TALE OF TWO KITTIES** is notable for being the first appearance of Tweety. But the stars of the picture (and it would be wrong to refer to any Warner Bros. cartoon as anything other than a "picture," because that's what the characters always called them when they were in one of their frequent postmodern-before-postmodernism-existed moods) are Babbitt and Catstello. The pair were, of course, based on Bud Abbott and Lou Costello, the most popular comedy team of that era.

Although I am a huge Abbott and Costello fan, I am the first to admit that most of their pictures aren't very good (*Abbott and Costello Meet Frankenstein* being a major exception). Instead, the first season of their television show fully displays their greatness. I wonder what their pictures would have been like if they had gotten to work with great directors. But as *A Tale of Two Kitties* demonstrates, the great comedy directors of those years—Bob Clampett as well as Friz Freling, Chuck Jones, and Tex Avery—were all working in animation. Although Frank Tashlin made the transition to live action, I feel his best stuff by far was his cartoon work; nevertheless, I would have loved to have seen him direct an Abbott and Costello feature.

Tweety's appearance in **A TALE OF TWO KITTIES** had the same impact that Abbott and Costello had in 1940's *One Night in the Tropics*: Both were supporting, star-making performances that stole the show.

The Three Little Bops

"I WISH MY BROTHER GEORGE WAS HERE!"

A narrator sings of the Three Little Pigs, "One played a pipe while the others danced jigs."

Today, the pigs are a hot jazz band, and their "cool, cool" music rocks the land.

They're playing at a club called the House of Straw when in comes the wolf with horn in paw.

Rather than eat his old-time foes, he'd join their band—but his blows are low.

The wolf plays trumpet like a total square. The pigs throw him out; should they have dared?

DIRECTOR: FRIZ FRELENG **STORY:** WARREN FOSTER **ANIMATION:** GERRY CHINIQUY, BOB MATZ **LAYOUT:** HAWLEY PRATT **BACKGROUNDS:** IRV WYNER **FILM EDITOR:** TREG BROWN **VOICES:** STAN FREBERG **MUSIC:** SHORTY ROGERS

For the wolf, not allowed to "go to town," huffs and puffs and blows the house down!

And it happens again at the House of Sticks: Wolf in; wolf out; House takes its licks.

So the pigs move their act to a brick-built club. The wolf breaks in; the wolf gets snubbed.

Says wolf, if the pigs won't let him play, he'll use TNT to blow them away!

But the blast takes the bad wolf out instead. He descends to hell; it appears that he's dead.

Yet his ghost returns to play music cool! "He had to get hot"—now he's learned the rule!

DANIEL GOLDMARK, professor of musicology
This cartoon comes along at a time when Warner Bros. had seemingly gotten out of the jazzy cartoon business. In the 1930s, the studio frequently used jazz or swing hits in cartoons or based a story on a nightclub or jazz spot, but the practice waned in the 1940s. **THREE LITTLE BOPS** is a return to the swinging sounds that once dominated the Warner Bros. cartoons. Los Angeles boasted a thriving jazz scene in the 1950s, so not only was the studio able to feature trumpeter Shorty Rogers, it also made great use of comedian (and voice artist) Stan Freberg as the cartoon's hep narrator. The entire cartoon is told in scatlike rhyme, and the pigs really play some smokin' jazz—as does the wolf once he finally gets "hot" down in hell.

JERRY SAYS Scored by jazz composer-trumpeter Shorty Rogers, **THREE LITTLE BOPS** is one of the few Warner Bros. cartoons to feature a "The End" title card rather than "That's all Folks!" Some 1940s cartoons got the same treatment on reissue, but **BOPS** had it from the start.

Thugs with Dirty Mugs

"I'M GOING TO TAY-ELL...I'M GOING TO TAY-ELL."

It's police chief Flat-Foot Flanigan vs. gangster Killer Diller (played by "Ed G. Robemsome"). Diller, as we are told via a succession of newspaper headlines, has robbed the First National Bank, the Second National Bank, and so on. ("13th National Bank Skipped—Killer Superstitious" reads one headline). It soon becomes clear that Diller's gang has robbed 87 banks in one day. The hunt for the bank robbers leads to a dozen gags based on classic crime movie clichés. For example, we see a silhouette of Chief Flanigan, apparently grilling a suspect behind closed doors, threatening, "I'm gonna pin it on ya!" We go inside to catch Flanagan playing pin the tail on the donkey. Diller is finally foiled in the middle of a heist at the estate of Mrs. Lotta Jewels, ratted out by a member of the audience who's seen this cartoon before. Killer ends up behind bars with a "long sentence": He has to write "I've been a naughty boy" on a blackboard one hundred times.

GREG FORD, animation historian Director Tex Avery's cartoons confirm that many of the characteristics of 1960s-era New Wave cinema—notably the plays on movie syntax and the numerous distancing techniques—were in fact invented, and used for purely comic effect, in animated cartoons. In **HAMATEUR NIGHT** (1939), for instance, a string of hootably bad amateur acts are each ushered in, listened to, hissed and booed, and given the hook with such frenetic rapidity that the short prognosticates the jump cut, a technique much used by Jean-Luc Godard. Still more radically

MERRIE MELODIES DIRECTOR: FRED AVERY **STORY:** JACK MILLER **ANIMATION:** SID SUTHERLAND **VOICES:** MEL BLANC (AGENT 2 3/8TH, BANK TELLER, HENCHMAN, MAN IN AUDIENCE), DANNY WEBB (KILLER DILLER, LONE RANGER VOICE), JOHN DEERING (FLAT FOOT FLANIGAN), TED PIERCE (SECOND HENCHMAN) **MUSIC:** CARL STALLING

distanced than that cartoon is **THUGS WITH DIRTY MUGS**, an Avery treatise on movie gangsterdom that insightfully satirizes the live-action crime thrillers being made at the Warner Bros. studios during this period. In **THUGS**, a dog-faced mobster holds up a phone booth ("Hello, Operator? This is a stickup, see! Shell out, sweetheart!"). Killer Diller leads his shifty fellow gangsters to crack a safe but tells their German expressionist shadows to stay behind ("You shadows stay back and watch the door, see!").

In the end, Diller gets turned in by an eyewitness in the theater's second row ("I sat through this picture twice," the patron tells the police-dog, "and the Killer's going to be at Mrs. Lotta Jewels'"). This eyewitness is seen in full-shadowed outline. He moves along the bottom of the frame, supposedly a "real" audience member silhouetted against the movie screen. The silhouette (usually a rotoscoped version of cartoon

storyman Ted Pierce) was one of Avery's most masterful distancing devices, allowing the characters onscreen to flagrantly, hilariously intimidate the viewer. In **THUGS**, even Inspector F. H. A. (Sherlock) Homes expresses his displeasure with the viewer's tattling, and the incarcerated Diller sticks his tongue out at the audience just before the iris-out.

The real secret behind **THUGS WITH DIRTY MUGS**' durability lies not in its impudent, intentionally trivializing quotations from pop songs ("Flat-Foot Floogie with a Floy Floy," anyone?),

nor in its references to top-rated radio broadcasts (*The Lone Ranger, The Fred Allen Show*), but rather in the spot-on accuracy with which the cartoon reconstructs the trappings of Warner's gangster films. Genuine filmmaking savvy prevails in the cartoon's great gag involving the phone conversation in which a snitch tips off the cops and the desk sergeant leans over and violates the split-screen: The setup is rendered with such exactitude that the split-screen's diagonal partition is painstakingly airbrushed in graded grays to look like a poor process shot.

From its title (a sarcastic spin on Michael Curtiz's 1938 film *Angels with Dirty Faces*) through its montage of newspaper headlines spiced with a soupçon of exaggeration ("87 Banks Robbed Today!"), to its atmospherically lighted, interior-overhead perspective on the gangsters' fateful last heist, **THUGS WITH DIRTY MUGS** builds up convincing compositions and dramaturgy—only to sabotage them unceremoniously.

Tin Pan Alley Cats

"GIMME THAT OLD-TIME RELIGION; IT'S GOOD ENOUGH FOR ME!"

It's a swingin' Saturday night as jolly Cats Waller swaggers down the boardwalk looking for girls and fun. As he heads for the jive-jumpin' Kit-Kat Klub, there's only one fly in the ointment: the revival singers next door at Uncle Tomcat's Mission. These Puritans call the Kit-Kat a "den of iniquity" and warn Cats that he'll be "tempted by wine, women, and song." "What's the matter with that?" our hero asks. Cats enters the Kit-Kat and joins the gang for a rousing round of "Nagasaki." Telling a trumpeter to "send me out of this world,"

Cats revels in the noisy, hot licks; what *could* be the matter with this? The answer comes when the intense music really does send Cats out of this world. Our hero lands in a hallucinatory wartime fantasyland where swinging rabbits, rubber bands, and cat-dogs are supplemented by butt-bumping Axis leaders. Scared out of his wits, Cats begs the trumpeter to bring him back down to earth—where he joins Uncle Tomcat's dumbfounded revival singers for the iris-out.

WILL FRIEDWALD, author and music critic It's hard to imagine how popular the singer-pianist-composer-bandleader Fats Waller was in the

DIRECTOR: BOB CLAMPETT **STORY:** WARREN FOSTER **ANIMATION:** ROD SCRIBNER **VOICES:** HARLAND C. EVANS (FATS); LEO WATSON (SCAT SINGING); CLIFFORD HOLLAND (PREACHER); EDDIE BEAL, CARL JONES, AUDREY FLOWERS, EDDIE LYNN (SINGERS); MEL BLANC (RUBBER BAND) **MUSIC:** CARL STALLING **MUSICIANS:** EDDIE BEAL (LEADER/PIANO); VERNON H. PORTER AND ULYSSES LIVINGSTONE (GUITARS); JOHN E. MILLER (BASS); LEO WATSON (DRUMS)

1930s. Radio had made him a national star, and by the start of the swing era, many musicians were already leading small combos inspired by his band, Fats Waller and His Rhythm. Known for singing with riotous and irreverent asides, Waller essentially made every song—even some of the sad ballads—into a party. Bebop trumpeter Dizzy Gillespie later said that Waller was as much a part of his foundation as Louis Armstrong.

Waller famously appeared in three major Hollywood feature musicals, and his voice and image were also unofficially reproduced in a series of MGM cartoons that paid homage (in a refreshingly respectful way) to African-American entertainers. By the time of his tragically early death at age thirty-nine in 1943, anyone who listened to the radio or frequented the record shops knew who Fats Waller was.

He was a natural inspiration for animated characters; the major difficulty was in coming up with a caricature that was more outrageous than the flesh-and-blood Waller. In truth, director Bob Clampett's version of Waller in this short is at once neither broad enough nor subtle enough, failing to capture the real Waller's creation of

long before he went to work for Warner Bros. but owned by the studio just the same. The animation for the number is surprisingly tame; it may seem like Clampett had a less fertile imagination for visuals for music than Warner Bros. directors Tex Avery or Frank Tashlin did. Not so. The director is merely being cagey—he's holding back. The musical number is a mere prelude for **TIN PAN**'s climactic sequence, in which the Waller cat goes on what seems like a narcotics-induced hallucination, actually set off as a kind of musical delusion. As ardent Looney Tunes fans would know, the cat has been transported to Wackyland, the same place Clampett had sent Porky Pig to six years earlier (**PORKY IN WACKYLAND**, 1938). Some of the earlier film's gags have been cannibalized and colorized, not to mention given a topical slant: There are now images of Adolf Hitler and Emperor Hirohito of Japan doing a dance of bumping keisters, and then of Adolf getting his butt kicked by Stalin. One forgives the borrowing, especially since the best gag in the sequence—the marching Rubber Band, allowing Mel Blanc to do a clever bit imitating elastic instruments—is original.

Once returned from his bad trip, the hero bolts from the nightclub and is delighted to take his place banging the drum for the mission band. The prodigal returned, the sinner reformed, Cats Waller gets his own tagline thrown back at him: "Well, what's de mattah with him?" The only thing that's the matter is that **TIN PAN ALLEY CATS** represents a near last stand for both black characters and extended musical numbers in the Hollywood cartoon.

comedy through intimate nuances such as the way he would wag his eyebrows. The whole cast is caricatured as blackface pussycats, and **TIN PAN ALLEY CATS** is an animated equivalent to the live-action features *Stormy Weather* (1943) and *Cabin in the Sky* (1943), which represented both the climax and the conclusion of the all-black Hollywood musical spectacular. The tone of **TIN PAN** is rather moralistic, and its plot has to do with an irrepressible party animal deciding between sin and salvation, precisely the same dilemma delineated by Eddie "Rochester" Anderson in *Cabin*.

Musically, **TIN PAN** is on solid ground: Clampett later recalled that the soundtrack was recorded under the supervision of pianist and musical director Eddie Beal, one of many black Los Angeles musicians who was under-recorded and underdocumented. All the voices sound like genuine African-Americans—the gruff Cats Waller character, a singing trumpeter (a cross between Hot Lips Page and Leo Watson), the vocal quartet inspired by the Mills Brothers, the Salvation Army–type band.

The main number in the nightclub, "Nagasaki," was a jazz standard composed by Harry Warren

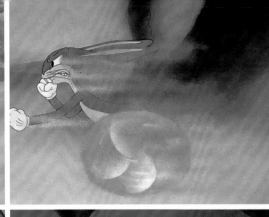

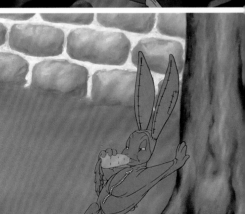

Tortoise Wins by a Hare

Bugs Bunny is watching archival footage from his and Cecil Turtle's previous encounter (Tex Avery's **TORTOISE BEATS HARE**, 1941). In a beautifully animated and acted soliloquy by Rod Scribner, Bugs is stupefied at how a tortoise could beat a rabbit at racing ("I got an ath-a-lete's physi-que!...I even got ath-a-lete's foot!"). Bugs vows that he'll find out what Cecil's secret is if it's the last thing he does. So, disguised as an old man, the rabbit visits Cecil to ask the secrets behind his victory. Cecil strings Bugs along and tells him that it has to do with the turtle's modern design and streamlined "air-flow chassis" shell. "Rabbits aren't very bright, either," he concludes.

As Bugs builds his own metal tortoise shell for the big race, we find out that there is much hype over the rematch. The rabbit mafia is involved, seeing to it that the turtle won't even finish. Shortly after the start of the race, Bugs dons his secret weapon and zips ahead. His jubilation is short-lived, as the bunny gangsters ambush Bugs, mistaking him for the "toitle." Cecil, now disguised as a rabbit, agrees with their conclusion.

"YOU FOOLS! WHAT ARE YOU DOING? I'M THE RABBIT!"

Bugs escapes their clutches and makes tracks, getting ahead of Cecil once again. Still in his metal shell, though, Bugs is kept from finishing the race by the mobsters, while the rabbit-eared tortoise is carried over the finish line. Bugs has a nervous breakdown and strips off his costume, revealing in tears that the mob has made a mistake. "Now he tells us!" sigh the gangsters, before killing themselves in one clean shot.

DIRECTOR: ROBERT CLAMPETT **STORY:** WARREN FOSTER **ANIMATION:** ROD SCRIBNER, ROBERT MCKIMSON **VOICES:** MEL BLANC (BUGS, CECIL TURTLE, GANGSTER BOSS), KENT ROGERS (LOOKOUT) **MUSIC:** CARL STALLING

JERRY BECK One of the things that most fans of director Bob Clampett's cartoons relish is that he would do almost anything to create a funny cartoon. That meant he would violate established character personality traits and traditional story points to get laughs. Here, he not only shreds the Aesop fable and Disney's 1935 short **THE TORTOISE AND THE HARE** but also Tex Avery's send-up of this famous race. The results are priceless. This sequel to Avery's picture is one of Clampett's best and contains perhaps Mel Blanc's greatest vocal performance as Bugs Bunny. The manic energy in the animation is matched only by Blanc's frantic ravings. He particularly surpasses himself in the scene at the end when the tortoise-shelled Bugs nears the finish line, delirious with joy, only to flip out, desperately screaming out his true identity, when the mobsters hold him down. Sheer lunacy—and perfect Looney Tunes. Only Clampett could twist his characters into such pretzels, and put them through the emotional wringer, with such hilarious results.

Tree for Two

"GO GET 'IM, SPIKE! GO GET 'IM!...SPIKE IS MY HERO!"

A fierce black panther has escaped from the zoo. But the news has yet to reach Spike the Bulldog and Chester, Spike's hero-worshipping fan. As the two dogs stroll downtown, Chester busily suggests typical canine pastimes such as car-chasing and ball-playing, all of which Spike rejects until Charlie proposes beating up a cat. *Cat?* Cue a singing Sylvester, a frenzied chase, and an escape through a vacant lot. Hey, where'd that cat go? the two dogs wonder. There's a black, furry tail in the shadows behind some crates. ROAR! It's the panther, of course, but hidden so nobody ever sees him. All the dogs know is that each time Spike tries to pull "Sylvester" out, the bulldog gets savaged; meanwhile, when little Chester confronts the real Sylvester, he effortlessly clobbers the cat. "If I can do it, you can," Chester encourages Spike. But try as he might, Spike gets sliced like bologna! In the end, Sylvester decides he must really be a killer. Chester flattens Sylvester anyway, and everyone simply concludes that some dogs have it and some dogs don't. So Chester becomes the

DIRECTOR: I. FRELENG **STORY:** WARREN FOSTER **ANIMATION:** KEN CHAMPIN, VIRGIL ROSS, ARTHUR DAVIS, MANUEL PEREZ **LAYOUT:** HAWLEY PRATT **BACKGROUNDS:** IRV WYNER **VOICES:** MEL BLANC (SPIKE, SYLVESTER), STAN FREBERG (CHESTER) **MUSIC:** CARL STALLING

new tough guy on the block, and Spike the gushing hero-worshipper.

MARK EVANIER, comic book writer Friz Freleng loved plots like these involving mistaken identity. Usually, he depicted Sylvester under the impression that, for example, the baby kangaroo that was knocking the tar out of him was a giant mouse. In **TREE FOR TWO**, two street hounds think they're going to beat up a cat. They believe Sylvester is doing unto them as they wanted to do unto him, when actually it's an escaped black panther.

What makes the comedy work are the vocal performances. Mel Blanc was the bulldog who, in keeping with cartoon bulldog naming conventions, was called Spike. Stan Freberg, sped up

ever so slightly, played Chester, who worshipped his big buddy to the point of shoving him back to face the cat, over and over. Freberg only received screen credit on one Warner Bros. cartoon wherein he soloed sans Blanc (**THREE LITTLE BOPS**, 1957). It's a shame because Freberg was always brilliant, matching Blanc for comic timing and infusing a spoken line with character. Mel could play opposite himself, serving as his own straight man, but it was usually better when someone else did the honors so as to ratchet up the contrast. You've got to feel a little sorry for Sylvester. Even when he isn't trying to eat anyone, he still gets flattened to a pulp. Always.

JERRY SAYS Director Friz Freleng's classic case of mistaken identity is also a fascinating study of bad-guy character types. "Puny" Chester worships Spike's strength and longs to be his pal—even though Spike is quite plainly a lazy, bullying thug who treats Chester badly.

Wabbit Twouble

"WEST AND WEWAXATION AT WAST!"

Elmer up. "How time fwies!" he says, surprised. While Fudd is lathering up his face, Bugs uses the branch with Elmer's towel hanging on it to lead him over the edge of the gorge.

Elmer gets wise to Bugs's shenanigans and goes for his gun, but immediately encounters a grizzly bear. Consulting his camping guide, Elmer plays dead, and the repulsed bear leaves the scene. Bugs has some fun mauling Elmer while he is playing possum. Just as Elmer swings his gun at Bugs, the real bear returns, and Fudd bashes the bear over the head. After a zany chase through the trees, Elmer gets back into his jalopy and zooms out of the park, stopping in time to destroy the Jellostone sign promising "a restful retreat."

Conveniently, Bugs has brought this act of vandalism to the attention of the park ranger, and in the final scene we find Elmer locked away in a cell. Elmer is at least relieved that he is finally rid of the pests, only to find that his cellmates are Bugs and the grizzly bear, both of whom ask, "Pardon me, but how long ya in for, doc?"

DAVID GERSTEIN, animation historian Online pop culture websites sometimes refer to "the Bugs Bunny" as a basic fictional character type. Generally a laid-back, retiring fellow, "the Bugs" bears no ill will to anyone—until an outsider invades his world and dares to pester him. Then it's doomsday for the pesterer, because a wronged Bugs is a force to be reckoned with.

But this character type only reflects a popular understanding of the later 1950s Bugs—which is not, in fact, the only celebrated Bugs. Robert Clampett's first Looney Tune, **WABBIT TWOUBLE** (in which the director is listed in the credits as "Wobert Cwampett"), represents a variant on the trickster of fable and myth who doesn't wait to pester first. Clampett's Bugs invades others' lives for the fun of it—especially when those others seem, like Elmer, to be easy targets. This Bugs, too, has his fans. He represents as logical a development from Tex Avery's 1940 cartoon **A WILD HARE** (Bugs Bunny's first appearance) as does

Elmer Fudd is driving to Jellostone National Park for "west and welaxation." He makes the mistake of setting up camp in the proximity of Bugs Bunny, who immediately steals Elmer's tent and ties it in knots. Fudd boards up the rabbit hole, but it doesn't stop Bugs. Bugs places opaque glasses over the napping Elmer's eyes, leading the dope to believe he's overslept and that it's already nighttime. Once he's asleep in his tent, Bugs takes the glasses back and crows like a rooster to wake

DIRECTOR: WOBERT CWAMPETT **STORY:** DAVE MONAHAN **ANIMATION:** SID SUTHERWAND **VOICES:** MEL BLANC (BUGS BUNNY), ARTHUR Q. BRYAN (ELMER) **MUSIC:** CAWL W. STAWWING

the later, self-defensive Bugs. In fact, the visual design of Bugs Bunny in **WABBIT TWOUBLE**, and the presence of former Avery animators on the cartoon's crew, suggests that Avery's unit may have begun work on **TWOUBLE** before the director's departure from Warner Bros.

"I do this kind of stuff to him all through the picture," the **WABBIT TWOUBLE** Bugs confides to the audience at one point, fully aware of his heckler role. Bugs has immediately identified Elmer as the perfect patsy and mocks his girth and mannerisms. From the point of view of the classic trickster, some people simply deserve a hard time. Elmer needn't even present a threat, and tellingly carries no rifle at first.

The only drawback to centering the story around a heckler hero is that at times he is less than sympathetic. Perhaps that's why the **WABBIT TWOUBLE** Elmer verges on becoming the figure the viewer identifies with most closely; interestingly, during Fudd's frenzied pursuit by the bear, Bugs is mostly absent.

JERRY SAYS In **WABBIT TWOUBLE**, Robert Clampett has redesigned Elmer Fudd, modeling the character after his portly voice artist, Arthur Q. Bryan. Fudd would appear in this form for four cartoons before returning to his svelter self.

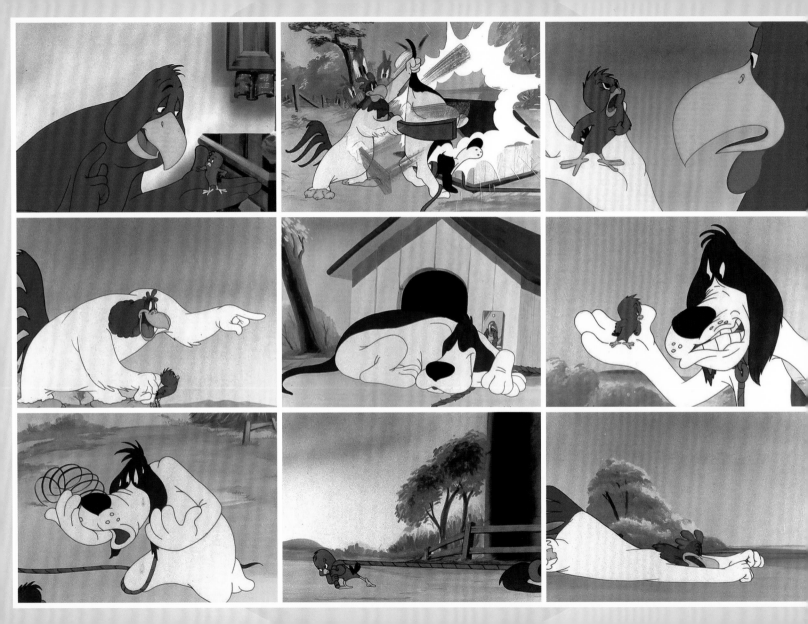

Walky Talky Hawky

"ONE OF THESE THINGS, I SAY, ONE OF THESE THINGS HAS GOT TO BE A CHICKEN!"

Henery Hawk is the featured star of this cartoon, but Foghorn Leghorn (in his debut appearance) steals the show. When Little Henery gets a father-son talk about life, he learns that as a chicken hawk he should crave chicken. So he goes off to find one. However, Henery doesn't know what a chicken looks like. The local farmyard has two suspects: a loud-mouthed rooster (patterned after radio comedian Jack Clifford's blustery Sheriff Claghorn character on the *Blue Monday Jamboree*) and a barnyard dog. The two are already caught up in a bitter war against each other. Each insists to the hawk that the other is the real chicken. After letting them fight it out in the barn, Henery ultimately grabs the whole lot of them (including a horse) to sort out later.

PAUL DINI, TV animation producer Bugs and Porky—indeed, most of the classic Warner Bros. characters—underwent years of refinement before they became stars. Not so Foghorn Leghorn, who

DIRECTOR: ROBERT MCKIMSON **STORY:** WARREN FOSTER **ANIMATION:** RICHARD BICKENBACH, CAL DALTON, DON WILLIAMS **VOICES:** MEL BLANC (HENERY HAWK, FOGHORN LEGHORN, DOG, POPPA HAWK) **MUSIC:** CARL STALLING

exploded fully formed and bellowing in **WALKY TALKY HAWKY**. Though he soon lost his realistic chicken squawks, Foghorn retained his bellicose personality and barrel-bellied design for the remainder of his theatrical career.

Animals in appearance only, Foghorn and his eternal nemesis, Barnyard Dawg, behave like frat boys gleefully bent on each other's destruction. Though aided and abetted on occasion by miniscule chicken hawks, salivating weasels, and even Daffy Duck, Foghorn and Dawg need no outside help to remain each other's worst enemy and, in a strange way, best friend.

McKimson's comic equation of rooster plus board plus dog's butt may lack the poetic elegance of comic-strip artist George Herriman's mouse plus brick plus Krazy Kat's head. However, the merry brutality worked well enough to ensure seventeen years of constant laughs—and in the case of **WALKY TALKY HAWKY**, an Academy Award nomination.

What's Opera, Doc?

"OH, MIGHTY WARRIOR OF GREAT FIGHTING STOCK / MIGHT I ENQUIRE TO ASK, EH, WHAT'S UP, DOC?"

In an exaggerated, stylized Wagnerian musical world, Elmer "Siegfried" Fudd plans to catch a rabbit with his spear and magic helmet, the latter a fearsome item of headgear that lets its wearer command the weather. But Bugs suckers Siegfried, first by running away, then by costuming himself as the gorgeous (?) Brunhilde, grandly riding in on a massively fat horse. Elmer serenades "her" with "Return, My Love"...until Brunhilde's blonde wig and headdress fall off. Enraged, Elmer tries to "kill the wabbit" with magical north winds, south winds, lightning, hurricanes, and even (shudder) smog. When all is said and done, Bugs seems dead, and stoic Siegfried bears him off toward the horizon. But is he really dead?

MIKE BARRIER, animation scholar **WHAT'S OPERA, DOC?** bridges the yawning gap between high culture, as represented by the operas of Richard Wagner and ballet, and popular culture,

DIRECTOR: CHUCK JONES **STORY:** MICHAEL MALTESE **ANIMATION:** KEN HARRIS, ABE LEVITOW, RICHARD THOMPSON **LAYOUT:** MAURICE NOBLE **BACKGROUNDS:** PHILIP DEGUARD **FILM EDITOR:** TREG BROWN **VOICES:** MEL BLANC (BUGS), ARTHUR Q. BRYAN (ELMER) **MUSIC:** MILT FRANKLYN **"RETURN, MY LOVE"** **LYRICS:** MICHAEL MALTESE

as represented by Looney Tunes and Disney's **FANTASIA** (which the cartoon mercilessly lampoons). The principal parties involved—director Chuck Jones, writer Michael Maltese, and layout designer Maurice Noble—make it clear throughout that they respect culture of both kinds. The score quotes or parodies elements of *Der Ring des Nibelungen*, *Tannhäuser*, and *The Flying Dutchman*, but there's no sneering at Wagner. Neither is there any embarrassment about Bugs Bunny and Elmer Fudd. **WHAT'S OPERA, DOC?**

delights in the comic possibilities when the two are juxtaposed, culminating in Bugs's address to the camera just before the iris-out: "What did you expect in an opera, a happy ending?" Not in most of Wagner's operas, certainly; but in a Merrie Melody, yes. And since Bugs has supposedly been killed when he speaks to us, and the distraught Elmer is carrying him away, Bugs's brief return to life permits this very clever cartoon to have it both ways.

JERRY SAYS Arguably the most famous of Warner Bros. cartoons, and certainly the most honored, this short took much longer to complete than others of its era—the extra work hours being surreptitiously billed to a Road Runner cartoon, **ZOOM AND BORED** (1957), that was comparatively made in a rush.

Wholly Smoke

"LITTLE BOYS SHOULD NOT SMOKE!"

The church bell is ringing, and it's time for Porky Pig to go to Sunday School. His mama gives him a nickel for the collection plate, but on the way to the church Porky encounters a little cigar-smoking hooligan who can do all sorts of tricks with his puffing. He calls Porky a "puny puss," and the pig retaliates by betting the street tough a nickel that he can smoke a cigar. Porky fails miserably at the same tricks and only succeeds in getting violently ill. Cigar still in hand, the pig staggers into a smoke shop, where he collapses; an impish puff of smoke shrinks Porky down to the puff's size. He introduces himself as Nick O'Teen and plans to give Porky all the "smoking [he] can handle," strapping him to a box of pipe cleaners. What follows is a wonderfully surreal rendition of the 1930s standard "Mysterious Mose" as Porky is force-fed multiple cigars and chaws. He meets the Pittsburgh Stooges (Curly, Larry, and Moe), the Crooner-Crooners (Bing Crosby and Rudy Vallee), and a Cab Calloway pipe cleaner. Porky frees himself from Nick's clutches and returns to consciousness. He skedaddles back to church, but realizes, as the collection plate nears him, that the bully still has his nickel. He goes and retrieves it, shoving the cigar in the hooligan's face. Porky makes it back in time to make his donation. He vows, complete with halo over his head, that he will "neyuh-neyuh-never smoke aguh-aguh-aguh-again!"

DIRECTOR: FRANK TASHLIN **STORY:** GEO. MANUELL **ANIMATION:** ROBERT BENTLEY **VOICES:** MEL BLANC (PORKY, TOUGH KID, KORN KOBB), TED PIERCE (PORKY'S MOM, NICK O'TEEN SPEAKING), CLIFF NAZARRO (CROSBY), BASIN STREET BOYS (QUARTET) **MUSIC:** CARL STALLING

DAVID GERSTEIN, animation historian It's easy to laud this Frank Tashlin classic for its most celebrated elements: its wild "Mysterious Mose" anti-smoking tune, for instance, or its walking, talking tobacco paraphernalia. But it's easy, too, to overlook something else that **WHOLLY SMOKE** represents: Warner Bros.' most successful effort to capture what it's like to be a child. **WHOLLY SMOKE** isn't just a morality tale or just another wacky Warner flight into dreamland. It's also the surprisingly real story of a little boy—our Porky—and his struggle with a larger world. Through masterful staging and timing, Tashlin introduces Porky as a young artiste, not just sliding down the banister but whipping down at wild speed, then making an impossible, perfect stop just inches short of a vase. The instant impression is that of a clever kid who has fully mastered his domain. But moments later, the would-be sharpie is reduced to carrying out mama's orders: "It sure is a lot for a little fellow like me to remember," he says. Young Porky is really the master of very little.

By first showing us Porky's idealized self, then his less impressive reality, Tashlin endears him to us as in few other shorts. And that's all the setup we need when Porky enters conflict with the bully. It's not just that this bully smokes per se. Rather, smoking represents to Porky the power and maturity he wants. The bully is "mature" even in his sarcastic fawning over Porky's nickel. Whereas a lesser cartoon might have made the bully a simple tough guy at this point, Tashlin wisely gives him the air of a sophisticated con artist.

The conflict is powerful enough to resonate even after the fantasy sequence takes over. Though the morality-tale formula demands that Porky repudiate smoking and be punished for his misdeeds, he is also given a chance to choke the bully with his own cigar—establishing his relative power in the kiddie realm even in the act of rejecting vice.

A Wild Hare

"WHAT'S UP, DOC?"

In the forest, Elmer Fudd beckons to us: "Be vewy, vewy quiet!" he whispers. "I'm hunting wabbits!" He tracks one rabbit to its hole in the ground and places a carrot as bait. The rabbit, proving smarter than Elmer expected, manages to tie his rifle barrel in a knot. So Elmer burrows in after, and out of another hole whirls Bugs Bunny. Casually munching on a carrot and pointing down the hole, he asks Fudd, "What's up, doc?"—and thus creates cinema history. Bugs leads the hunter on, asking him to describe a "wabbit." As Elmer lists the essential characteristics, Bugs helps by illustrating each: long ears, fluffy tail, hopping on all fours. Elmer catches on and tells Bugs he looks just like a rabbit. Bugs divulges that "confidentially—I AM A WABBIT!"

Bugs ducks behind a tree and covers Elmer's eyes to play "Guess Who." Hedy Lamarr? Carole Lombard? Rosemary Lane? Olivia de Havilland? Bugs ducks back into his hole, so Elmer sets a box trap. It works, and catches a skunk, who elucidates that he has B.O. Bugs tells Elmer that the rabbit has had his fun and wants to let the hunter take a good shot at him. Bugs poses himself in front of a tree (first stepping away from under some birds so they won't poop on him), and Elmer shoots Bugs. The rabbit hams it up in a dramatic death scene. "Everything's gettin' dark!" he cries pitifully. "I can't see! Don't leave me!" Elmer mourns over what he's done, not realizing that Bugs was just faking, and the rabbit gives him a swift kick in the rear. Elmer breaks down and leaves the forest in anguish, howling, "Aw, wabbits, wabbits, guns, wabbit twaps, cawwots, wabbits!"

DIRECTOR: FRED AVERY **STORY:** RICH HOGAN **ANIMATION:** VIRGIL ROSS, BOB MCKIMSON, ROD SCRIBNER **VOICES:** MEL BLANC (BUGS, SKUNK), ARTHUR Q. BRYAN (ELMER), MARION DARLINGTON (BIRD WHISTLING) **MUSIC:** CARL STALLING

MARK KAUSLER, animator A WILD HARE marks the appearance of the key element that makes Bugs Bunny's personality coalesce, even though the hare is not named in the film. That element: the underplayed, tough, Brooklyn-Bronx voice that Mel Blanc gave to the rabbit in this cartoon. The humor of the "What's up, doc?" line and the "You know, you look just like a wabbit" routines seem a little familiar to us—those bits were done so much faster and better in later cartoons. However, the personalities of the outrageously stupid Fudd and the resourceful Bugs dominate the story and keep us entertained.

Johnny Johnson's lush oil backgrounds are breathtaking in Technicolor. They are often so beautiful that they take the viewer's mind off the underlying vulgarity and silliness of the gags. For instance, the staging of the bird routine in which Bugs yells "Hold it!" to Elmer and steps out from underneath a pair of birds might have been funnier and clearer without the beautiful point-of-view shot looking up at the birds singing sweetly in the branches. The beauty of the setup (and the length that it's held) don't match the bathroom humor that's struggling to emerge, something that animator Ub Iwerks never had any trouble with in his Flip the Frog cartoons.

There are a lot of wonderful scenes that presage many later Bugs Bunny cartoons, such as the protracted and well-acted death scene, animated by Bob McKimson. What really makes this work is that Elmer is completely taken in by Bugs's melodramatic screed; McKimson makes Elmer look so sad, you'd think he was holding his dying grandmother instead of the crafty hare he's been trying to kill.

Rod Scribner's drawings of Bugs are the sharpest and funniest in the scenes where the bunny demonstrates his rabbit attributes to Elmer, hopping all around him, as well as the final scene, when Bugs confides to the audience, "I think the poor guy's screwy!" and then disappears into his den, playing "The Girl I Left Behind Me" on his carrot flute. The *oo* sound in "screwy" sounds funny and sarcastic as hell. Scribner's drawing of Bugs holding his ears out, with those wide, almost pie-cut eyes, hit a peak of comic intensity. The pose pointed the way to the mischievous gremlin-like face that Bugs developed when McKimson redesigned him in 1943.

JERRY SAYS Though the rabbit was identified as Bugs Bunny in promotional trade ads for two earlier films, **A WILD HARE** is unquestionably the first short in which all the elements of his character came together. They served as a template for most of the Bugs shorts that would follow over the next twenty-three years. Note that in the 1944 Blue Ribbon reissue of the short, "Carole Lombard" was replaced with "Barbara Stanwyck" in light of Lombard's 1942 death in a plane crash.

You Ought to Be in Pictures

"HE'LL BE BACK!"

DIRECTOR: I. FRELENG **STORY:** JACK MILLER **ANIMATION:** HERMAN COHEN **VOICES:** MEL BLANC (PORKY, DAFFY, GUARD) **LIVE ACTION ROLES:** LEON SCHLESINGER (HIMSELF), MICHAEL MALTESE (STUDIO COP), GERRY CHINIQUY (MOVIE DIRECTOR), HENRY BINDER (GRIP) **MUSIC:** CARL STALLING

In live action, the staff of Leon Schlesinger's cartoon studio storm out to lunch and Daffy Duck and Porky Pig come to life. Daffy tells Porky that he's a fool to be working in cartoons, and that he'd be a shoo-in to play Bette Davis's leading man at $3,000 a week. He goads the pig into going over to the big boss, Schlesinger himself, and telling him that he's quitting. "What's Errol Flynn got that I haven't?" Porky demands. So Schlesinger tears up the pig's contract. They shake on it, and Porky leaves disoriented, leaving Leon certain that he'll be back soon. After Daffy sends Porky off to the Warner Bros. studio, the duck tells us that now's his chance to become the resident Termite Terrace star (Termite Terrace is the nickname given to the animation studios).

The studio cop (played by Mike Maltese and voiced by Mel Blanc) won't let Porky or his car in, however. Porky returns, disguised as Oliver "Babe" Hardy, but the cop gets wise and goes after him. Porky hides on a closed ballroom set and ruins the footage by sneezing. The musical's director (Gerry Chiniquy) has Porky thrown back onto the lot, where the cop resumes the chase. After running into a stampede of horse and carriages from a Western, Porky decides that he's not cut out for features and returns to Schlesinger. Meanwhile, Daffy is hamming it up for a big raise, showing off his wacky dancing skills and singing to an uninterested producer. Porky arrives just in time and beats Daffy senseless for all the trouble he's caused. Porky tells Leon that he was only fooling about his resignation; so was the boss, and Porky's contract is still intact. When Porky returns to the drawing board, Daffy, bandaged with arm in sling, tries goading the pig into quitting again to play opposite Greta Garbo. Porky hurls a tomato at the duck's face.

JERRY BECK Predating **WHO FRAMED ROGER RABBIT** by several decades—in fact, it's credited with inspiring the 1988 film—**YOU OUGHT TO BE IN PICTURES** is one of the most memorable of the black-and-white-era Porky Pig cartoons. It's also one of the funniest. Director Friz Freleng cleverly made use of a 35mm motion-picture camera that the Schlesinger studio normally used for shooting reference footage or live action to be rotoscoped. The studio had previously made several "Christmas reels," live-action gag films shot around the studio, with the staff all pitching in on camera and behind; these shorts were shown each year at the studio Christmas party. In fact, the footage of the animators running out for lunch came from one of the gag reels.

YOU OUGHT TO BE IN PICTURES was Freleng's third film upon his return to Schlesinger's studio, just back from an unhappy year spent at MGM, where he toiled on a series of bland Captain and the Kids cartoons. He said he made this film as a way of saying "Thank you for having me back." In addition to Leon Schlesinger, Gerry Chiniquy, and Michael Maltese, other staffers pictured on screen include animator Fred Jones (no relation to Chuck) drawing Porky in the first scene; checkers Gladys Hallberg and Paul Marin; and executive Henry Binder. Stock footage lifted from the 1936 Dick Foran B-movie *California Mail* is used in the scenes when Porky drives through the Western's back lot. Freleng's experience making this film came in handy in later years—he mixed Bugs Bunny with Doris Day in **MY DREAM IS YOURS** (1949) and created a TV pilot blending live action and animation, **PHILBERT**, in 1963.

Contributors

LIA ABBATE is an artist and writer who has worked in production management, recruiting, and casting at Sony Pictures Animation, Walt Disney Animation Studios, Warner Brothers Feature Animation, and Universal Studios.

MIKE BARRIER is a historian of animation and comics. His books include *Hollywood Cartoons*, *The Animated Man*, and *The Smithsonian Book of Comic Book Comics*. He blogs at www.michaelbarrier.com.

JERRY BECK is the author of fifteen books, including *The Hanna-Barbera Treasury*, *The Animated Movie Guide*, and *The Art of Madagascar*. He co-writes the animation blog Cartoon Brew at www.cartoonbrew.com.

DAVID BOWERS is a writer, director, animator, and story artist. His most recent work includes directing the DreamWorks-Aardman film *Flushed Away* and writing and directing Imagi's feature adaptation of Osamu Tezuka's classic manga *Astro Boy*.

JOHN CANEMAKER is an educator, animation historian, and Academy Award–winning filmmaker. His books include *Disney's Nine Old Men*, *Felix: The Twisted Tale of the World's Most Famous Cat*, *The Art and Flair of Mary Blair*, and *Winsor McCay: His Life and Art*.

CHARLES CARNEY is an author and animation writer whose books include *The Acme Catalog: Quality Is Our #1 Dream* and *Space Jammin': Michael and Bugs Hit the Big Screen*.

ROB COLEMAN is an Academy Award–nominated animation director whose credits include the three *Star Wars* prequels, *Men in Black*, and many other films; he is currently working on *Happy Feet 2*.

FRANK CONNIFF is a writer and comedian best known for his role as Frank on TV's *Mystery Science Theatre 3000*. He was also the head writer on the Nickelodeon series *Invader Zim*.

PAUL DINI is writer of live-action and animated movies and TV series, as well as comic books. Best known for his role as writer and co-producer of *Batman: The Animated Series*, he has also written for *Lost*, *Duck Dodgers*, *Pinky and the Brain*, *Superman*, and *Star Wars: Clone Wars*.

MARK EVANIER is a noted writer of comic books and animated TV series, including *Garfield and Friends* and *Dungeons & Dragons*. In comics, he collaborates with Sergio Aragonés on *Groo the Wanderer* and has authored *Kirby: King of Comics*, a biography of the legendary Jack Kirby. Evanier blogs at www.newsfromme.com.

ANDREW FARAGO is the curator of San Francisco's Cartoon Art Museum. He has written for publications including *The Comics Reporter*, *The Comics Journal*, and *Animation World Network*, and is the creator of the online comic *The Chronicles of William Bazillion*. He blogs at andrewfarago.livejournal.com.

GREG FORD is a New York–based filmmaker and the animation writer, director, and producer of numerous Warner Bros. shorts and features, including *Daffy Duck's Quackbusters*, *Invasion of the Bunny Snatchers*, *Night of the Living Duck*, and *Blooper Bunny*. Currently, he is independently producing Mark Kausler's *There Must Be Some Other Cat*.

WILL FRIEDWALD is a noted authority on music and animation. His books include *Sinatra: The Song Is You*, *Stardust Melodies*, *Jazz Singing*, and the biography of Tony Bennett, *The Good Life*. He writes regularly on jazz for the *Wall Street Journal*.

SHAENON GARRITY is an award-winning webcartoonist best known for her strips *Narbonic* and *Skin Horse*. She works as a manga editor for Viz Media and has written for Marvel Comics.

DAVID GERSTEIN is a comic book writer and editor and animation historian. His books include *Mickey and the Gang: Classic Stories in Verse* and *Walt Disney Treasures—Disney Comics: 75 Years of Innovation*. He can be found online at www.cartoonresearch.com/gerstein and ramapithblog.blogspot.com.

ERIC GOLDBERG is a director and animator at Walt Disney Animation Studios. He was supervising animator for the Genie in *Aladdin* and co-directed the feature *Pocahontas*. He also directed the animation in *Looney Tunes: Back in Action* and is the author of *Character Animation Crash Course!*.

DANIEL GOLDMARK teaches music history at Case Western Reserve University. His books include *The Cartoon Music Book* and *Tunes for Toons*.

MARTIN GOODMAN is an animation historian and critic who currently writes a monthly column on cartoons and culture for the online *Animation World Network* (www.awn.com).

YVETTE KAPLAN is an animation director, writer, and creator. She co-directed *Beavis and Butt-head Do America* (1996) and was head of story for *Ice Age* (2002).

MARK KAUSLER is a veteran animator whose credits include Disney's *Beauty and the Beast* and *Who Framed Roger Rabbit*, Warner Bros.' *Looney Tunes Back in Action*, Ralph Bakshi's *Heavy Traffic*, and Nickelodeon's *Ren & Stimpy*.

EARL KRESS is a prolific writer of animation and comic books. His credits include *Tiny Toon Adventures*, *Pinky and the Brain*, and *Animaniacs*.

MIKE MALLORY is a mystery writer, animation historian, and pop-culture geek. His books include *Iwao Takamoto: My Life with a Thousand Characters*, *Marvel: The Expanding Universe Wall Chart*, and *Universal Studios Monsters: A Legacy of Horror*.

MARK MAYERSON is an animator, producer, and director. He created the TV series *Monster by Mistake* and teaches animation at Sheridan College in Oakville, Ontario. He blogs at mayersononanimation.blogspot.com.

HARRY MCCRACKEN is the founder and editor of the tech news site Technologizer (technologizer.com), and was formerly editor of *PC World* and *Animato*. He blogs about cartoons at www.harrymccracken.com.

MARK NEWGARDEN is a cartoonist and author. He created *The Garbage Pail Kids* for Topps Co. He is also the author of *We All Die Alone*, *Cheap Laffs*, and *Bow-Wow Bugs a Bug*.

STEPHAN PASTIS gave up a career as a litigation attorney to create the comic strip *Pearls Before Swine*, which has garnered two National Cartoonists Society Newspaper Comic Strip awards.

STEVE SCHNEIDER is a writer, music critic, and film historian.

KEITH SCOTT, an Australia-based voice actor and the voice of Bullwinkle J. Moose, is also an animation historian specializing in early voice artists. He wrote *The Moose That Roared*, the definitive history of Jay Ward cartoons.

J. J. SEDELMAIER is an award-winning producer, designer, and director of TV commercials and animated series such as *Saturday TV Funhouse* on *Saturday Night Live* and the pilot episode of *Harvey Birdman, Attorney at Law*. He can be found online at www.jjsedelmaier.com.

LINDA SIMENSKY is the vice president of children's programming for PBS and has previously developed animation for Nickelodeon and Cartoon Network. She is also a past president of ASIFA-East and the founder of the New York chapter of Women in Animation.

TOM SITO is an animator, teacher, and author. His most recent book is *Drawing the Line: The Untold Story of the Animation Unions from Bosko to Bart Simpson*. He can be found online at tomsito.com.

JEFF SMITH is the creator-writer-artist of the comic *Bone*, which has garnered ten Eisner Awards, ten Harvey Awards, and the National Cartoonists Society's award; *Bone* was also named one of *Time* magazine's "Top Ten Graphic Novels of All Time."

MICHAEL SPORN is an award-winning animator and animation director. His films include *The Man Who Walked Between the Towers*, *Whitewash*, and *Dr. DeSoto*. He blogs at www.michaelspornanimation.com/splog.

DARRELL VAN CITTERS is an animation director and producer who runs his own studio, Renegade Animation, in Glendale, California. He has also written the book *Mr. Magoo's Christmas Carol: The Making of the First Animated Christmas Special*.

CRAIG YOE is a cartoon historian and award-winning graphic designer. His resume includes being a toy designer, the creative director and later VP/general manager of *The Muppets*, and author of several books including *The Art of Mickey Mouse* and *Secret Identity: The Fetish Art of Superman's Co-Creator Joe Shuster*. He can be found online at www.yoe.com.

Index

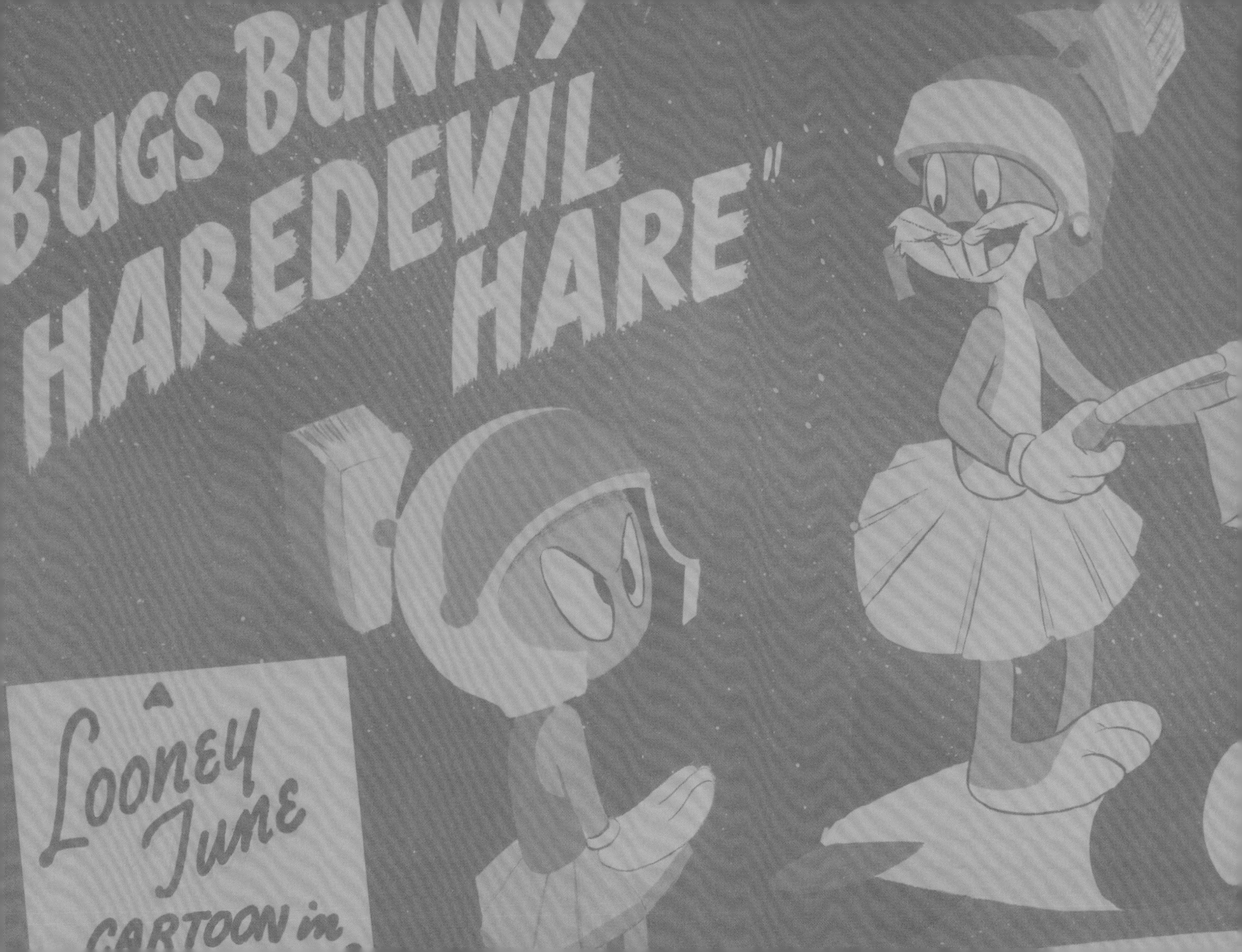
Bugs Bunny
HAREDEVIL HARE"
A Looney Tune
CARTOON in

Acknowledgments

Like Ringo, I get by with a little help from my friends. Actually, this book would not exist without *a lot* of help from *a lot* of my friends and esteemed colleagues, along with hundreds of fellow Looney Tunes enthusiasts and animation historians all around the world. I'd like to thank each and every one of them for contributing to this book.

Special credit must go to Keith Scott for sharing his research into the unsung voice talents behind many Loony Tunes characters; many of these actors finally get their due in this volume. And thank you to Daniel Goldmark and Will Friedwald, who identified all the music cues, songs, and merrie melodies that Carl Stalling and Milt Franklyn stuck in our heads in our childhoods.

David Gerstein and Thad Komorowski went above and beyond the call of duty in lending special assistance to this project. Their expertise in animation research is only matched by their enthusiasm for all things Looney. This book would not be as authoritative, accurate, or fun without their input.

I especially want to thank Yvette Kaplan, Amid Amidi, Leonard Maltin, and Mark Kausler for all kinds of additional help, as well as their ongoing moral support of my many crazy cartoon-related projects. My personal thanks to Ruth Clampett and Mike Van Eaton for help in locating graphics, and to Elaine Piechowski, Melanie Swartz, Kevin Bricklin, and Victoria Selover at Warner Bros. Global Publishing for their invaluable service to the cause. And a large shout out to editors Mark Burstein and Kevin Toyama, copyeditor Jonathan Kauffman and proofreader Mikayla Butchart, designer Michel Vrana, and production manager Anna Wan.

Hundreds of people responded to our initial **100 GREATEST LOONEY TUNES** poll on Cartoon Brew (www.cartoonbrew.com). This book is the end result of their cumulative opinion. Thank you to the following pollsters:

Mariah Abell, Stephano Alba, Alec, Tortstein Adair, Daniel Adler, Pat Adler, Nicole Alvarado, Vincent Alexander, Andrew, Jason Anders, Lynn Anderson, Anna, Benjamin Archand, Christopher Atkins, Autumn, Eric B., Vlad B., Jamie Badminton, Bakamintai, B. Baker, Callum Barker, Floyd Bishop, Lawrence Boocker, K. Borcz, Boxmyth, Brandon, Brannon, Jay Brennan, Brenton, Jim Bricker, Brian, Brien, Grian Browe, Shelia Brol, Curt Brown, Joe Budda, Andrew Burt, Buzz, Ian Cairns, Paul Camp, Dominck Cancilla, Frank Capalbo, Mike Caracappa, Steve Carras, Sammy Castanon, John Chadwick, Charles, Chill, Chris, Tony Claar, Henry Cline, Stephen Coats, Zack Cole, Gary Conrad, Cowmix, Edward R. Cox, Brian Crist, Norman L. Cook, Chris Cressionnie, David L. Crooks, Bill Cross, Crystal, Dani Cuttler, Clinto D., Daffy 47, "Uncle" Wayne Daigrepont, Michael Dambrot, Daniel, Tommy Day, David, David Dean, Koen Dekonick, Daryl Della, Charles DeWitt, Paul Dini, Mark C. Dooley, Donald, Donna, Ann E.R. Duff, Doug Edwards, EGM, Glen Ehlers, Greg Ehrbar, Michael E. Ellis, El Kabong, Emilie, Erik, Paul Etcheverry, Dave Flilipi, Sam Filstrup, Firefly, Melanie Fletcher, Joseph Fobbs, Rich Fogel, Justin Foley, Bob Ford, Aaron Foster, Kurt Frank, Scott French, Jake Friedman, Duane Fulk,

Asitya Gadre, Sam Gaffney, Jeff Gardner, Gavin, gdx, Larry Geng, David German, Andrew Gilmore, Lorretta Giron, Glowworm, Emmett Goodman, Scott Graham, Harley Green, Gregs, Marc Greisinger, Darryl Grossi, Jack Gruber, Jorge Gutierrez, Terry Guy, Guy, Merlin Haas, Joe Harmatink, Harris, John Hartnett, Tommy Hawkins, Joe Hefferman, Ted Hering, Ted Herrmann, Hhex65, Ian W. Hill, Robert Hill, J. Hobart, Gary Hoffman, Mike Hollingsworth, Mike Holsather, Tom Holste, Joe Horne, Ryan Howard, Clark Humphrey, J.J. Hunsecker, Jeff Hunsel, Matthew Hunter, Alan Hutchinson, Iain, Daniele Iaschi, Andrea Ippoliti, Ira, Susan J., Charlie Jacob, Jason, Jeff, Jim Chig, Mike Johnson, DJ Jonas, Jonathan, Donovan Jones, Jpdj, Jpox, Martin Juneau, Corey K., Jeff K., Randy K., Kal, Robert Kass, Kel, Scott Kelly, Yves Kerremans, Kerry, Sandra Khoo, Chuck King, Ed Kirk, Alex Kirwan, Tiffany Knoell, Zane Kohler, Jeff Kovel, Nic Kramer, Joshua Kreitzer, Kris, TV's Kyle, Chris L., Rod Ladouceur, Windy Lawley, Jack Lechner, Mark Lensenmayer, Larry Levine, Jeffery Lewis, Lucas Libanio, JC Limoges, Peter Lish, Lloyd, Jeanne Loewenstein, Steve Losco, Looney Lover, Chris Luna, Robert M, Dave Mackey, Marbles, Todd Masters, Joe Mathis, Matt, Maxpower, Sean McAlpine, Tony McCarson, Merril McCarthy, Jon Melhorn, Will Mendes, Greg Method, Michael, Milena, Alfonse Moline, Molly, Motherbear, Sean Montgomery, Mrgoberg, Paul Mular, Captain Murphy, Tony N., Roberto Naldi, Paul Nass, Peter Neski, Ian Neumann, Rachel Newstead, Eric Noble, Nicole, Pat Nolan, Elizabeth Oaks, OM, Pay O'Neill, Trevor Orsztynowicz, Austin Papageorge, John Papovitch, Fred Patten, PC Unfunny, Patrick Peters, Mike Pelensky, Bill Perkins, Naomi Perl, Tony Perodeau, Tom Pope, Ted Pratt, Precode, Ken Priebe, Jesse Price, Ron Price, Thom Purdy, Robert Pusani, Chuck R., Rachelle, Randy, Patrick A. Reed, Robert Reynolds, Nick Reymann, RJ, Robbo, Roberto, Roman, Michael Rosenberg, Rosscott, Anthony Russo, Carl Russo, Dennis S., Sam, Saturnome, Robert Schaad, Nick Schfer, Brian Scott, Paul Scrabo, Steve Segal, Mr. Semaj, David Sendker, Hameed Shaukat, Mark Sheldon, Norin Shirley, Steve Siegert, Mark Simons, Tom Sito, Jonathan Sloman, Mike A. Smith, Smitty, Chris Sobieniak, Mark Sonntag, Danny Spellman, Spencer, Brian Stanley, Michael Stewart, Sunday, BJ Swartz, Darryl T., Tallman, Vincent Tang, Jennifer Tangeman, Nicholas Tan, Jake Tashjian, Zoran Taylor, Robert Taylor, Tony Teresa, Terry, Tex, Juliet T. Thornae, Justin J. Times, Andrew Tisher, Rob Tomshany, Tony, Tommy, Tor, Grant Tregloan, Raymond Tucker, Joonas Vainikainen, Joe Valdivia, Ben Varkentine, Death Vegas, Stephanie Vincent, Virgilio, Vince, Ben W., Joey Waggoner, DaVon M. Walker, Has Walther, Stu West, Peter Whitaker, Whit, Gary Wolff, Kevin Wollenweber, Eric Wood, Woody NYC, Jonny Yeah, Frank M. Young, Matthew Yorstein, George Zadorozny, Zavkram, J.B. Zimmerman, and Edward Zuk. And last, but certainly not least, my gratitude to Martha Sigall, who helped create the magic at Termite Terrace. —JERRY BECK

Colophon

INSIGHT EDITIONS

Publisher ★ RAOUL GOFF
Creative Director ★ IAIN R. MORRIS
Managing Editor ★ KEVIN TOYAMA
Acquisitions Editor ★ JAKE GERLI
Project Editor ★ MARK BURSTEIN
Copyeditor ★ JONATHAN KAUFFMAN
Designer ★ MICHEL VRANA
Design Assistant ★ DAGMAR TROJANEK
Production Manager ★ ANNA WAN

INSIGHT EDITIONS would like to thank Victoria Selover at Warner Bros.; Mikayla Butchart; and especially Jerry Beck, the Bob Clampett Collection, Paul Bussolini, Eric Calande, Ruth Clampett, and Mark Newgarden for sharing their wonderful collection of vintage Looney Tunes art with our readers.

Images for **ROBIN HOOD DAFFY** (p. ii), **CANNED FEUD** (p. iii), **MEXICALI SCHMOES** (p. iv), **BUNNY HUGGED** (p. v), **BUGS GETS THE BOID** (p. viii), **LITTLE RED RIDING RABBIT** (p. x), **ALI BABA BUNNY** (p. xiii), **LONG-HAIRED HARE** (p. xiv), **A WILD HARE** (p. xxiv), **BIRDS ANONYMOUS** (p. 21), **BULLY FOR BUGS** (p. 30), **CINDERELLA MEETS FELLA** (p. 39), **8 BALL BUNNY** (p. 68), **LITTLE RED RIDING RABBIT** (p. 113), **NASTY QUACKS** (p. 121), **OLD GLORY** (p. 124), **THREE LITTLE BOPS** (p. 184), **HAREDEVIL HARE** (p. 211), and **RABBIT FIRE** (p. 215) courtesy of Jerry Beck (cartoonbrew.com)

Image for **COAL BLACK AND DE SEBBEN DWARFS** (p. 41) courtesy of the Bob Clampett Collection

Images for **EASTER YEGGS** (p. 64), **ONE FROGGY EVENING** (p. 129), and **WHAT'S OPERA, DOC?** (p. 199) courtesy of Paul Bussolini

Image for **ITCH IN TIME** (p. 109) courtesy of Eric Calande (warnerart.com)

Image for **THE GREAT PIGGY BANK ROBBERY** (p. 79) courtesy of Clampett Studio Collections (clampettstudio.com)

Image for **BEAR FOR PUNISHMENT** (p. 17) courtesy of Mark Newgarden (laffpix.com)

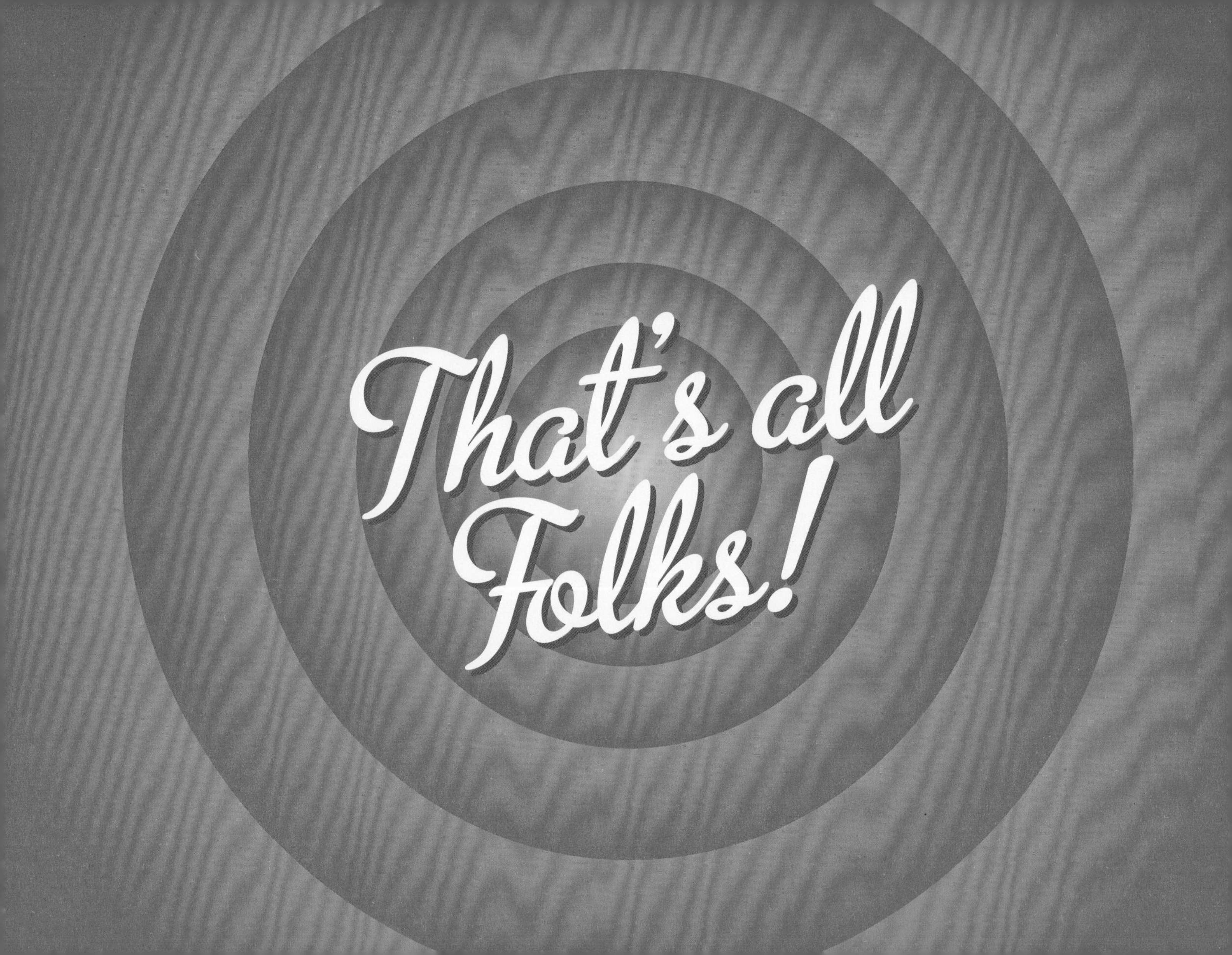
That's all
Folks!

A LOONEY TUNE
CARTOON IN
COLOR BY
TECHNICOLOR
'FAST AND FURRY-OUS